The Search for Mabila

D1526646

The Search for Mabila

The Decisive Battle between Hernando de Soto and Chief Tascalusa

Edited by Vernon James Knight Jr.

THE UNIVERSITY OF ALABAMA PRESS
Tuscaloosa

Copyright © 2009
The University of Alabama Press
Tuscaloosa, Alabama 35487-0380
All rights reserved
Manufactured in the United States of America

Typeface: Bembo

∞
The paper on which this book is printed meets the minimum requirements of American National Standard for Information Sciences-Permanence of Paper for Printed Library Materials, ANSI Z39.48-1984.

Library of Congress Cataloging-in-Publication Data

The search for Mabila : the decisive battle between Hernando de Soto and Chief Tascalusa / edited by Vernon James Knight, Jr.
p. cm.
Papers originally delivered at the conference "The Search for Mabila : A Three-Day Multidisciplinary Workshop", held at the University of Alabama, Sept. 28–30, 2006.
Includes bibliographical references and index.
ISBN 978-0-8173-1659-4 (cloth : alk. paper) — ISBN 978-0-8173-5542-5 (pbk. : alk. paper) — ISBN 978-0-8173-8242-1 (electronic) 1. Soto, Hernando de, ca. 1500-1542—Congresses. 2. Mabila, Battle of, Ala., 1540—Congresses. 3. Southern States—Discovery and exploration—Spanish—Congresses. 4. Tuskaloosa, Chief—Congresses. 5. Spaniards—Southern States—History—16th century—Congresses. 6. Choctaw Indians—First contact with Europeans—Congresses. 7. Spaniards—Southern States—Antiquities. 8. Choctaw Indians—Antiquities. 9. Excavations (Archaeology)—Alabama. I. Knight, Vernon J.
E125.S7S43 2009
970.01′6092—dc22

2008050482

To the searchers. For the search is a metaphor for what is really important.

Contents

Illustrations

FIGURES

TABLES

Introduction

Vernon James Knight Jr.

One of the most profound events in sixteenth-century North America was a ferocious battle between the Spanish army of Hernando de Soto and a larger force of Indian warriors under the leadership of a feared chieftain named Tascalusa. The site of this battle was a small, fortified border town within an Indian province known as Mabila. Although the Indians were defeated, the battle was a decisive blow to Spanish plans for the conquest and settlement of what is now the southeastern United States. For in that battle, De Soto's army lost its baggage, including all proofs of the richness of the land—proofs that would be necessary to attract future colonists. Facing such a severe setback, De Soto led his army once more into the interior of the continent, where he was not to survive. The ragtag remnants of his once mighty expedition limped into Mexico some three years later, thankful to be alive. The clear message of their ordeal was that this new land, then known as La Florida, could not be easily subjugated.

But where, exactly, did this decisive battle of Mabila take place? The accounts left by the Spanish chroniclers provide clues, but they are vague ones. They are so vague and lacking in corroboration that without additional supporting evidence, it is impossible to trace De Soto's trail on a modern map with any degree of certainty. Nonetheless there is a long history of conjecture about the battle locality based on these historical clues, going back well over two hundred and fifty years. Hundreds of native archaeological sites in the general area have been located and explored, yet none of them to date has produced definitive evidence to show that it was the battle site. Although there is a widespread consensus that the event took place in the southern part of what is now Alabama, the truth is that to this day, nobody knows where Mabila is—neither the editor, nor any of the fifteen contributors to this volume, nor any of the historians and archaeologists, amateur and professional, who have long sought it. One can rightfully say that the lost battle site of Mabila is the predominant historical mystery of the Deep South.

Many care deeply about this mystery, particularly in south Alabama, and they have done so for a long time. There is a natural curiosity to know where an event of great historical importance took place. Where under different circumstances such localities are known, as at Gettysburg or the Little Bighorn, we tend to set these grounds aside as national parks and national monuments and to provide them with facilities for visitors so that their story can be properly told on the very ground on which it happened. History enthusiasts visit such places by the tens of thousands every year, and schoolteachers bring busloads of children to visit them as part of their education in American history. All of this is expected among a people who are curious about their heritage. Up to the present, such an experience has been impossible for Mabila.

But it would be improper for us to seek Mabila solely in order to satisfy local pride or to turn it into a tourist destination. There are legitimate reasons to know exactly where the battle of Mabila was fought. These are scholarly reasons; they arise from our belief that its discovery and careful exploration will lead to an improved account of what happened there. For "what happened" is not at all certain.

The chroniclers who wrote about the De Soto expedition, for example, all expressed the view that chief Tascalusa deceived the Spaniards and led them into an ambush, planned long in advance. But was that really the case? At least one scholar, historian Jay Higginbotham, sees evidence in the chronicles that there was no ambush; that the Mabilians actually intended to receive De Soto peaceably. In Higginbotham's view, the fight nonetheless broke out because of cultural misunderstandings and nervousness on both sides.[1] If so, the Spaniards later rationalized the outbreak of violence and subsequent slaughter by falsely accusing the Indian leader of treachery.

There is, in fact, room for doubt about Tascalusa's treachery and many other things. For, as we will see in the chapters of this volume, each of the Spanish chroniclers whose accounts have come down to us saw things a little differently from the others. And each account is far too sparing in detail to tell us a lot of what we would like to know.

A central scholarly issue has to do with the handling of archaeological and historical data. For well over a century, southeastern archaeologists have been compiling information about Indian settlements of the period of early European contact. In a slow process of collecting data on site locations, excavating sites, defining artifact types, and improving chronologies, archaeologists have built up a substantial picture of native life during the early Contact era. This picture is not just about artifacts; archaeologists today are reasonably informed about such things as population size, areas of dense and sparse habitation, the nature of towns, agriculture and diet, social relationships, trade, and the size of political chiefdoms. But something important is still missing. In most cases, we cannot yet say with certainty that particular groups of archaeological sites on a map are equivalent to the "provinces" of towns mentioned in the De Soto chronicles. Until we are able to do so, neither source of information, archaeological or historical, can truly illuminate the other. We realize that a satisfactory reconciliation of both could be much more powerful. As Waselkov and colleagues (chapter 15, this volume) remark, "We prefer to treat these two forms of evidence, the documentary and the material, as complementary but distinct—to pay particular attention to areas where these independent sets of data seem to coincide or seem to contradict—and thereby extend the insights of each to achieve a better understanding of the past."

This elusive reconciliation of independent forms of evidence could yield what anthropologist Charles Hudson has called the "social geography" of the native Southeast at the time of European contact. This would be a geography of real archaeological sites on a real landscape that have been given their proper names for the first time. And with that accommodation, by adding in everything archaeologists have learned about these native societies, the initial chapter of the history of the Old South could then be properly written.[2]

Thus it is not our quest to walk in the exact footsteps of De Soto from motives of zealousness, quaint curiosity, pride of discovery, or local boosterism. It really does not matter to us in the slightest way which modern town or city can lay claim to having Mabila in its backyard. Our desire is simply to learn more about a fascinating but keenly intractable period of early American history. And we are openly optimistic that it is possible, using an enlightened approach, to find these sites and thus finally to put together the pieces of this puzzle. As Charles Hudson notes in the closing passage of *Knights of Spain, Warriors of the Sun,* "I do not think it is at all far-fetched that in coming years we may expect to find one or more of the following: Mabila, Chicaza, Utiangüe, and Aminoya. And of these, the site that will do the most in anchoring a long stretch of the De Soto route will be the site of Mabila."[3] The approach we recommend toward that end is laid out in this book.

What have scholars concluded over the years about the location of Mabila? A map of identified localities drawn from a variety of published sources (Figure I.1)[4] shows potential Mabilas distributed in a broad swath, ranging from Hale and Greene counties in the north to Mobile and Baldwin counties in the south. The distance between the northernmost and the southernmost of these is about 106 miles. Locations near the Alabama, Tombigbee,

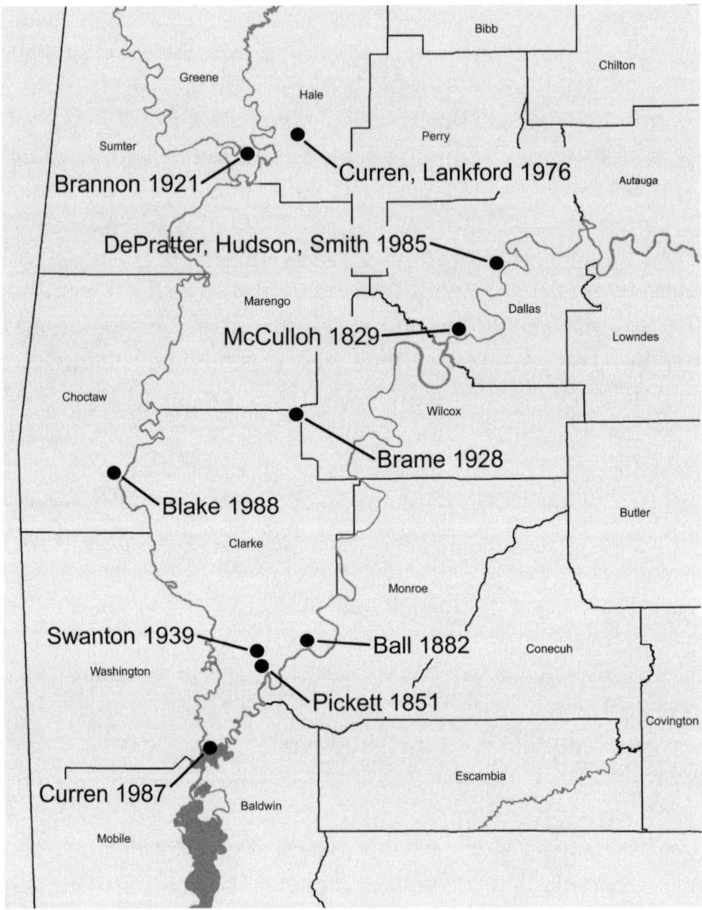

Figure I.1. Proposed Mabila locations, 1829–1988.

and Black Warrior rivers have all been proposed at different times. Looking at the dates associated with these, there is no gradual convergence of opinion in favor of any particular locality. Within the eight-county area defined by this distribution, there have been proponents of northern, southern, eastern, and western localities all within the last thirty-five years. Curiously, despite this divergence of opinion, many of these identifications have been expressed in a highly confident tone. For example, Peter Brannon and his colleagues considered Mabila and several other towns along De Soto's route as "definitely located"—Mabila being at the Forkland Mound site in southern Greene County.[5]

Despite the fact that these opinions are literally all over the map, it is possible to narrow the search area to something much smaller. As is spelled out in chapter 11, "Seeking Methods That Work," some of us are convinced that there are right and wrong ways to go about locating the routes of conquistadors. Some are "right" in the sense that they use all of the modern approaches available to us: historical, linguistic, geographic, and archaeological, not to mention technological resources like Geographic Information Systems (GIS). Because no one can reasonably claim to command all these disciplines and technologies, one of the "right" things to do, it seems to me, is to make the search a multidisciplinary, group effort. This would maximize the contributions of various specialists, each of whom brings a different perspective to the problem. At the same time, the dynamics of group discussion serve to counteract the effects of personal and local biases, which heretofore have done little but cloud the topic with acrimony.

Having discussed all of this with Dr. Douglas E. Jones in the spring of 2006, we took the next step and decided to co-organize and convene such a multidisciplinary group. We submitted a proposal to Dean Robert F. Olin of The University of Alabama's College of Arts and Sciences, who generously granted monetary support for a three-day workshop as part of the celebration of the 175th anniversary of the college. Our Mabila conference was to complement one held twenty-five years earlier in 1981 on the occasion of the 150th anniversary of the university. That previous conference, titled "Alabama and the Borderlands," featured distinguished lectures on the history and archaeology of our region in the context of the old "Spanish borderlands." An outstanding result of the 1981 conference was a volume edited by Reid Badger and Lawrence Clayton and published by The University of Alabama Press.[6]

Thus, "The Search for Mabila: A Three-Day Multidisciplinary Workshop" came to pass during September 28–30, 2006, at the Ferguson Center on The University of Alabama campus. Our panel included, in addition to the organizers, fourteen invited participants including a mix of professional scholars and avocational students of the problem. Disciplines represented in the mix included history, folklore, geography, geology, and archaeology. In preparing the list of invitees, we made a deliberate effort to identify new voices, as opposed to those with well-known, published opinions on De Soto's route. While this decision involved something of a learning curve for those not previously immersed in the minutiae of everything De Soto, it enlivened the discussion by encouraging fresh perspectives. The participants were Dr. Kathryn E. Holland Braund, Dr. Lawrence A. Clayton, Ms. Linda K. Derry, Dr. Robbie Ethridge, Mr. Ned J. Jenkins, Dr. Douglas E. Jones (co-

Figure I.2. Participants in the 2006 "Search for Mabila" conference at The University of Alabama.

organizer), Dr. Vernon James Knight Jr. (co-organizer), Dr. George E. Lankford, Dr. Neal G. Lineback, Mr. E. Mason McGowin, Dr. Michael D. Murphy, Dr. Amanda L. Regnier, Dr. Craig T. Sheldon, Mr. Donald E. Sheppard, Dr. Gregory A. Waselkov, Dr. Eugene M. Wilson, and Dr. John E. Worth (Figure I.2).

A collection of resources for the use of participants was posted on-line, prior to the conference, including links to the complete De Soto and Luna chronicles plus a number of relevant maps and manuscripts in Spanish, Portuguese, and English.[7] A small library of books was assembled for the workshop, including a complete run of the De Soto Working Papers published in the 1980s by the Alabama Museum of Natural History (see chapter 10, this volume). During the conference, the resources of The University of Alabama Map Library and the Cartography Laboratory of the UA Department of Geography were generously made available to us. Four students from the UA Department of Anthropology were selected to attend and assist the conference, performing such duties as note-taking, library research, scanning, photocopying, computer support, and the all-important job of keeping the participants sated with coffee, donuts, and box lunches. These students were Erin Phillips, Megan Batchelor, Jeremy Davis, and Paul Noe.

We divided the conference into two main components. The first was an inaugural series of slide-illustrated position papers on several key topics. This portion of the meeting was advertised and open to the public. The presenters each agreed to circulate drafts of their presentations in advance for the benefit of the other participants, and this was done by posting these drafts online. This public component of the conference was well attended, attracting representatives of the news media. For the public segment, a display case was set up in the Ferguson Forum containing illustrative examples of sixteenth-century Spanish and native American artifacts from the collections of the Alabama Museum of Natural History.

The second part of the conference was a closed-door workshop. In this workshop, the invited participants were divided into three working groups, each assigned to a general theme: (a) issues of historical interpretation (convened by Robbie Ethridge), (b) issues bearing on the physical environment (convened by Eugene Wilson), and (c) archaeological traces (convened by Gregory Waselkov). Each working group was provided with its own conference room, all within easy reach of one another and convenient to the Ferguson Forum, in which the larger group could convene as needed. Each of the three working groups was provided beforehand with a list of questions for investigation, intended as discussion starters. With this framework, the groups sequestered themselves, working until the third day of the meeting toward consensus on a variety of matters. For the final hours of the workshop the larger group was reassembled in the Ferguson Forum, and each working group presented its conclusions to the larger body, subjecting these conclusions to broader questions and commentary. Our sense was that substantial progress was made on each theme, and there was a good discussion of possibilities for follow-up meetings and a field survey to begin examining some of our results.

Reflecting the structure of the conference from which it came, this book is divided into two parts. Part 1, titled "Background," includes the ten original position papers presented at the public symposium on the first day of the conference, revised by their authors for publication. To this introductory section I have added an English translation by Dr. John Worth of Luys Hernández de Biedma's eyewitness account of the battle of Mabila. I include this short account for the benefit of readers who may not be familiar with the details of the battle, or for those who may simply need a refresher. Part 2, "Conference Results," includes papers representing the conclusions of each of the three workshop groups.

Although the workshop format in which these essays were originally conceived works toward consensus building, the reader will not find complete agreement among the authors on all topics. This is to be expected. I have not made any determined effort to reconcile these differences of opinion. On the contrary, they have been allowed to stand, as I believe they reflect legitimate scholarly differences and healthy debate. Much as Kathryn Braund notes in chapter 13 that the De Soto chroniclers of the sixteenth century have left us a story "with Rashomon-like, multiple realities," so too do our colleagues, who in spite of our extended conversations leave us with different takes on where De Soto went and what it all means.

These chapters represent a useful summary of the Mabila problem as it currently stands. The results should be helpful to all who have an interest in this fascinating topic. Offering this material to a broad readership has been my main objective. If Mabila were to be found using some of the strategies found in this book, that would be an additional benefit.

The book ends with a postscript, which is a brief update on the post-conference activities of some of the participants.

Finally, a note on spellings. There are no standard spellings for many proper names found in sixteenth-century sources, especially for the names of Indian towns, provinces, and rivers. In this volume, of the ones mentioned in the De Soto chronicles, I have used those in the Rangel account (but making the orthographic substitution "s" for "ç"), because in my opinion Rangel had a slightly better ear for what was being heard in the unwritten Indian languages than did his companions. I have spelled Hernando de Soto's surname *De Soto* when standing by itself, simply because that is the most common form in English-language sources. Others, legitimately, use *Soto.*

Notes

1. Higginbotham, *Mauvila.*

2. Hudson, *De Soto in Alabama,* 10.

3. Hudson, *Knights of Spain, Warriors of the Sun,* 481.

4. The sources for these map locations are Ball, *A Glance into the Great South-East,* 672–74; Blake, *A Proposed Route for the Hernando de Soto Expedition,* 13–14, map III-E; Brame, "De Soto in Alabama, 1540"; Curren, *The Route of the Soto Army through Alabama,* 45; Brannon, "The Route of De Soto"; DePratter, Hudson, and Smith, "The Hernando de Soto Expedition," 123; Lankford, "A New Look at DeSoto's Route through Alabama," 31–32; Pickett, *History of Alabama,* 36; and Swanton, *Final Report,* 16–40, 217. The location at Big Prairie Creek in Hale County was proposed for a time by Caleb Curren and George Lankford, and was subsequently abandoned after testing the site. See Curren, *The Protohistoric Period in Central Alabama.*

5. Brannon, "The Route of De Soto." In placing Mabila in southern Greene County between the Black Warrior and Tombigbee rivers, Brannon closely follows the earlier logic of T. H. Lewis ("The Narrative of the Expedition of Hernando de Soto by the Gentleman of Elvas," 189n1). See also the opinion of the Swiss ethnologist Albert Gatschet in *A Migration Legend of the Creek Indians,* 1: 110.

6. Badger and Clayton, *Alabama and the Borderlands.*

7. I wish to thank John Worth for his energetic assistance in assembling many of these resources.

I
Background

1

An Account of the Battle of Mabila, by an Eyewitness

Luys Hernández de Biedma, translated and edited by John E. Worth

[I have chosen to begin with John Worth's translation of the Biedma account for the benefit of readers who may be new to the Mabila story line or may need a refresher.[1] Biedma is chosen because it is short, is the earliest known account, is the least controversial, and is the only one we have in manuscript. This extract begins at Cosa and ends at Chicasa. —The editor.]

From here [the province of Cosa] we headed south, drawing near the coast of New Spain, and we passed several towns until we arrived at another province that was called Tascalusa, of which the cacique was an Indian so large that, to the opinion of all, he was a giant. He awaited us in peace in his town. We made much festivity for him when we arrived and jousted and had many horse races, although he appeared to think little of all this. Afterward we asked him to give us Indians to carry the burdens, and he responded that he was not accustomed to serving anyone, rather that all served him before. The Governor commanded that he not be allowed to go to his house, but rather that he should be detained there; as a result he felt that he was detained among us, and because of this he committed the ruin that afterward he inflicted on us.

Because he said that he could not give us anything there, that we should go to another town of his, which was called Mabila, and that there he would give us what we requested of him, we headed for there, arriving at a large river, which we believe is the river that flows into the bay of Achuse. Here we had news of how the boats of Narváez had arrived in need of water, and that here among these Indians remained a Christian who was called Don Teodoro, and a black man with him. They showed us a dagger that the Christian had. We were here two days making rafts to cross this river, during which the Indians killed a Christian who was one of the Governor's guard. In a fit of anger, he [the Governor] treated the cacique badly and told him that he was going to burn him unless he gave him the Indians that had killed the Christian. He said that in his town of Mabila he would give them to us.

This cacique was an Indian who brought along many other Indians who served him, and he always walked with a very large fly-flap made of feathers, which an Indian carried behind him in order to block the sun. We arrived at Mabila one day at nine in the morning. It was a small and very strongly palisaded town, and was situated on a plain. There were some Indian houses on the outside of the palisade, but we found that the Indians had demolished all of them to the ground in order to have the field more clear. Some important Indians came forth to us upon seeing us, and asked the Governor, through the interpreter, whether he wished to spend the night there on that plain or if he wished to enter within the town, and said that in the afternoon they would give us the Indians for the burdens. It seemed to the Governor that it was better to enter in the town with them, and he commanded us all to enter in there, and so we did it.

Having entered within, we were walking with the Indians, chatting, as if we had them in peace, because only three hundred or four hundred appeared there, but there were a good five thousand Indians in the town, hidden in the houses. We did not see them, nor did the Indians appear. As they made festivity for us, they began to do their dances and songs. In order to dissemble, they had fifteen or twenty women dance in front of us. After they had danced a little while, the cacique arose and entered one of those houses. The Governor sent a message for him to come outside, and he said that he did not wish to. The Captain of the Governor's guard entered to bring him out, and he saw so many people within, and so ready for war, that he thought it a good idea to go out and leave him, and he said to the Governor that those houses were full of Indians, all with bows and arrows, ready to do some treachery.

The Governor called to another Indian who was passing by there, who likewise refused to come. A nobleman who found himself alongside him seized him by the arm in order to bring him, and then he [the Indian] gave a pull that set himself free. Then he [the nobleman] put hand to his sword and gave him a slash that cut off an arm. Upon wounding this Indian, all began to shoot arrows at us, some from within the houses, through many loopholes that they had made, and others from outside. As we were so unprepared because we thought that we had met them in peace, we suffered so much damage that we were forced to leave, fleeing from the town, and all that the Indians brought us in our loads remained within, as they had unloaded it there. When the Indians saw us outside, they closed the gates of the town and began to beat their drums and to raise banners with a great yell, and to open our trunks and bundles and display from the top of the wall all that we had brought, since they had it in their possession.

As soon as we left the town, we mounted our horses and encircled the entire town, so that the Indians might not get away from us on any side, and the Governor decided that sixty or eighty of us should dismount, those of us who were best armed, and that we should form ourselves in four squads and assault the town on four sides, and that the first to enter should set fire to the houses, so that they might not do us more damage from within, and that we should give the horses to other soldiers who were not armed, so that if some Indians should come forth from the town in order to flee, they might overtake them. We entered within the town and set fire, where a quantity of Indians were burned, and all our supplies were burned, so that not one thing remained.

We fought that day until it was night, without one Indian surrendering to us, rather they fought like fierce lions. Of those who came out, we killed them all, some with fire, others with swords, others with lances. Later, near nightfall, only three Indians remained, and they took those twenty women that they had brought to dance and placed them in front of themselves. The women crossed their hands, making signs to the Christians that they should take them. The Christians came to take them, and they turned aside, and the three Indians who were behind them shot arrows at the Christians. We killed two of the Indians, and one who remained alone, in order not to surrender to us, climbed a tree that was in the wall itself, and removed the cord from the bow and attached it to his neck and to a branch of the tree and hanged himself.

This day the Indians killed more than twenty of our men, and two hundred and fifty of us escaped with wounds, for we had seven hundred and sixty arrow wounds. We treated ourselves that night with the adipose tissue of the dead Indians themselves, since we had no other medicine, because all had burned that day. We stayed here treating ourselves twenty-seven or twenty-eight days, and thank God we all healed. We took the women and divided them among the most seriously wounded, in order that they might serve them.

We heard through news from the Indians that we were up to forty leagues from the sea. Many wished that the Governor would go to the sea, because they [the Indians] gave us news of the brigantines, but he did not dare, for the month of November was already half over and it was very cold, and he felt it advisable to look for a land where he might find provisions in order to be able to winter. In this [land] there were none, because it was a land of little food. We turned again north and walked ten or twelve days' journey, with great hardship from cold and from waters that we crossed on foot, until we arrived at a province, well-provisioned and with plenty of food, where we could halt while the fury of the winter passed, because more snows fell there than in Castille.

Note

1. This material was previously published, with minor editorial differences, in Clayton, Knight, and Moore, *De Soto Chronicles,* 1: 232–36.

2

The Battle of Mabila in Historical Perspective

Lawrence A. Clayton

One of the first questions I asked myself when preparing this chapter will perhaps sound subversive: who cares about the battle of Mabila, and, secondarily, even if we have some interest, who cares on what abandoned field or overgrown, weed-infested lake in south-central Alabama it may be located?

These are seditious questions indeed for readers such as professional archaeologists, geographers, and historians, as well as aficionados of all stripes, desirous of the latest developments in finding Mabila. It is similar to asking Da Vinci code fanatics, both pro and con, who cares about finding the Holy Grail?

Nonetheless, as we get closer to finding Mabila, we ought to ask these questions. We need to make our search worthwhile, in the many nuances of that word. Otherwise it boils down to a simple exercise in antiquarianism, or perhaps an effort to satisfy a local chamber of commerce interested in promoting tourism in county x or y or a local historical society curious to prove that town or city z or q really has a long history that reaches all the way back to the great De Soto expedition that came through Alabama in the summer and fall of 1540, four hundred and sixty-eight years ago from the time of this writing.

Why indeed do we want to be associated with, or know more about, a battle almost half a millennium ago that had no redeeming value (at least none that I have discovered over the years)? It did not end an evil, or defend a good, or promote a value we esteem. Let me add some perspective here as we search not only for the site of Mabila but for its ultimate significance in the long historical record of man on earth.

In the summer of 2006 while I was visiting one of my daughters and her family in Portland, Oregon, we all went to Cannon Beach for a few days. I then proceeded to drag my family to Fort Clatsop, where Meriwether Lewis and William Clark wintered in 1805 and 1806 after crossing the continent on their monumental expedition. Actually, I'm being unfair; the family went quite willingly, since I have long been known to have an affinity for visiting historical sites on travels and they have become accustomed to it.

Let us cut to the quick here. The Lewis and Clark expedition accomplished an admirable scientific end, observing the continent, its people, and its flora and fauna in meticulous detail, harming no one in particular, being careful to observe and record rather than thrust and conquer, which was the goal of the De Soto expedition. What redeeming value was there in slaughtering native Americans, stripping them of their livelihood, their lives, their mothers and daughters, and forcing them to submit to a foreign conqueror?

As I walked around the museum and site of Fort Clatsop, and as I finally read *Undaunted Courage* by Steven Ambrose, I discovered an immense appreciation for the Corps of Discovery.[1] As I contemplate Hernando de Soto and his epic streak across the New World, I find—at first glance—little other than greed, cupidity, and brutality inflicted on native Americans with a ferocity that still appalls us today when we read the firsthand accounts of the conquest of America. I am not excusing our forebears, especially in the second half of the nineteenth century when they, too—George Custer and his troops excepted—practiced a form of genocide on the frontier of North America. Lewis and Clark may have been the outriders of the arrival of Euro-American civilization on the frontier, but they did not conceptualize themselves as conquerors.

I must admit a prejudice here. I have finished writing a biography of Father Bartolomé de las Casas (1485–1566), who was the defender/protector of American Indians, the author of the Black Legend, and the man most associated with indicting the Spanish conquistadors for the very evils I have just attached to De Soto.[2] Las Casas was, in fact, as I label him, the "anti-conquistador" who championed the rights and liberties of Indian peoples in the face of the Spanish onslaught, even with all his warts, which were considerable.

De Soto and Las Casas were at opposite ends of the spectrum of the Spanish conquest of the New World. They may have crossed paths at some time in the Americas, and if they did, I am certain Las Casas would have lumped De Soto into the same band of criminals led by Francisco Pizarro, who ravaged the Peruvian empire of the Inca in the 1530s and murdered the emperor Atahualpa in return for an immense ransom in gold and silver.[3] And De Soto was among the principal beneficiaries, a lieutenant in Pizarro's army as it brought the Incas to their knees. Pizarro and his followers were excoriated by Las Casas, held up as the worst of the worst, and no doubt the bold

De Soto, before he perished on the banks of the Mississippi in 1542, was held equally accountable.

As we explore the context of the battle of Mabila a bit more, it begins to take on an aspect much wider than a simple battle. It lasted for a full day and into the night and was indeed not simple in its origins and development on this edge of the frontier between European outriders and native American peoples.[4] Nor was it important because, as is so often advertised, it was the largest battle between Europeans and European descendants and Indians east of the Mississippi, including Andrew Jackson's conquest of the Upper Creek Indians at the Battle of Horseshoe Bend in the spring of 1814.

It becomes apparent that the battle of Mabila was much larger than an episode in the De Soto *entrada* (or armed expedition) into North America, more than the efforts of Chief Tascalusa and his people to crush the invaders, and more than the valor shown by the invaders, who, in spite of their motives, demonstrated the capacity of the Spanish soldier of the sixteenth century to prevail. It is more than a mystery that brought together this conference on the search for Mabila.

The battle symbolizes two distinct sides of the Spanish coin of the era of Conquest: one image is of a Spanish soldier, sword in hand, crushing the Indian beneath his foot, claiming "a la espada y al compás, y más, y más, y más!" (the sword and the compass, and more, more, more!);[5] the other image is of the fiery Las Casas, standing between Indians and the soldiers, hand up to shield them from further abuse, debasement, and destruction.

For, as many appreciate, and perhaps others are first realizing, the Spanish conquest was indeed a nuanced affair. Mabila was but one battle of the many waged by Spaniards on the Indians, beginning as early as 1493. In fact, this first "battle," or campaign, was not even a battle about which we know any details, nor was it a Spanish victory. The first battle went to the Indians. When Columbus's *Santa Maria* shipwrecked on Christmas Eve 1492 on the north coast of Hispaniola, Columbus was forced to leave some of his crew behind when he returned to Spain. So was born the little settlement of La Navidad.[6] Columbus returned to the islands in 1494 and searched for his crew and settlement. The settlement was gone, the crew nowhere to be found. The Indians had taken care of these early looters, who were interested largely in gold and the Taínos' work and women.

We are used to framing the Encounter (a more fashionable label for the Conquest) within the spectacular campaigns of a Hernán Cortéz in Mexico or a Francisco Pizarro in Peru, all driven by Spanish steel while the Indian will to resist was undermined by such killers as smallpox. Indeed, a best-seller like *Guns, Germs, and Steel: The Fates of Human Societies* by Jared M. Diamond reinforces that stereotype.[7] But in-depth research in the last several generations has probed more closely, and in many of the battles and clashes of the Conquest native Americans gave as much as they got, diseases played only small roles, and it was not invariably European weapons and tactics that prevailed. George Raudzens's edited volume, *Technology, Disease, and Colonial Conquests, Sixteenth to Eighteenth Centuries: Essays Reappraising the Guns and Germs Theories,* demonstrates how guns and germs certainly helped carry the day, but the simple growth of the European population also ground down Indian resistance.[8] It was demographics, not arquebuses and fevers, that prevailed.

We know that Indian rivalries and subjugated peoples also contributed mightily to the Spanish victories. Neither Cortéz nor Pizarro would have had much luck in their adventuring had they not made strategic alliances with disaffected peoples within the very hearts of the Aztec and Inca empires. That the Spaniards were incredibly bold and a people trained by half a millennium of fighting Moors to know and practice warfare with great skill and courage is undeniable. They were groomed to win, and their leaders, such as De Soto, did not enjoy the title of Adelantado for nothing. It comes from the root word *adelante,* which means "forward." But it is preposterous to think that Pizarro conquered the Inca Empire with 162 men and a few horses. Disaffections, civil war, and internecine and interregional rivalries ran like fissures through the Inca political and military empire, and bold, wily, ambitious, totally ruthless warriors like Pizarro exploited these divisions brilliantly. That Pizarro had learned from Cortéz in Mexico, and that Cortéz had learned from his experiences in the islands, all added to the thread of experience that ran through the Spanish conquistadors. De Soto served both Pizarro in Peru and other successful conquistadors in Nicaragua and Panama. He was bold to a fault and knew how to exploit Indian weaknesses. Providence put him in Peru with Pizarro, where he was rewarded with a fortune in Inca gold and silver. Less providential was his appointment as governor of Cuba and Adelantado of La Florida in 1537 and 1538. He anticipated another Peru; what he found was a vast country, thinly populated compared to the highlands of Peru or the central valley of Mexico, and not particularly rich in the way he desired.

At the same time De Soto crossed the southern Appalachians into Georgia and then Alabama in the spring and summer of 1540, the Dominican friar Bartolomé de las Casas embarked on the fleet returning from Veracruz on the coast of New Spain (Mexico) to Seville, with a stop in Havana to make the final preparations for the long transatlantic crossing. De Soto battled the Indians of Alabama at Mabila in the fall (October) of the year, while Las Casas was back in Spain in winter (December), preparing for the monumental task of stopping the destruction of Indians by fellow countrymen such as Hernando de Soto.

De Soto's star was descending, while Las Casas's was rising.[9] In 1542 Emperor Charles V (King Charles I of Spain) signed the New Laws of 1542 that radically restricted the privileges and rights the conquistadors and settlers had largely taken for granted in subduing and governing the Indies and the Indians. Indian slavery was prohibited, the encomiendas were largely stripped from the descendants of the encomenderos, and the worst and most abusive practices of the settlers were curtailed or forbidden. At the heart of the New Laws of 1542 was Las Casas, the spiritual, if not in many ways the actual, author of the laws. That the New Laws produced a violent reaction among the settler/conquistador class across the Indies attests to their vitality and profoundly reformist nature. In New Spain the officials charged with enforcing the New Laws simply did not publish or try to enforce them in the face of near universal rebuke. In Peru, the Pizarrista faction rose in actual rebellion and killed the king's representative. It would be several years and several wars later before the Crown reestablished firm control over Peru. Las Casas himself was in 1544 appointed Bishop of Chiapa in southern Mexico in recognition of his service to the Crown as protector of American Indians.[10]

Two years earlier, in 1542, De Soto had died as his depleted army crisscrossed the South, maybe even plunging as far north as the Midwest, looking for another Atahualpa, another Peru, another Mexico. Mabila was the turning point of his expedition's *entrada* into the land the Spaniards knew as La Florida, or *tierra incognita del norte.* After that battle, he never recaptured the élan or momentum that fueled his desire for fame and fortune.

Here we need to take stock of how that battle fit into the larger scheme of empire presided over by Charles V. We tend to view the expedition of Hernando De Soto rather myopically. Hundreds of skirmishes and scores of major battles left trails of blood and memories of anguish, defeat, and triumph in their wake. Mabila was but one of them. For those of us in the United States, it has taken on an importance perhaps disproportionate to how the battle fit into the minds of contemporaries of De Soto who either fought in the battle or read about it years later through accounts or chronicles recorded by either eyewitnesses or historians at a distance from the actual events.

While Mabila was a guarded victory for the Spanish army, it cost De Soto a great deal. It was, in fact, a bloody win, achieved at such great expense of dead, wounded, and momentum that it did not emerge in the chronicles of the time as something worth remembering. When De Soto died in May 1542 along the banks of the great Mississippi, his expedition had already failed. So it is not surprising that the battle of Mabila was but a footnote in the Spain of Charles V. Grand victories were celebrated. Defeats were buried.

Charles V, the Holy Roman emperor, was more concerned with defending his empire across Europe and the Mediterranean from Suleiman the Magnificent and his robust Ottoman Empire. All the while he was dealing with his main competitors, the French, in Europe, as well as the English under the volatile King Henry VIII. Add the ambitious popes, and the Reformation triggered by the German Augustinian friar Martin Luther for good measure, and one realizes that while the progress of the conquest and subjugation of the Indies sometimes rose to the fore of the emperor's attention, it did not happen often. A few Spaniards lost in the wilderness of the Indies, a band, or "army," making its way through vast plains, mountains, and jungles, conquering and enslaving a strange people—these reports appeared as blips on the emperor's radar, far off and of small consequence. What did make a difference was the treasure, for the wily *adelantados* such as Hernán Cortéz and Francisco Pizarro sent back much gold and silver looted from the Aztecs and Incas to ensure the emperor's good will.

So, while the doings of captains and soldiers in the far Indies was not inconsequential, it just seemed to Charles in the late 1530s and early 1540s that other more pressing business needed to take precedence. The historic Council of Trent called by Pope Paul III in 1545 to deal with the Reformation that had so broken the unity of Christendom was but one example. It was almost precisely at this juncture that the remnants of the De Soto expedition floated and stumbled back into New Spain in September 1543. Coincidentally, totally apart from the De Soto odyssey, one of the greatest tales of the Encounter was published in Spain in 1542.

Álvar Núñez Cabeza de Vaca, one of four survivors of a failed expedition that had landed on the Florida coast in 1528 led by Pánfilo de Narváez, published his memoirs called *Naufragios,* or *Shipwrecks.* There he recounted seven years of wandering through the "wilderness" of what is today Florida to Texas and northern Mexico before finding his way back to the northern reaches of New Spain in 1537.[11]

Following the failed Narváez expedition, Hernando de Soto and his army sailed from Spain in 1538 bound for Cuba and La Florida. De Soto's expedition, in fact, represented but one of numerous Spanish probes and *entradas* manned by Spanish mariners, soldiers, adventurers, friars, bishops, and an occasional representative of Emperor Charles V into the world we now know as the Americas.

The same year that De Soto's expedition sailed, Charles's attention had been drawn momentarily to the Indies. In 1538 Pope Paul III issued a decree,

Sublimis Deus, which championed the American Indians as perfectly rational people, quite capable of accepting and understanding Christianity (the Catholic brand, of course). Charles thought this a reasonable premise but banned the bull in his empire since the pope had overstepped the boundaries of what Charles thought a pope should be adjudicating. The affairs of the Indies—both those of the Church and the Crown—were the business of the king of Spain, and the pope was instructed to get his nose out of the tent.

How did the battle of Mabila fit into this "big picture"? How do the chroniclers fit into the context of the expanding Spanish empire of the sixteenth century?

Today the narratives of conquest are analyzed for more than mere narrative accounts of an expedition's doings. Rolena Adorno has described Cabeza de Vaca's *Naufragios* as a source of insight and for discussions into areas such as "quest and adventure, freedom and bondage, empire and colonialism, miracles and shamanism, sacrifice and survival, transcendental good and evil, or human gain and loss."[12] She also mentions "mediation, marginalization, liminality, and multilingualism" as subjects springing forth from a deeper study of not only Cabeza de Vaca but also his contemporaries, such as the very chroniclers of the De Soto expedition.[13]

In a sense, the chronicles, and the chroniclers, were reborn and rediscovered in the twentieth century as historians, language scholars, anthropologists, and others shifted their gaze from a Eurocentric view of the world to one more focused on the Americas, and as they developed new prisms (postmodernism, deconstructionism, and so on) to view and interpret the past. The failed battle of Mabila, so little regarded by Charles (if he even knew of it) as he dealt with Protestant heretics, Muslim expansionism, and French competitors, emerges as a touchstone and entry into our own history. The chronicles become the keys to "finding Mabila" in two ways: one, finding the actual physical location of the site; and two, informing us in a larger sense of issues that transcend time as Adorno and other recent scholars have suggested. From the chronicles and the story of De Soto and Mabila arise questions of good and evil, morality, truth, justice, and, indeed, humanity's correct relationship to God. On the surface, however, they tell the story of an odyssey of near epic proportions. That story is compelling enough by itself to draw us into this drama that played out in the fall of 1540.

While De Soto was attempting to carve out his new empire in the wilderness of La Florida from the hides of American Indians, Las Casas was moving in the exact opposite direction, defending them with equal conviction and fervor. The New Laws of 1542 marked the continuation of a spectacular trajectory that Las Casas had embarked on years before as protector of American Indians. As noted above, the open rebellion and sedition in the colonies that greeted the New Laws only confirm the reformist message and spirit of the laws. While some Spaniards like De Soto waged detestable war on native Americans, others like Las Casas fought the conquistadors and defended Indians from within the context of Christendom, helping create the modern origins of human rights, based on Christian doctrine and natural law. Instead of submission demanded by the De Sotos of the era, Las Casas and his fellow activists thought of freedom and liberty. Instead of crass exploitation, Las Casas and other brother Dominicans and Franciscans promoted evangelization and conversion. The struggle continued for the rest of the sixteenth century.[14]

All was not black and white in this competition for the minds, bodies, and souls of the American Indians, not to speak of their silver and gold. Like all great contentions, it was settled only in part. Neither De Soto nor Las Casas triumphed in absolute terms.

De Soto died along the Mississippi River and his body was sunk ignominiously in its deep, flowing waters to prevent desecration of the Adelantado of La Florida by native Americans. After fourteen more months of wandering to the west of the Mississippi searching for an overland route to Mexico, the remnants of the once great expedition returned to the Mississippi and oared down the river into the Gulf of Mexico, fleeing from the abysmal defeat they had suffered in their four-year odyssey across much of the southeastern United States.

No sooner had Las Casas reached his bishopric in Chiapa than he was engaged in a bitter dispute with the encomendero/conquistador class. He excommunicated virtually all of the most offensive ones; some emboldened ones then attacked him in his quarters, and as modern slang goes, it all went south from there. Las Casas forbade his fellow Dominicans and priests from hearing the confessions of the most unrepentant settlers, they called for his resignation, and Las Casas returned to Spain in the late 1540s, determined to wage his war against the encomenderos all across the Indies by appealing directly to the Crown.

In 1550 Charles V stopped all expeditions of exploration and conquest and convened a scholarly committee to rule on the justness and legality of the conquest of the Indies. It was an unprecedented moment: an empire on the make stopping the very engine of expansion and profit to debate the higher issues of justice, spirituality, liberty, and the nature of humanity. That much of the New World had already been conquered and incorporated into the growing Spanish Empire makes the convening of this committee perhaps a

Figure 2.1. Bartolomé de las Casas, in a portrait in the Capitol painted by Constantino Brumidi in the mid-nineteenth century. One can easily note the obvious symbolism of Las Casas's title as "protector of American Indians" that inspired the painter. Photo by Andy Tuttle, by permission of Stephen T. Ayers, Architect of the Capitol.

bit disingenuous. De Soto's brother conquistadors had already done much of their work, but the reformers also had their day.

As we put the battle of Mabila into historical context, it is obvious from this short overview that the battle represented more than the clash of arms. In the context of the times, it was a waypoint in the struggle for human rights, for decency, and for liberty. Without Mabila, without the demographic disaster that befell the Indians of the islands of the Caribbean within a generation of the Columbian voyages, without the capture and murder of the Inca emperor Atahualpa at Cajamarca in Peru, without the methodical killing of Aztecs in Tenochtitlan in 1520 and 1521 by Cortéz, and without the cruelty

Figure 2.2. Bartolomé de las Casas, late in his life, in a portrait painted sometime between 1548 and 1558, by the artist N. Albítez. Photo by L. Clayton.

of the encomienda we would have had no Las Casas and fellow reformers. Nobility is always born in adversity, and the nobility of purpose that Las Casas and like-minded thinkers represented is testimony to how the quality of goodness is so often, and remarkably, born and reborn in trying times.

In modern times, Mabila has taken on new meaning. In the nineteenth century De Soto was resurrected from the historical record and given a patina of respect and even admiration as one of the early European explorers of these young United States. In the search for a myth, American historians sought ties with men such as Columbus and De Soto, whose larger-than-life deeds were seen as prophetic of a new people on the make, themselves embarked on an enterprise of Herculean proportions, making a modern republic that would rise to world dominance.

The romance with De Soto continued into the twentieth century, at least through the 1930s with the United States De Soto Expedition Commission's report on the expedition's route through the United States (see chapter 10, this volume). By the second half of the twentieth century, archaeologists were becoming more actively engaged in trying to determine the De Soto route, but they were motivated by a different set of goals: the use of the De Soto chronicles as snapshots into the native American culture of the period. Led by such anthropologists as Charles Hudson of the University of Georgia, they sought to marry the archaeological record with the historical accounts with precision. If they could but fix places on the route described by the chroniclers with certainty to archaeological sites, then the chronicles could help them re-create the culture of that region. They slowly began to nail down the pieces. The winter camp of the expedition in 1539–40 was discovered in downtown Tallahassee, while progress was made on the route through the Carolinas and down the southern Smokies into Tennessee, Georgia, and then Alabama.[15]

But the battle site of the great confrontation between the Spaniards and the Indians at Mabila remained elusive. In the search for precision, all of the chronicles were once again retranslated or edited and annotated with almost clinical precision to achieve absolute accuracy with the originals—the goal being, of course, theoretically unattainable.[16] De Soto himself was revised by modern historiography and his darker side as a brutal and ruthless adventurer who represented the ugly side of an empire on the rise in the sixteenth century came to the fore.

At the same time Las Casas was rescued from relative historical anonymity by historians of many nationalities in the mid-twentieth century. The author of the Black Legend was revealed as an imperfect but passionate defender of American Indians. The elusive Mabila emerged as a representative example of a European-Indian "encounter," a term much favored by postmodern scholars who preferred it to the culturally loaded Conquest. But the term *encounter* is a banal and sanitized word for what happened at Mabila, a bloody battle between an invading army and a people attempting to defend their lives and freedom.

This battle was but one event in the long and often violent history of the Encounter/Conquest. Many, if not most, of the Spanish soldiers were no doubt ashamed of what they did at Mabila. The slaughter of Tascalusa's people continued until nightfall; few were spared from the sword and the lance and the flames.

Read one chronicler's comments on the general nature of Spanish conquistadors in the Indies:

> As to where they were going, neither the Governor [De Soto] nor they knew, except that his intent was to find some land so rich that it might sate his greed. . . . Oh, lost people; oh, diabolical greed; oh, bad conscience; oh, unfortunate soldiers; how you did not understand in how much danger you walked, and how wasted your lives and without tranquility your souls! . . . Listen well, Catholic reader, and do not lament any less the conquered Indians than their Christian conquerors, or killers of themselves and of those others, and attend to the incidents of this ill-governed Governor, instructed in the school of Pedrarias de Avila, in the dissipation and devastation of the Indians of Castilla de Oro, graduate in the killing of the natives of Nicaragua and canonized in Peru, according to the Order of the Pizarros. And freed from all those hellish passages, and having gone to Spain loaded with gold, neither as a bachelor nor a married man could he rest, nor did he know how to, without returning to the Indies to spill human blood.[17]

Whether these were the words of Rodrigo Rangel, the private secretary of De Soto on the expedition who left us his account, or the interpolation of Gonzalo Fernández de Oviedo y Váldes, the sixteenth-century historian who had the Rangel account before him and included it in his massive *Historia General y Natural de las Indias,* we cannot be sure. Oviedo may have interviewed Rangel in Santo Domingo, but Oviedo himself authored the narrative and sometimes included his own comments, which ranged far and wide over the moral, legal, ethical, and religious issues involved in the conquest and settlement of the Indies. Some readers find these comments extraneous and discursive. In fact, they can give us valuable insight into the frame of mind of those participating in the events. Oviedo himself was a conquistador and longtime traveler and resident of the Indies and thus brought an eyewitness's validation to his observations.

The account of the end of the battle by Luys Hernández de Biedma, a royal official (factor) assigned to the expedition, is no more noble in its recollection (see chapter 1, this volume). The original was composed about 1544 as testimony before the Council of the Indies in Spain. It is often thought of as the most "reliable" of all the chronicles. In it, Biedma says that the Indians "fought like fierce lions," without surrendering. But "we killed them all," he says coldly, "some with fire, others with swords, others with lances," until the last defender remaining alive hung himself from a tree with his bowstring.[18]

Two decades later, when the Tristán de Luna expedition (1559–61) went ashore at Pensacola and sent reconnoitering expeditions into the interior to the north—and a number of De Soto's veterans were on the Luna expedition—no mention was made of Mabila in their reports and chronicles.[19] It sank from history for over four centuries, but it needs to be remembered, and it needs to be located to give us a piece of ground, a small lake, a place where we can once again rekindle our ties with our past. Perhaps it is not the hallowed ground of a Gettysburg, but it opens a window into the past, revealing a panorama of what the human heart is capable of feeling and doing, for great evil and for great good.

Notes

1. Ambrose, *Undaunted Courage.*

2. L. A. Clayton, *Bartolomé de las Casas,* manuscript submitted to The University of Alabama Press.

3. For a good history of this conquest where De Soto marched with Pizarro see Hemming, *The Conquest of the Incas.* For details on De Soto's life, see Lockhart, *Men of Cajamarca.*

4. For the best overall study of this expanding Spanish frontier in North America, see Weber, *The Spanish Frontier in North America.*

5. Vargas Machuca, *Milicia y Descripción de las Indias.*

6. A good introduction to Columbus and some of the vast literature on the subject, including these early contacts, is Phillips and Phillips, *The Worlds of Christopher Columbus;* see also Deagan and Cruxent, *Columbus's Outpost among the Tainos.*

7. Diamond, *Guns, Germs and Steel.*

8. Raudzens, *Technology, Disease, and Colonial Conquest.*

9. Two modern biographies of De Soto are Hudson, *Knights of Spain, Warriors of the Sun,* and Duncan, *Hernando de Soto.*

10. The literature on Las Casas is almost overwhelming. "Standard" biographies include those by Gutierrez, *Las Casas;* Wagner and Parish, *The Life and Writings of Bartolomé de las Casas;* Alvaro Huerga, *Fray Bartolomé de las Casas* (vol. 1 of the *Obras Completas*); and the many works, in English at any rate, by Lewis Hanke, Helen Rand Parish, and Benjamin Keen where their introductory notes are often little less than mini-biographies. See, for example, Hanke, *The Spanish Struggle for Justice in the Conquest of America;* Freide and Keen, *Bartolomé de las Casas in History;* and Parish,

Bartolomé de las Casas. For those who read Spanish and want the complete works of Las Casas, see *Fray Bartolomé de las Casas: Obras Completas.* And for the latest works as of this writing, see Castro, *Another Face of Empire,* and Merediz and Arias, *Teaching Las Casas.*

11. As a close student of *Naufragios* observed, Cabeza de Vaca and the three companions who survived with him experienced "the areas of the future United States as no natives of Europe or Africa had previously done," traversing from the Gulf Coast of northern Florida all the way to modern Mexico. See Adorno, "Álvar Nuñez Cabeza de Vaca, Relación."

12. Ibid.

13. Clayton, Knight, and Moore, *The De Soto Chronicles.*

14. The photograph of this painting (also a photograph) was taken by L. Clayton, Managua, Nicaragua, July 2004, in the LaSalle Brothers Retreat at a meeting of Dominican historians on Las Casas. The original is located in Ottawa, Canada, according to the curator who put on this display of Las Casas portraits for this meeting.

15. See Ewen, "Anhaica."

16. See Clayton, Knight, and Moore, *De Soto Chronicles,* 1:xxvii–xxx, for the goals of the editors.

17. Clayton, Knight, and Moore, *De Soto Chronicles,* 2: 289–90.

18. Ibid., 1: 235–36.

19. For the Luna expedition, see Priestley, *The Luna Papers.* The complete Luna Papers are on-line at the Florida Heritage Collection, http:*//purl.fcla.edu/fcla/dl/SNWF000009.pdf.* See the PALMM Project at http://www.palmm.fcla.edu.

3
How Historical Are the De Soto Chronicles?

George E. Lankford

To raise the question of the historical accuracy of the chronicles of the sixteenth-century expedition of Hernando de Soto is to confront a pragmatic problem in reconstructing the past. Although the issues embedded in the question are philosophically complex, the problem is not, for it is the fundamental problem of trustworthiness. To what extent can the four chronicles serve as accurate descriptions of the events of the first major European journey through the Southeast in 1539–43?

The problem is remarkably similar to that of the historicity of the gospels of the New Testament. Although there are four accounts enshrined in the canonical authority of the New Testament of the Christian church, there are other accounts known by full documents or fragments or references to their former existence. So, too, there are four De Soto chronicles in full or partial text, but there are fragments like the Cañete and Argote documents that hint at the possibility that more accounts may still lurk in archives and family collections, awaiting discovery.[1] The problem of historicity in both chronicles and gospels is made inescapable because of their fourness. There are obvious disagreements of fact among the four gospels and the four chronicles, and they cannot be harmonized satisfactorily.

Moreover, even a cursory examination of the two foursomes reveals a categorical split in each. In the gospels the similarity of three (Matthew, Mark, and Luke) has been noted from the beginning, leading to their characterization as "synoptic" gospels. The fourth gospel stands apart from the others in details, structure, and language. Among the four chronicles, Garcilaso de la Vega's *La Florida del Inca* has always been recognized as different because of its length, details, and narrative quality. Recognizing these disharmonies at a superficial level is simple, but explaining them is extraordinarily complex.

Scholars who have devoted themselves to gospel research have through the last two centuries developed a set of questions and procedures that have guided the discussion, and that framework may be useful in organizing this survey of the debates over the historicity of the De Soto chronicles. The first issue is the history of the document, insofar as that can be determined—its age, editions, versions, translations, and publications. The second concern is the identification of the author, which in many cases has turned out to be an unanswerable question but a fruitful inquiry nonetheless. The third concern is to identify the literary genre into which the document falls, an important issue in determining the best approach to interpretation. With the gospels this is almost tautological, since they define the "gospel" genre, but the question serves to highlight the document's literary characteristics. In the case of the De Soto chronicles, the question of genre has proved to be very important. The final area of examination—empirical analysis of the text—is a multifaceted one. The issue of language, which is important in gospel research for helping determine the date and author, is useful in the chronicles primarily for translation problems. Other textual approaches, however, have been important in the discussion of the chronicles: the identification and separation of the contents into coherent units, the determination of antecedent sources of the material (both other chronicles and external influences), and the elucidation of the presuppositions and peculiar emphases of the authors.

This list of issues will serve as an organizational guide in summarizing the conclusions, debates, and problems that have emerged thus far in the recent examination of the Soto chronicles. This survey will not try to be exhaustive in examining the work of all the scholars on the topic but will attempt to include all the major issues of the discussion.

Dating of the Chronicles

Biedma

Only one of the four chronicles passes muster by modern historical standards as a primary source. Luys Hernández de Biedma's "Relation of the Island of Florida" still exists as a copy of an original 1544 document in the Archivo General de Indias in Seville.[2]

Elvas/Burgos

"The Account by a Gentleman of Elvas" was published in Portuguese in Evora in 1557.[3] Fifty years later, in 1609, it was published in English and has remained generally available.[4] It must be considered a secondary source despite its early date because it was published as an "as-told-to" account, and there is no extant primary source document.

Rangel/Oviedo

The report of Rodrigo Rangel, which would have been an important primary source as the diary of an eyewitness, does not exist as an original document. It is purported to be embedded—with unknown accuracy and in a fragmentary state—in the text of the second volume of Gonzalo Fernández Oviedo y Váldes's *Historia General y Natural de las Indias.*[5] A draft of the volume was apparently completed before 1549 and left with the publisher in Spain, but it was not published until 1851.[6]

Garcilaso

Finally, *La Florida del Inca* has little claim to be a primary source, other than the author's assertion that he learned his material from a survivor of the expedition.[7] It was written in Spain over a period from the 1560s to 1589, when it was probably completed. The author, Garcilaso de la Vega, El Inca, was born in Peru the year the De Soto expedition began. The lengthy work was published in Spain in 1605.

These basic facts make it clear that only one primary source for the expeditions exists, the Biedma chronicle, the briefest of the four. The others, as they exist at this point, are secondary sources, which means that any claim to historical veracity must be established by scholarly endeavor.

Authorship

Biedma

About Luys Hernández de Biedma there is little to say. The details of his life both before and after the expedition are unknown. He apparently served as the king's factor on the expedition, and he was therefore one of three such officials whose duties included reporting to the Crown. It is thus no surprise that he seems to have kept notes on the journey and apparently composed his report soon after the expedition's arrival in Mexico, knowing that he would be called upon for an official account.[8] Having submitted his report, he vanished from history.

Elvas/Burgos

If Biedma has only a faint presence in history, "the Fidalgo of Elvas" has none. His identity is unknown. The name on the chronicle is at best a nom de plume, at worst a hoax. Because the book was published in Portugal and the author identified as a gentleman from that country, the name has generally been supposed to represent one of the eleven Portuguese officers on the expedition. That supposition has been called into question, however, as will be seen.

Rangel/Oviedo

Rodrigo Rangel has a firmer footing in the historical record. He was listed as De Soto's personal secretary on the expedition, and Oviedo claimed that he had kept a diary on the journey and made a report to the Audiencia at Santo Domingo after the return from La Florida. The Audiencia then ordered him to turn his materials over to Oviedo, who was the commander of the fortress at Santo Domingo.[9] Rangel later became the mayor of Pánuco in Mexico, but he never had any further control over the fate of his chronicle, which had gone to Spain with Oviedo in 1546.

Garcilaso

The author of *La Florida del Inca* has never been in question. Garcilaso's authorial voice is present throughout, even when he claims to be passing on narratives and details learned from his informants who had been on the expedition. The only issue regarding authorship is the degree to which Garcilaso was really transmitting the information he had gathered from the oral tradition of De Soto's men.

Genre

In regard to the literary genre of the four gospels, there is little question, since the four canonical New Testament books, together with the other lesser-known similar writings, define the "gospel" genre. In clear contrast to that situation, the question of genre classification for the Soto chronicles is not only a topic for debate; it also is a clear signal of important differences between them.

Biedma

The most straightforward genre is that of Biedma, who produced a bureaucratic report with details of geography and numbers of leagues and casualties.

Elvas/Burgos

In Elvas, by contrast, what has been produced is a popular narrative. That is suggested by the fact of early publication by the private printer André de Burgos, but it is demonstrated by the expanded narratives of events and personal characterizations of various figures. The expedition in Elvas became a much longer story with entertainment value, an account suitable for sale in the book market.

Rangel/Oviedo

If the Rangel passages in Oviedo's work are taken as transmission of Rangel's own writing, then the genre appears fairly close to the Elvas narrative, for it is full of details, characterizations, and anecdotes. The genre question becomes confused in this case, however, because the Rangel account is embedded (if it is truly quoted) within the larger framework of Oviedo's production of a "general history" of the New World. One feature of that history is the highlighting of moral issues involved in Spain's treatment of native peoples in the New World and the behavior of her representatives, the conquistadors. With two authors involved in this narrative, it is probably fair to suggest that the genre is confused, since it consists of a popular narrative serving the more solemn purposes of a historian with moral arguments suffusing his work.[10]

Garcilaso

In *La Florida del Inca* the popular narrative of Elvas and Rangel has been raised to an altogether new level. Garcilaso's work deserves to be considered a historical novel, "an adventure tale with a hero," as Galloway has termed it.[11] David Henige has classified it simply as a "literary history" or "fiction posing as history."[12] Whether the genre emphasis should be placed on the historical side or the literary side is a serious issue that has resulted in much discussion and will probably continue to do so.

Textual Analysis

Examination of the chronicles for the purpose of identifying separate clusters of text, possibly indicating different original sources, has been done by various scholars with somewhat different conclusions.

Biedma's account has received little attention from this viewpoint. It seems generally agreed that it is what it appears to be: a single-source primary document quickly written and quickly placed in reposit.

The Elvas document is another story. It appears to be a Portuguese document, in that it was published in Portuguese, bears a Portuguese nom de plume, and has two major episodes focused on the Portuguese (an account of the initial muster when the Portuguese outshone the Spanish forces, and the appointment of André de Vasconcelos as master of horsemen). These Portuguese aspects have led to the traditional supposition that the anonymous author was one of the Portuguese officers, an assumption that leaves hanging the question of why there was a need for anonymity, especially when the narrative could use some authoritative backing.

Galloway has summarized the arguments supporting a view that the account is rooted in the Rangel narrative. She has stressed the common sequence of events, noting that Elvas's structure "exactly duplicates" that of Oviedo/Rangel, even to the point that Elvas's longer chapters (13–17) match Oviedo's longer ones.[13] She examined several examples of close Elvas-Rangel parallels, especially the "Mala Paz" episode, the descriptions of mulberry bark clothing and native fortifications, and the use of the Nahuatl word "petaca" (container).[14] She buttressed the argument for a connection between Rangel and Elvas by emphasizing the sixteenth-century role of printing shops as literary centers for the gathering of authors and manuscripts, a context in which Oviedo's manuscripts could have been available for scrutiny during the decade after 1546. That fact, when added to the fact that Burgos had served as a publisher for Oviedo in earlier years, thus indicating a personal relationship between them, opens the possibility that the Rangel chronicle could have provided the basic structure of the Elvas chronicle.[15] Galloway also concluded from various episodes and details included in Elvas but not present in Rangel/Oviedo, such as the detachment that returned to Apalache and details of the battle at Mabila, that there was another independent source blended into the Rangel-based narrative, "probably a military man active in the expedition," possibly even "a trusted comrade of Añasco."[16] She also indicated the addition of literary episodes, particularly in the story of Juan Ortiz.[17] She left open the question of how much of this writing and editing was done by Burgos, who may have been much more than just a publisher.

A separate examination of the Elvas chronicle has yielded somewhat different results. The scholarly team of Martin Malcolm Elbl and Ivana Elbl agree with Galloway's conclusion that Elvas is not really very Portuguese, and they suggest that the false name disguises the gathering of information about the expedition from various sources that were not necessarily Portuguese.[18] They disagree with the conclusion that the Rangel chronicle was the major source, however. They dismiss the shared descriptive texts, such as the mulberry clothing, as "meaningless for establishing intertextual linkages," since they might easily be reflections of widely shared commonplaces.[19] After a lengthy comparison of the two chronicles, they argue that claims for Rangel as the source are not strong enough. They do agree, however, that there was "an unknown source close to Hernando de Soto's inner circle."[20] They also agree that there was a literary influence evident in the chronicle, but they go further and seek to identify its nature. The scholars argue that the influence was García de Resende's *Vida e Gradissimas Virtudes del Rey Dom Joam II.* They point out that Resende was "easily the most prominent local humanist in Evora" and that "Burgos was close to a powerful Resendian coterie."[21]

They shift the focus from Burgos himself, however: "Given the mechanical aping of García de Resende, it is probable that we have here the work of an amateur or beginner, lacking the self-assurance to reshape more profoundly the base account."[22] Their final conclusion is surprising, for it offers a new argument for the historical importance of the Elvas chronicle.

> We clearly have here a composite work, consisting of at least two layers of text. The first layer appears to be an account similar to that of Rangel, but reflecting the attitudes and values of the Estremaduran soldierly core of Soto's followers. It diverges from book 17 of Oviedo's *Historia* in too many respects to be a mere elaboration of the latter. . . . [The other layer is the Resendian "literary beautification."] On balance, and until new research provides answers to the numerous riddles, the *Relaçam* thus ought to rank as a source at least as authentic as Oviedo, and infinitely more so than Garcilaso.[23]

This summary leaves several textual issues about the sources of the Elvas chronicle unresolved, and it also raises the issue of whether the Rangel chronicle served as a basis for Elvas or whether Elvas influenced Oviedo's use of Rangel.

Two of the difficulties in examining Rangel are that the putative original does not exist for comparison and that there was clearly a lengthy time in which the Oviedo version was available for perusal and use by others, such as Burgos and Garcilaso. The important role of Oviedo in the presentation of the Rangel material has never been hidden, however. His obtrusive opinions and commentary throughout the volume are obvious to even the casual reader.

Galloway has pointed out that there are at least two kinds of Oviedoan presence in the chronicle. The first is "framing" information, the supplying of contextual information for an episode, including moralistic interpretations of events and providential history. The consistent thread of condemnation of De Soto for his poor treatment of natives runs through the chronicle, and it seems to be the work of Oviedo rather than Rangel. The other is the more covert work of selection of material (a difficult argument from silence, since there is no original) and the adding of emphases to Rangel's narrative.[24]

Galloway concludes her brief survey of the issues concerning the Rangel/Oviedo chronicle by offering what she considers some "safe assumptions": (1) Oviedo did not tamper with Rangel's sequence, but he did add structure and emphasis to what was there in the text; (2) Oviedo added covert and overt commentary throughout the narrative; and (3) the version as it now exists, with its missing two final chapters, is the result of problems inherent in the sixteenth-century publishing process.[25]

The disagreement between Galloway and the Elbls is not the only viewpoint in the Elvas-Oviedo/Rangel problem. Charles Hudson is one of the leading spirits of the Soto 450th anniversary research, and the route proposed by him and his colleagues is generally accepted as the most accurate yet devised. In a final chapter to his detailed presentation of the proposed itinerary, he made it clear that he considers the two documents to be separate accounts. As he commented, "Whereas I take the agreement between the Rangel and Elvas narratives to be evidence that they are two different accounts of the same string of experiences, Galloway takes this to be proof that Elvas is cribbed from Rangel. Since these antithetical conclusions follow from precisely the same evidence, other kinds of evidence must be sought. . . . I see no merit to Galloway's argument that Elvas's chronicle is derived from Rangel's, and several indications that it was not so derived. To the extent that Elvas and Rangel agree, they corroborate each other."[26] Hudson follows his conclusion into extended use of archaeology to broaden the database from which hypotheses about the journey must be drawn.

It is the fourth chronicle that has attracted most of the attention through the years. Garcilaso's *La Florida del Inca* is in a category by itself—in length, literary quality, and dramatic presentation. It is clearly the work of a master, a major production that, when coupled with Garcilaso's even more important work on the history of the Incas, has commanded attention from scholars for centuries.

Textual analysis of *La Florida del Inca* is accordingly different from what is called for in examining the other chronicles. Here it is not a matter of discerning other hands on the pen, for Garcilaso is the narrator, and he dominates center stage. The question then becomes how Garcilaso, a non-witness to the events he describes, knew what he told the reader. He claimed that he had three primary sources—an unnamed veteran of the Florida expedition and two unpublished manuscripts by expedition veterans Alonzo de Carmona and Juan Coles. The anonymity of the first continues to be a problem, because the identification of him as Gonzalo Silvestre was easily done by careful reading of the text at an early date. The ease of that detective work raises the questions of why Garcilaso did not do the naming himself and whether the whole thing was some sort of devious setup by the clever author. Carmona and Coles were used sparingly, with their contributions seemingly labeled carefully whenever they appeared, usually as corroboration of the main narrative. As corroboration, of course, they share the difficulty of being sources seen only by Garcilaso, which is hardly corroborative.

If the goal is to isolate the historical material, and thus to reconstruct the claimed "historical source" behind Garcilaso's narrative, then one of the tasks is to identify the paragraphs and episodes that are not likely to have come from the mind of an informant like the old soldier Silvestre. Analysts of *La Florida del Inca* have inevitably been thrown into the arena of literary sources for sixteenth-century writing. Galloway has pointed out some of the classical motifs and parallels embedded in the story—the barge of the Lady of Cofachiqui, the failure of the Indians to attack at crucial junctures, the "temple" at Talomeco, the lion in Ortiz's cemetery, and others.[27] Lee Dowling, who wrote a dissertation on the subject of the literary sources of *La Florida del Inca,* went much further.[28] A short list of the background materials includes the romances of chivalry (with special reference to the Ortiz story), the Byzantine novel, the Italian novella, Thomas More's *Utopia,* myths, and legends.[29] Dowling notes that the efforts of modern analysts of Garcilaso "have revealed sufficient traces in it of a variety of contemporary genres to qualify *La Florida del Inca* as virtually a literary mosaic."[30] If those genres were used as a filter to remove passages influenced by them from *La Florida del Inca,* the chronicle would be a great deal shorter.

I have attempted a different approach to the same problem.[31] I have hypothesized that the memories of the expedition in the minds of the survivors would first have taken the form of memorates (personal experience narratives); then as they were told and performed around the campfire those stories would have been altered and smoothed into tellable legends acceptable to the group. Moreover, in the years of the expedition such legends would have changed even the memorates into more standardized legend forms so that ultimately the soldiers would have emerged from the experience with roughly the same body of lore committed to memory by repetition. If Garcilaso was honest in his claims to have learned his material from the one (or more) old soldiers, then he would likely have gained information organized in legend—story—form, and they would look a lot like the stories strung together in *La Florida del Inca.* I drew up a list of eighty-two stories from Garcilaso that appear to be legendary narratives and offered them as a hypothetical corpus of legendary "history" from the expedition. Many of the narratives are the same ones that figure in other analyses as Garcilaso's stories drawn from literary sources. The experiment in folkloristic reconstruction thus attempts to take the concern about the trustworthiness of Silvestre's three- or four-decades-old memory to a new level—a discussion of memory and legend as the raw materials of Garcilaso's literary artistry.

The other major source that may lie hidden within *La Florida del Inca* is the origin of the sequence of events. If an old soldier like Silvestre (granting for the moment that he was the informant) is likely to recall the expedition from decades earlier in legend form, there is likely to be no trustworthy timeline or sequence of events on the journey. Many analysts believe that the source of that missing sequence was the Elvas chronicle.[32] It is almost impossible to believe that the 1557 publication was not part of Garcilaso's library after his arrival in Spain in 1560, and it may even have been part of the putative conversations between the author and his Soto informant. There may also have been other documents available; at his death there were four books "about Florida" listed in Garcilaso's personal library.[33] If they included Elvas and perhaps the *Naufragios* of Cabeza de Vaca, what were the other two?

The hypothesis that Garcilaso utilized the sequence of Elvas as his basic structure permits the legendary memories of Silvestre and other veterans to be fitted into the framework with some ease. The literary influences could then have easily altered the telling of the stories to fit the literary styles, and all that remained would be the contribution of Garcilaso's own mind. Those contributions were certainly not inconsiderable. Commentators have made much of Garcilaso's facile supplying of Inca information to fill out the ethnographic picture for the Southeast. Galloway has referred to his "uniformitarian" understanding of New World cultures, a belief that permitted him to supply alien data to complete his sketch.[34] That belief was part of his larger theological approach to the providential history embedded in both the *Comentarios Reales* and *La Florida del Inca*. From that perspective he saw the New World natives as spiritually and culturally advanced, ready to receive the Christian gospel, a process that was hidden behind the Conquest and the divine task that was set for the Spanish conquistadors.[35] The consequences of that understanding are readily seen in the portrayal of advanced Indian cultures, the nobility of the Indian warriors and rulers, and the enthusiastic reception accorded crosses and prayers.

This survey of sources and influences in *La Florida del Inca* is so complex that it is difficult even to summarize it. Galloway attempted it when she described the work as based on Elvas for its "main armature," a book he also used in his discussions with Silvestre. The memories of the latter, along with those of Coles and Carmona, were folded in, and the whole was completed by Garcilaso's own Inca memories and his theology of history.[36] Dowling would probably reply that she is underrating the importance of Garcilaso's dual mestizo identity—his descent from the Inca royal family, leading to his self-determined role as spokesman for the New World inhabitants, and his European Renaissance heritage, leading to his achievements as one of the leading humanists and writers of the age. For Dowling, *La Florida del Inca* "qualifies superbly as an early work of Chicano literature."[37] Henige, taking primarily a historian's approach, does not bother to sift the literary influences so carefully.

The predominance of those forces was clear enough for a verdict: "*La Florida del Ynca* bears innumerable hallmarks of being largely a work of tautological fiction based on the *Relaçam* (1557) of Elvas, the only account of the expedition published in the sixteenth century; on other since-lost sources; and on revivified and embellished oral recollection." He concludes that it would be "fatuous" to rely on *La Florida del Inca,* a book of "no demonstrable historical worth."[38]

Concluding Thoughts

Where, then, does all this leave the quest for the historical journey? Certainly with some shadows of doubt cast across the chronicles as historical sources. Here is a brief list of tentative conclusions that are intended more as guides to discussion than as firm results of this inquiry.

1. The most trustworthy source for numbers is Biedma. His report is apparently based on notes he made during the journey, and there is no reason to expect fraudulent accounting to the Audiencia. Rangel/Oviedo is usually taken as an accurate source for the same reason, but that assertion has to be tempered by the lack of his diary or any original report. Then, too, there is a three-century hiatus when the security of the document cannot be guaranteed, and even the manuscript from which the published version was made is not available for examination of interlinear alterations and marginalia.
2. The use of Garcilaso for historical details places a great reliance on legendry over primary documents. The amount of time elapsed between event and purported interviews, the legend-making process, and the literary intentions of the author all combine to make confidence in this secondary source a risky business.
3. The disagreement between Galloway and Elbl and Elbl over the relationship between Elvas and Rangel/Oviedo is important, because the basic issue is whether they represent two different sources. If that could be taken as true, then their agreement on details would carry far more weight when they stand against the primary source authority of Biedma. The possibility that Galloway is correct in seeing interdependence of the later sources, however, leaves them in a weak position over against Biedma. It would be helpful if other scholars would weigh in on this debate.
4. Native speeches should never be taken as literal translations of communication between the Indians and the Spaniards. The ethnographic evidence of native oratorical skill suggests that the chroniclers had a warrant for imputing such flowery speech to the native leaders, but the range of interpre-

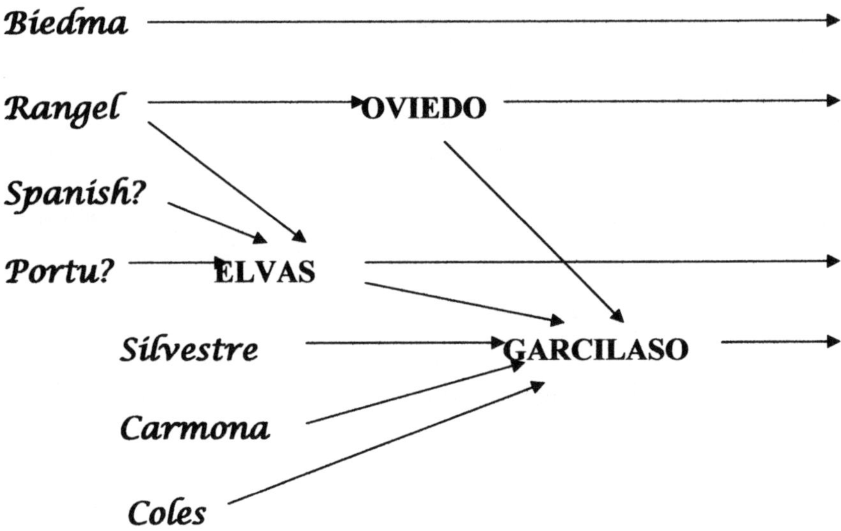

Figure 3.1. The sources and their possible interrelationships.

tation of each such example ranges from sheer literary fiction to an earnest attempt to impart the gist of the communication (or at least what the Spaniards understood it to be). Thus any attempt to interpret a speech as hard evidence should be defended from the viewpoint of communication difficulties on the expedition. That situation leads to another reflection.

5. In connection with the problem of the trustworthiness of language in Spanish encounters with the natives, what is needed is a thorough linguistic examination of the possibilities of clear communication throughout the journey, based on who could have been present at each encounter and how long the translation chains were in each case. Such an endeavor might serve to strengthen the arguments in some cases that the Spanish understood what their informants were saying.
6. All the ethnographic information has to be taken as resulting from the process of passing through the double filter of Spanish worldview and New World (Mexican, Central American, and Peruvian) experience. Any claims to trustworthy use of the data as reportage should be supported by careful argument.

The negative tone of these propositions is not intended as a defeatist conclusion. The list is, instead, offered as an indication of the difficulties of using the chronicles as simple historical sources (Figure 3.1). It is not to say that they are not good sources, nor is it a judgment that they are inherently untrustworthy. It is to say that the use of them involves a significant amount of historiographical examination, together with forthright statement and clear argumentation in defense of the assumptions made by modern students of the De Soto expedition. It would probably be a sound practice for current appeals to the chroniclers as evidence to be accompanied by assessments of the risks involved in doing so.

Notes

1. Lyon, "The Cañete Fragment."
2. Biedma, "Relation of the Island of Florida"; Altman, "Biedma Account."
3. Elvas, "The Account by a Gentleman from Elvas"; Elbl and Elbl, "Gentleman of Elvas."
4. Elbl and Elbl, "Gentleman of Elvas," 86.
5. Oviedo y Valdés, *Historia General y Natural de las Indias;* Rangel, "Account of the Northern Conquest and Discovery of Hernando de Soto"; Avalle-Arce, "Gonzalo Fernández Oviedo y Valdés"; Galloway, "Incestuous Soto Narratives," 12–18.
6. Turner, "The Aborted First Printing of the Second Part of Oviedo's *General and Natural History of the Indies.*"
7. Garcilaso de la Vega, "La Florida."
8. Altman, "Biedma Account."
9. Galloway, "Incestuous Soto Narratives," 12.
10. Ibid., 12–18.
11. Ibid., 33.
12. Henige, "The Context, Content, and Credibility of *La Florida de Ynca,*" 5, 8.
13. Galloway, "Incestuous Soto Narratives," 21–22.
14. Ibid., 15–16, 23–25.
15. Ibid., 22–23.
16. Ibid., 16, 26.
17. Ibid., 25.
18. Elbl and Elbl, "Gentleman of Elvas."
19. Ibid., 55–56.
20. Ibid., 63.
21. Ibid., 66–67.
22. Ibid., 72–73.
23. Ibid., 73.
24. Galloway, "Incestuous Soto Narratives," 14–15.
25. Ibid., 18.
26. Hudson, *Knights of Spain, Warriors of the Sun,* 446–47.
27. Galloway, "Incestuous Soto Narratives," 35.
28. Dowling, "*La Florida,*" 101, 106–14, 116–18.
29. Ibid.
30. Ibid., 110.

31. Lankford, "Legends of the Adelantado."

32. Galloway, "Incestuous Soto Narratives," 27; Henige, "'So Unbelievable It Has to Be True,'" 161.

33. Galloway, "Incestuous Soto Narratives," 35; Durand, "La Biblioteca del Inca."

34. Galloway, "Incestuous Soto Narratives," 28, 39.

35. Ibid., 30–33; Henige, "'So Unbelievable It Has to Be True,'" 159.

36. Galloway, "Incestuous Soto Narratives," 39.

37. Dowling, "*La Florida,*" 139.

38. Henige, "Proxy Data, Historical Method, and the de Soto Expedition," 156.

4
The De Soto Map and the Luna Narratives

An Overview of Other Sixteenth-Century Sources

Kathryn E. Holland Braund

In addition to the standard De Soto narratives, a number of other sixteenth-century sources that postdate the expedition deserve close scrutiny for possible additional information and insight about De Soto's route, as well as the impact of the expedition on the sixteenth-century Southeast. Among the most important of these additional sixteenth-century sources are the so-called De Soto map and documents detailing the failed expedition of Tristán de Luna y Arellano.

The De Soto Map

The De Soto map (Figure 4.1) is an unsigned, undated manuscript map, some 23 1/2 × 17 1/2 inches, that depicts, quite unmistakably, the southeastern United States from approximately the Cape Fear River in North Carolina to the Panuco River in Mexico and stretches from the Gulf Coast northward to what would be modern Tennessee. As Louis De Vorsey has written, "It is also the only extant contemporary map attempting to illustrate the country explored by de Soto (1539–43), a fact that has contributed largely to its fame and frequent reproduction."[1] Emphasis should be placed on the phrase "attempting to illustrate," for it is immediately obvious to modern viewers that although the outline is familiar, the interior is scarcely recognizable. Nonetheless, as Barbara Boston wrote in 1941, "it is the first known graphic reproduction of the interior of the southern United States. On it is found for the first time the nomenclature of the interior."[2]

The map carries a descriptive inscription on its reverse, which modern cartographers use as the map's title: "Mapa del Golfo y costa de la Nueva España desde el Rio de Panuco hasta el cabo de Santa Elena & De los papeles

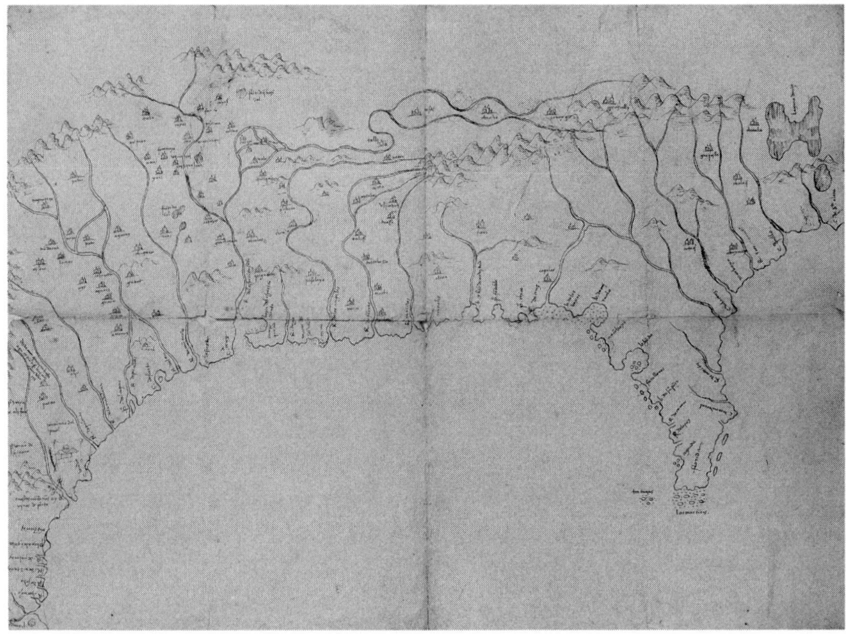

Figure 4.1. The De Soto Map. Undated original manuscript map owned by Archivo General de Indias, Seville. Photograph copy from the Library of Congress, Lowery Collection.

que traxeron de Seuilla de Alonso de santta cruz" [Map of the Gulf and coast of New Spain from the Panuco River to the cape of Santa Elena & from the papers that they brought from Seville of Alonzo de Santa Cruz]. Alonzo de Santa Cruz, of Seville, was cartographer to Charles V. He died in November 1567 and his maps were inventoried in 1572. Since the map is undated, scholars have relied on internal information to ascertain when it was drawn. Because the map contains geographical information obtained by De Soto's *entrada,* but no information that might have been derived from the Luna expedition of 1559, and fails to note the settlement of St. Augustine, which occurred in 1565, scholars assume that the map was completed prior to Luna's return. Scholars generally agree on a date of 1544 as the logical time frame for the map's production.[3]

A number of reproductions of the map are available for scholarly study, as well as the original, still held at the Archivo General de Indias in Seville.[4] The original map shows signs of being folded into quarters at one time, and the fold obscures some detail, including a town name that would be interesting to Alabamians. Scholars have frequently used tracings of the original or tracings of a photograph, and some published editions contain errors in drafting as well as transcription. Perhaps the most useful modern tracing of the map was produced to accompany James A. Robertson's edition of the *True Relation . . . by a Gentleman of Elvas,* published by the Florida State Historical Society in 1932. The carefully reproduced map contains a tissue overlay with the names and legends neatly reproduced so they are clearly visible for study.[5] Photographic reproductions of the map are found in William P. Cumming and Louis De Vorsey Jr.'s *The Southeast in Early Maps,* and more recently in *Charting Louisiana,* edited by Alfred E. Lemmon, John T. Magill, and Jason R. Wiese. A high-resolution digital version of a photographic copy is now available for download from the Library of Congress.[6]

The map is a blend of two sources of information about the Gulf Coast and its interior: charts and sailing directions (sometimes known as a rutter) and information obtained by members of the De Soto expedition from personal observation as well as from Indian informants.[7] More properly, we might deem this "map" more a "chart," for it is as much the product of maritime exploration as inland discovery. At the time the De Soto map was constructed—and for a good number of centuries following—the art of pilotage required a number of specific skills. These included the ability to recognize terrestrial features by sight as approached from the sea, to know the distance from one anchorage to another as well as the sailing course, the location of shoals and obstacles, and the location of freshwater and safe harbors; it extended to such things as a knowledge of tidal flow and coastal depths and bottoms. Common navigation or pilotage, as opposed to grand navigation involving ocean crossings, was a skill set essential for any mariner. Simple coastal drawings had a long tradition and were developed to a fine art in the Mediterranean basin. Simple charts, accompanied by written directions or oral tradition, were essential for coastal navigators.[8]

There is little debate among scholars as to the reason the map was created, for in 1508, the Casa de la Contratación (House of Trade) began to collect geographic data from pilots in order to produce an accurate master map. The most famous early effort was the 1529 map by Diego Ribero, the cosmographer to the king of Spain.[9] Spanish geographers would have eagerly sought out the reports of De Soto survivors for information about the interior of North America and likely questioned some of the men in person. The now famous "De Soto" map is assumed to have resulted from such an effort to capture geographic data from the expedition for incorporation into the master map or *patrón general*. Thus, the route taken by the expedition—of supreme interest to scholars today—was of only tangential interest to the Spanish mapmakers.[10]

While the majority of the coastal features predate De Soto, the information about the interior is clearly derived from the expedition. And most likely, the information was not compiled in map form during the expedition but recalled from memory for trained cartographers afterward. Louis De Vorsey Jr., the preeminent historical geographer of the Southeast, points out that more information from the later stages of the expedition is depicted than from the earlier stages, thus lending credence to the idea that it is a "memory map." Since the De Soto expedition produced over 250 survivors, there were ample informants. Luis de Moscoso, who led the expedition after De Soto's death, is generally believed to have been a chief informant for the mapmaker.[11]

In all, there are 127 names and legends on the map. By the date the De Soto map was drawn, Spanish cartographers had compiled an impressive knowledge of the Gulf of Mexico from earlier expeditions, some of which had specifically been dispatched to obtain information about the Gulf Coast, including that of Alvarez de Pineda in 1519.[12] Indeed, most of the coastal names (rivers and bays) are found on earlier Spanish maps. And as Paul Hoffman has shown, Pineda's map and his rutter are the source for many of the places on the De Soto map.[13] On the map, fourteen rivers flow into the Gulf of Mexico, seven into the Atlantic, and the coastline is pocked by a variety of bays, inlets, and islands.[14] Mountains and lakes add interest as well as confusion. But the coastline is not unlike other Spanish maps of the period. Clearly, it is the interior that makes this map important. As they had with other maps of the period, geographers had to grapple with very thin data to produce a terrestrial map—and most were based on textual evidence. Without proper instruments to ascertain longitude, much less establish reliable distances from specific points of reference, such maps were more illustrative than instructive.[15]

Adding to the confusion as to the map's source is the fact that the spelling of all interior place-names depicted varies considerably from those in the standard sources about the expedition.[16] Barbara Boston, who wrote about the map in the 1940s, compared the names to De Soto chronicles and concluded that most were derived from Rangel's account. Her work has been largely accepted by later scholars and, in effect, provides the date for the map, since cartographers would not have had access to the Rangel account until 1544 or 1545. Indeed, it may be that the cartographers had the Rangel account and little else and thus selectively included what they deemed important. Yet a significant number of map place-names (27) are not found in any of the surviving De Soto narratives; thus it is obvious that survivors' memories or no-longer-extant accounts of the expedition were used by the map's maker as well.[17]

Another oddity regarding the map is the preponderance of place-names from the later stages of the expedition. The Florida peninsula is devoid of towns, and significant other locations are missing as well, including Mabila. Barbara Boston suggested simply that the map was in an "unfinished state" or that place-names in Florida were omitted for aesthetic reasons.[18] Yet these reasons fail to satisfy, for surely De Soto survivors would have remembered the site of their greatest battle, and other nearby town sites are included on the map. As Charles Hudson, whose work has established the most comprehensive consensus route of the expedition, notes, "the place name 'Mabila' does not appear on the map at all."[19] Perhaps, as many have suggested, the burned battle site and the hostile towns of La Florida did not interest the cartographer as much as the more promising locations actually shown on the map. But even that reasoning is not satisfactory, for the purpose of the effort, one is bound to assume, was to record vital information of all kinds about the interior and not simply locational information that offered promise as opposed to sites of disappointment.

If the map is informed by the written accounts or oral testimony of survivors, Louis De Vorsey also believes that much of the information that appears on the map was derived from Indian informants, particularly information about the river systems. These, upon first examination, seem peculiar indeed. De Vorsey points out that normally, streams are dendritic: "that is, small streams join to form larger streams that drain discrete basins and flow into the sea or other large bodies of water. On the De Soto map, however, some large rivers are shown to be anastomosed—connected to each other—a condition that almost never occurs in nature. Notice, too, that one large drainage system flows from the mountains to both the Atlantic Ocean and the Gulf of Mexico." De Vorsey reasons that "in European maps, asymmetrical or mixed networks tended to retain their characteristics to the extent that a particular map would allow. Trails or portages would be shown as different and distinct from the rivers in a region. With native American cartographers, however, such systems were usually shown as combined and undifferentiated. To them the overall transport system was of principal concern—not whether one segment had to be walked, while another required a canoe for passage." Thus, according to De Vorsey, "what the European author of the De Soto map depicted as anastomosed and weirdly forking rivers resulted from his misunderstanding of Indian route maps."[20]

The degree to which Indian informants helped shape the mapmaker's conception about the interior hydrography is perhaps debatable, but this much is certain: De Soto did not put a premium on producing a clear map of his travels or systematically attempt to record geographic knowledge—nor could he have done so with the technology and skills available to the best geographers at the time. But his expedition's path was determined by Indian informants, whose tales of gold and pearls (as well as food supply) sent him on an often erratic and rambling course.[21]

In addition to the oddly convergent river systems, another area of interest is the "laguna dulce" and a smaller lake underneath. These have been variously explained as the Okefenoke swamp and Lake Okeechobee or, more lately, a supposition by De Vorsey that the lakes are meant to represent the Great Lakes, notions of which the Spanish would have acquired from their Indian hosts.[22]

Rivers were of supreme interest to the Spaniards, based on the idea that gold and precious metals originated in mountains and might be washed into plains and valleys by rivers. Moreover, connecting interior rivers with coastal outlets made sense from a transportation and locational standpoint. Thus, rivers and mountains—the origin of the river systems—play an important role in the De Soto map and not merely by adding to geographic knowledge. For in naming and attempting to understand the landscape, the Spaniards were laying claim to the vast interior—the waterways if not the towns and people.

In her examination of the map, Patricia Galloway, whose expertise on the De Soto narratives and early maps is without equal, discerned "the possibility that it [the map] represents a real Spanish cognitive map of the interior" rather than imperfectly understood information gathered from native southerners.[23] As she attempted to understand the relationship between the map and the De Soto narratives, she became convinced that "the hydrography is not wholly imaginary . . . instead, it is an attempt to rationalize the narrative evidence."[24] In her words, "hydrography was deduced from the number of known rivers at the Gulf of Mexico in conjunction with river crossings and direction of travel; it is a picture of where the officials of the *Casa* thought the Spaniards had gone."[25]

Galloway believed that the explanation for the absence of some towns was a simple one: "the map's scale prevented it from portraying all the places mentioned in the narratives." Yet those that are shown are important, for as Galloway observes, "it does not exclude a single 'province' named by Biedma, who thought most thoroughly in *encomienda* terms (and named the fewest towns)."[26]

Galloway also carefully studied the use of symbology for Indian towns, comparing the De Soto map with derivative maps that followed it, specifically the 1584 printed map of La Florida by Ortelius based on a redrawing of the De Soto map by Hieronymo Chiaves and the 1597 version of the Chiaves map produced by Cornelius Wytfliet. As Galloway notes, the towns on the De Soto map are represented by similar-looking icons, usually of two or three buildings, that do "not differ from one another substantially." Since the De Soto map was the first map to portray the interior, it also features the first use of icons to indicate Indian town locations. Subsequent maps did not develop distinct icons to differentiate towns by size or importance. Galloway's study of seventeenth-century maps reveals that, generally speaking, "one sign was chosen to stand for an Indian town." This is, to Galloway, indicative of the fact that these earliest maps portray "an erroneous conception of social organization across the polities of the Southeast; these maps demonstrate graphically the early explorers' idea of one 'standard Indian polity.'"[27]

Galloway's interpretation regarding town placement and the seeming lack of hierarchal order evident in their display, thoughtfully developed from detailed study of period maps and consummate in its overall coherence, fails on one point: the town she identifies as Mabila is clearly on the wrong side of the river. In her schematic, Galloway identifies as Mabila the southernmost town on the Alabama River system—a town whose name is obscured by a fold line and is thus illegible on all published reproductions of the map. This town, south of Piachi ("tiachi" on the original map), is on the east side of what is the present Alabama River. Though obscured by the fold line, close scrutiny suggests that the first three letters could be "ach." If so, this could represent the town of "Achusy," an appropriate location for the town, which does not appear elsewhere on the map. By sight, "tiachi" is approximately midway between this town to the south and "tascalussa" to the north. In her schematic, Galloway lists "tascalussa" as "Athahachi" since Atahachi is the name of Chief Tascalusa's town.[28]

Further, in her schematic tracing of the map, Galloway omits the town of Nosco entirely. Nosco is the only town portrayed on the map in the general vicinity that various De Soto chroniclers place Mabila.[29] But as De Soto scholar Charles Hudson has observed in his attempts to reconcile the map with reality, "'Nosco' is by no stretch of the linguistic imagination 'Mabila.'"[30]

Yet Nosco was included by the cartographer for some reason—and the settlement name is not among those listed in the various De Soto chronicles. It might well be that the cartographers did indeed omit the battle site but included another town in the area, for the De Soto expedition, according to the Elvas account, marched "through a continuously peopled region" just prior to reaching Mabila. The account by Rangel mentions a "palisaded town" where the Spaniards received a present of chestnut bread just prior to entering Mabila. And, in the month following the battle, as they recuperated, the Spaniards pillaged and burned villages throughout the region. Survivors would likely have recalled larger towns from which food was procured or where they rested. Vernon James Knight suggests yet another less likely possibility: that Nosco is actually the correct name of the town known as Mabila. Knight notes that in other cases, the name of the town and the province have been conflated in period documents. Another possibility worthy of consideration is that Nosco represents Mosulixa, a town in Apafalaya province visited by the expedition before they reached the town of Apafalaya. Until new discoveries are made, "Nosco" and the town to the south of "tiachi" with an illegible name will remain riddles.[31]

Although a town named Mabila is missing from the map, the towns visited by De Soto on his journey toward that location are very well represented and include not only "provinces" but individual towns. From Chiaha to Piachi, every major town mentioned in the Rangel account is placed on the map, including Chiaha, Coste, Tali, Cosa, Itaba, Ulibahali, Tuasi, Talisi, Atahachi (town of Tascalusa), and Piachi. (These towns appear on the map as chiaha, coste, tallj, cossa, aytaba, vljbahalj, tuassi, talissi, tascalussa, and tiachi.)[32] Two towns present problems if one is attempting to reconcile river crossings to town location. The town of "neter" between Tali and Cosa is present on the map, but is not mentioned in the chronicles. On the other hand, Tasqui, a village where the Spaniards rested overnight, was not on the map.

The naming practice employed by the cartographer who constructed the map—that of retaining native place-names—is revealing and deserves special note. The act of naming was important from the standpoint of sixteenth-century Spanish-Catholic religion and also from the standpoint of legal formality, for naming conferred possession. Moreover, it conferred understanding and familiarity, as well as power over place.[33] In most cases, the Spanish renamed the lands they explored. As Stephen Greenblatt has so eloquently written, "The founding action of Christian imperialism is a christening. Such a christening entails the cancellation of the native name—and hence a kind of making new; it is at once an exorcism, an appropriation, and a gift. Christening then is the culminating instance of the marvelous speech act: in the wonder of the proper name, the movement from ignorance to knowledge, the taking of possession, the conferral of identity are fused in a moment of pure linguistic formalism."[34] In light of Greenblatt's observation, it is striking that virtually without exception, the coastal names are Spanish, while the interior names are not. As much as the errant rivers and the misplaced lakes and mountains, the aboriginal names that do dot the map reveal

Spanish recognition of De Soto's failure and the continuing hegemony of native peoples who survived him.

One note of lasting significance regarding the merger of early coastal surveys with De Soto expedition information is the identification of the Río del Espíritu Santo, or River of the Holy Spirit, a river of some debate among De Soto trackers. The river and its large bay first appeared in a map produced from a woodcut in 1524 and published in Nuremberg—the so-called Cortes map. The river was placed north of the west coast of Yucatán and roughly in the center of the northern Gulf Coast. According to Paul Hoffman's research, the Río del Espíritu Santo of the Cortes map—and its derivatives through the De Soto map—was actually the Sabine River of Texas, while the Mississippi, on this early map, would have been the Río de Flores. However, De Soto's men, as we learn in Biedma's account, dubbed their river of escape the Río del Espíritu Santo, a name quickly adopted by subsequent maps for the river we know as the Mississippi.[35]

The Luna Narratives

Another collection of documentary material that postdates the De Soto expedition but provides helpful evidence for De Soto route studies are the records generated by the colonizing expedition of Tristán de Luna y Arellano (1559–61). Luna's mission was to establish a colonial settlement along the Gulf Coast, set up Spanish mission towns at interior village sites as well as on the Atlantic seaboard, and link all these settlements via a road, thus securing Spain's claim to the region as well as providing bases for the protection of the treasure fleet. Planning for the Luna expedition depended heavily on intelligence from the De Soto survivors as to landing sites and likely interior locations for settlement. In addition, the expedition itself generated data on interior locations, some of which had been visited by De Soto, as well as refinement in knowledge of coastal areas by reconnaissance of the Gulf prior to the departure of the main expeditionary force.[36]

The most accessible and the most useful collection of Luna material is a two-volume collection translated and edited by Herbert Ingram Priestley, who was the librarian of the Bancroft Library and professor of Mexican history at the University of California–Berkeley. *The Luna Papers: Documents Relating to the Expedition of Don Tristán de Luna y Arellano for the Conquest of La Florida in 1559–1561* appeared in 1928, in a limited printing of 360 copies, most of which went to members of the Florida State Historical Society, the publisher of the work.[37] An accomplished linguist, as well as a well-respected scholar of the Spanish colonization of the southeastern United

States, Priestly provided each document in Spanish as well as English. The work contains a number of previously published documents, but is composed primarily of previously unpublished manuscript material from the Archivo General de Indias, as well as a small number of documents from the collections of the New York Historical Society. The majority of the documents from Spain were the result of Luna's attempt to regain the governorship of Florida after his colonization fiasco, as well as various other official (legal) papers.[38] Given that they are firsthand primary sources from a variety of people and not reminiscence-type documents, their value as sources is unmistakable.[39] Yet, while they do contain information concerning various activities of the Luna expeditionaries, they reveal more about the tensions and problems of the expedition than specifics about Indian town locations. Indeed, the surviving records do not provide a complete record of the expedition, and the extant documents are frequently imprecise or lacking important details.

The recent inclusion of Priestley's work as a full-text document through the digital Florida Heritage Collection makes the two volumes easily accessible to anyone with an Internet connection. However, a fluent Spanish linguist, with the sensitivity of a twenty-first-century documentary editor, might profitably examine the original archival documents and report on the translations as well as the transcriptions provided by Priestly, who worked in an age of different standards. As Priestly notes in his preface, he chose "intelligibility rather than literalness" when working on the documents. Moreover, he modernized names, including place-names of Indian towns. Thus, those whose Spanish skills force them to rely on translations are at a distinct disadvantage.[40] Finally, although Priestly made a concerted effort to locate materials in the Spanish archives (actually, the search was conducted by Miss Irene Wright), it would be a mistake for De Soto scholars to blithely assume that an earlier search, even an admirably exhaustive one, should preclude an undertaking in our own century given the greater ease of travel and improvements in finding aids that make new discoveries in Spanish papers a real possibility.[41]

Another frequently cited source is *Historia de la fundación y discurso de la provincia de Santiago de México,* including a history of the expedition produced by Fray Agustín Dávila Padilla and first published in 1596. Dávila Padilla's work is primarily concerned with documenting the works of the Dominicans in the region, and in it he uses the memorial of one of the members of Luna's expedition, Fray Domingo de la Anunciación. John R. Swanton published an English translation, by Ms. Fanny Bandelier, in *Early History of the Creek Indians and Their Neighbors.* There is no full, modern English translation of the pertinent parts of the original work.[42] Clearly, a modern translation of the

1596 work, carefully annotated and subjected to discourse analysis, would be a service to sixteenth-century scholarship. Two scholars, Patricia Galloway and Paul Hoffman, have made significant efforts in that direction.

Dávila Padilla's history has two major problems. First, Fray Anunciación's account was actually composed some thirty years after the expedition and was primarily intended to glorify his coreligionists. As Patricia Galloway writes in her assessment of the work, it is "so full of miraculous events that separating the real from the supernatural becomes difficult, and only the lack of an English translation of the entire history has kept this fact from being blatantly obvious to English-speaking researchers."[43] It seems clear that few who have used the document have bothered to critically analyze events and separate the real from the marvelous. And some of the events are clearly written to serve other purposes and were perhaps created as vehicles to demonstrate holiness rather than historical reality.[44] The usefulness of the history for route studies is compounded by the usual vague details and lack of specific locational references.

While all of these sixteenth-century sources raise problems of access and interpretation, they may perhaps provide clues in the search for Mabila's location, for Luna's party visited two major towns that had earlier played host to the De Soto expedition: Piachi and Cosa. Moreover, one important Indian town visited for a prolonged period by the Luna party, Nanipacana, claimed to have been damaged by the earlier expedition. And there is speculation that Luna's Atache is De Soto's Atahachi. However, Mabila is not specifically mentioned in any of the Luna material. It is not surprising in the least that, like those of De Soto, Luna's route and camp locations have created debate and controversy. Most of the controversy relates to Luna's activities in the south, along the Alabama River, and is pertinent to the search for Mabila in that if it were possible to pin down Luna's Nanipacana and Piachi, a better understanding of Mabila's location would emerge. Galloway and Charles Hudson, the key protagonists in the debate over Nanipacana's location, postulate vastly different locations for the site: Hudson near modern Camden (Wilcox or western Dallas County in modern Alabama) and Galloway considerably to the south, in the Mobile Delta.[45]

Considering the importance of the town of Nanipacana as a possible clue to the discovery of Mabila's location and the De Soto route in particular, a review of their arguments is in order. While both rely on the same documentary record, Hudson and his associates' reconstruction is driven by their commitment to pairing potential archaeological sites with the places mentioned in the documentary record, while Galloway is more sensitive to the topographic and toponymic details as revealed by the Luna material and later data.

Both base their reconstructions of the Luna party's route on the same incomplete documentary record provided by the *Luna Papers.* While this collection of documents is considered extremely reliable, it does not present a complete record of the expedition's activities. Indeed, there are major gaps, vagueness regarding sequences of events, and lack of specific details that present complications that frequently result in varying interpretations of the same document. Indeed, only a handful of documents survive that are related to the questions at hand. And scholars have frequently been tempted to state as fact what can only remain supposition.

One primary source about the discovery expedition to Nanipacana survives. In sworn testimony, Alonso de Montalván, a young horseman, related that following the hurricane that devastated the Spanish camp at Achuse (Pensacola Bay), Luna dispatched Mateo del Sauz, the sergeant major, and captain Cristóbal de Arellano with a party of roughly 150 footmen and horse soldiers together with two Dominican friars "to discover a town called Nanipacana of which they had heard." Montalván did not accompany that expedition but, like the others, waited "in great distress" as the expeditionaries failed to return within the thirty-day time allotted to them. Finally, after forty-five days, Cristóbal de Verdugo and twenty men returned with a letter for Luna indicating that they had found the town and that there were ample supplies of corn for the hungry settlement.[46] Montalván's testimony is brief and provides no clues on the direction traveled or other circumstances surrounding the journey.

The distance the expeditionary party traveled is supplied by Dávila Padilla. Though a problematic secondary source, his history does provide a relatively straightforward account of the expedition to Nanipacana. According to Dávila Padilla, after the hurricane, Luna ordered a substantial exploratory party of four companies to seek Indian towns. Fray Domingo de la Anunciación and Fray Domingo de Salazar accompanied the party, as noted by the testimony of Montalván. With only "limited rations," the men traveled with "extraordinary difficulty." They traversed a diverse landscape of "large unpopulated zones, hilly regions, and woods, of never-used roads." After traveling forty leagues, they came upon "a very large and deep river," and it was obvious to them that "according to the greatness of the river, and that of the fame that that land had, it was hoped there would be very large provinces of very populous cities in that place." Following the river, they shortly came to settlements described as "hunting camps," the largest of which was Nanipacana, containing eighty houses. There were "ruined buildings in the town," and the inhabitants informed the explorers that their town "had been famous, both in the number of people and in sumptuous building," but that other Spaniards who had been there earlier had been the cause of their decline.[47] Thus, Dávila Padilla's history, like Montalván's account, provides no direction of march, merely reporting that the explorers reached a large river after traveling forty leagues from their base camp at Achuse.

Hudson and his colleagues specifically identify this as "the River of Piachi," a designation employed by neither Montalván nor Dávila Padilla, although it clearly was that river: the modern Alabama River. Further, Hudson's group asserts that the party actually headed "northward," specifically "to search for Piachi and the River of Piachi" rather than Nanipacana, as Montalván's testimony states.[48] Hudson, recalling Biedma's testimony that "Mabila and Piachi were 40 leagues to the north of the coast," discerns importance in the specified distance mentioned by Dávila Padilla. But as Galloway notes, Biedma's account merely relates that at Mabila, the Spaniards "heard through news from the Indians that we were up to forty leagues from the sea."[49] In any case, the Luna party did not reach Piachi or Mabila but Nanipacana, which everyone agrees is south of Piachi. Questions of approximate distance and the length of a league aside, Hudson bases his northerly direction for the march solely on logic that Mabila was to the north of Achuse and south of Piachi and that De Soto survivors among the Luna expedition, as well as other intelligence gathered by Luna's parties, would have suggested to the Spanish that they head to the general region of Mabila for succor, having found corn and other food in abundance in the region previously. Previous explorations prior to the hurricane would have ruled out the Escambia as the riverway to Mabila (i.e., the Escambia River was not the "River of Piachi").[50]

Galloway, on the other hand, taking into account information from Indian informants about the richer lands around Mobile Bay and the growing realization that the expedition had landed on the wrong bay (Pensacola rather than Mobile), favors a westerly route for the exploratory party.[51] Thus, these two scholars arrive at divergent locations teased from limited evidence and a great deal of intelligent speculation. Galloway's interpretation finds ample support in the documents, for it is clear that Luna had almost immediately become disenchanted with his landing site, and by May 1560, explorations had definitively confirmed that the "Río de Piachi" (the modern Alabama River) flowed into Bahía Filipina (modern Mobile Bay) and that it was navigable from the region of "black and good" land expeditionary parties had discovered upriver around Nanipacana all the way to the sea, making possible the supply of a coastal as well as an inland settlement.[52]

Neither Hudson nor Galloway mentions the obvious route for interior exploration: an Indian trail leading inland from Achuse. Dávila Padilla, as noted previously, reported that the roads were overgrown. In fact, both extant primary accounts relating to the discovery and relocation to Nanipacana note that it was necessary for the road from Achuse to Nanipacana to be "opened," presumably implying that the overgrown path had to be widened in order to move the colonists with their baggage and animals. A systematic study of early Indian trails in this vicinity, on extant maps and through documentary records, might prove a useful undertaking for De Soto scholars.[53]

Other clues as to Nanipacana's situation are revealed by further expeditions after the Spaniards finally relocated to the town. By the time the colony relocated to Nanipacana, the Indians had abandoned the site and taken away the food supplies. At that point, another expeditionary party was dispatched to find other Indian towns (and corn). This party was led by Captain Alonso de Castilla, Captain Álvaro Nieto, and Alonso Pérez, the expedition's accountant general. Montalván reported that the expedition set forth "in two brigantines and two barks [which traveled] sixty or seventy leagues up the river." As they progressed, their reputation preceded them, and for the first thirty to thirty-five leagues they passed territory "occupied by houses and fields, but no people, it appearing that they [the Indians] had revolted and absented themselves." After that, the territory was depopulated. This party was away twenty-two days.[54]

Here, the interpretations of Montalván's testimony offered by Galloway and Hudson's team disagree significantly. While both acknowledge explorations of the "River of the Tome," Galloway asserts that the expedition described by Alonso de Montalván explored the Tombigbee River, not the Alabama River. Hudson's reading of Alonso de Montalván's account places the expedition on the Alabama River.[55] Given that the document records that the expedition set out from Nanipacana and went "up the river," it is apparent that the Alabama was indeed the river explored. And at least one other document would seem to confirm this, for the leading captains of the expedition, then residing on the Alabama River at Nanipacana, along with other notables, recorded "we know for certain that for sixty or seventy leagues up the river there is no food which can be found by marching the army inland."[56] Yet Galloway asserts that Hudson "unaccountably conflated" the expedition described by Montalván with yet another that explored the "River of Tome." Hudson mentions the separate exploration of the "River of Tome" and, like Galloway, identifies it as the Tombigbee River.

Other documents appear to shed light on the matter. On June 19, 1560, the Spaniards were in great distress and Luna's leadership was challenged. Ordered by the Crown to move inland toward Cosa and from thence to Santa

Elena, the expedition's leading military men and magistrates balked. Pointing to their almost complete lack of provisions, they recounted previous efforts to find relief and recalled explorations of "this river of Nanipacana and the Tome." This document names Captains Baltazar de Sotelo, Juan de Porras, and Diego Téllez as the leaders of the expedition(s), noting that they "went to these rivers, but returned with all their people dying of hunger, not having found one grain of corn: the cornfields had been pulled up, and all the fields burned and pulled up by the natives, [as had] even the wild herbs, which they had learned that we could make use of and which we eat."[57] The fixation on location rather than action overshadows the obvious: the Spanish were engaged in numerous—and desperate—attempts to find food. Moreover, at least to this reader, the imprecise language of the document suggests multiple attempts: "all the efforts possible have been made by sending captains with brigantines and barks to obtain them and to search for them on the rivers, the inlets and in the swamps, with great suffering on the part of the captains and soldiers, as is public and notorious."[58]

Regardless of the river meant by Montalván (and which he only reports secondhand since he was not a participant), Galloway's reading of all the documents leads her to conclude that Nanipacana was part of a thickly populated polity composed of numerous villages stretching along the alluvial floodplain. She believes that the "lower Tombigbee and the complex Mobile-Tensaw delta with its distribution of protohistoric sites fits this description very well and certainly offers many toponymic links with the Tohome and Naniaba Peoples later found settled there."[59] However, in Galloway's words, "the location of the Nanipacana town found by the exploration party in the delta is not immediately obvious."[60] Hudson, on the other hand, while acknowledging exploration of the delta, places the town farther north on the Alabama River and points to known archaeological sites in the region as possible candidates for Nanipacana.[61] Nanipacana, like Mabila, does not appear on the De Soto map.[62]

Luna material describing towns visited by both Luna and the De Soto expedition has also been used by Charles Hudson and his colleagues to help establish the location of Cosa, the most notable Indian town visited by both expeditions. Hudson's use of the Luna material to fix Cosa's location has not gone unchallenged in this case either.[63] Patricia Galloway, in particular, has written that Hudson's group employed "a dangerous circularity" in using De Soto and Luna material to help establish the route of Juan Pardo, who followed Luna chronologically, while at the same time using Pardo's travels to pin down "crucial locations" for the De Soto and Luna expeditions.[64] Thus, like virtually all sites associated with the two expeditions, Cosa—a key stop on De Soto's way southwest toward Mabila—remains a contested location.

Galloway's construction of the Luna route is more compact than that developed by Hudson and his partners, and places the Luna party's ultimate destination, Cosa, on the upper Coosa River in Alabama. Hudson's Cosa is located in modern Georgia, at the Little Egypt archaeological site.[65] In the absence of adequate records and convincing archaeological evidence, the locations of Nanipacana and Cosa—like other sites visited by De Soto and Luna—remain open to debate.

Conclusion

Many of the problems associated with the effective use of these sources for route studies stem not only from the vagueness of the geographical information but from problems of interpretation and comparative analysis. Perhaps a new generation of De Soto scholars, using a variety of tools, an interdisciplinary approach, the dispassionate employment of all the best methodologies, and, with luck, the discovery of new archaeological sites and documentary evidence, will, at last, solve the many mysteries surrounding the amazing journeys of sixteenth-century Spaniards through what is now Alabama.

Notes

1. Cumming and De Vorsey, *The Southeast in Early Maps,* 108.

2. Boston, "The 'De Soto Map,'" 243–44.

3. Cumming and De Vorsey, *The Southeast in Early Maps,* 108. For an extended discussion of the various attempts to date the map, see Boston, "The 'De Soto Map,'" 236–38.

4. Cumming and De Vorsey, *The Southeast in Early Maps,* 108–11.

5. Robertson, *True Relation of the Hardships Suffered by Governor Fernando de Soto.* The author has not had an opportunity to examine the original for this survey but has relied on published versions.

6. Cumming and De Vorsey, *The Southeast in Early Maps,* plate 5; Lemmon, Magill, and Wiese, *Charting Louisiana,* map 2, p. 24. The Library of Congress image available on-line is from a photograph in the Lowery Map Collection and can be accessed through the Map Collections home page of the LOC.

7. Hoffman, "Discovery," 7, credits "mostly Native American hydrography" as the source of interior information.

8. See excerpt from Michiel Coignet's 1581 treatise on navigation in Parry, *The Age of Reconnaissance,* 83.

9. Boston, "'The De Soto Map,'" 239–40.

10. Galloway, "*La Florida's* Route through Maps," 75. Of the survivors of the expedition, only fifteen made their way home to Spain. See Chang-Rodríguez, introduction, 26. For the fullest treatment of the survivors, see Avellaneda, *Los Sobrevivientes de La Florida.*

11. For the number of survivors, see Galloway, *Choctaw Genesis,* 144.

12. Galloway, *Choctaw Genesis,* 209; Hoffman, "Discovery," 8–9, notes that Pineda produced not only a map of the coast but a rutter with valuable information about the northern Gulf Coast.

13. Hoffman, "Discovery," 9.

14. Boston, "The 'De Soto Map,'" 243.

15. See Galloway, "*La Florida's* Route," 76, for an instructive discussion of mapmaking obstacles in the sixteenth century.

16. Cumming and De Vorsey, *The Southeast in Early Maps,* 108–09.

17. According to Boston, of the four primary De Soto narratives, it is possible that three could have been used as an aid in the construction of the map. That of the Inca did not appear until 1605, thus it appeared after the map is generally believed to have been completed. The accounts of Biedma and Rangel, likely available in manuscript form in the royal records, are assumed to have been available to court historians and cartographers, and the account of Elvas, which appeared in 1557, might also have been used. Boston counted 29 names from Rangel, 24 from Biedma, and 39 from Elvas. Her table lists 27 map names that have no expedition narrative equivalent. Boston, "The 'De Soto Map,'" 244–47.

18. Boston, "The 'De Soto Map,'" 244.

19. Hudson quoted in Jones, *Highway Route of the De Soto Trail,* 9.

20. De Vorsey, "Silent Witnesses," 716–17. De Vorsey's reasoning assumes that copies of such route maps made it back to Spanish territory or influenced earlier versions of the De Soto map that served as a base for the map under discussion.

21. Weber, *The Spanish Frontier in North America,* 55, makes this point.

22. Cumming and De Vorsey, *The Southeast in Early Maps,* 109–10. See Hoffman, *A New Andalucia,* for a discussion of early exploration, the acquisition of geographic knowledge, and the creation of mythical geographies.

23. Galloway, *Choctaw Genesis,* 213.

24. Ibid.

25. Ibid., 215.

26. Ibid.

27. Ibid., 215–17.

28. Ibid., map 6.5, p. 215. I am indebted to Jim Knight's keen eyesight for deciphering the first three letters of the obscured name of the town south of "tiachi."

29. Ibid. Sixteenth-century Spanish script presents some problems for modern English readers. Nosco is the generally accepted transcription of this town's name.

30. Hudson quoted in Jones, *Highway Route of the De Soto Trail,* 9.

31. See Clayton, Knight, and Moore, *De Soto Chronicles,* 1: 98, 292, 294. Knight's comments are from personal communication with the author, February 2007.

32. Transcriptions from Boston, "The 'De Soto Map,'" 246–47.

33. Greenblatt, *Marvelous Possessions,* 82, explores the implications of Spanish naming practices.

34. Ibid., 83.

35. Hoffman, "Discovery," 9–11.

36. Hudson et al., "The Tristán de Luna Expedition," provides the most concise overview of the expedition. For a fuller discussion of the expedition and its place in sixteenth-century exploration, see Hoffman, *A New Andalucia,* particularly ch. 7.

37. Robertson, "Review of The Luna Papers."

38. Priestley, *Luna Papers,* 1: ix–xv, lists and categorizes the documents.

39. Galloway, *Choctaw Genesis,* 145–60, provides an exhaustive analysis of the *Luna Papers.*

40. Priestley, *Luna Papers,* 1: xv.

41. Ibid., 1: xi.

42. Swanton, *Early History of the Creek Indians and Their Neighbors.* The translation appears on pages 231–39 and describes the expedition's journey to Cosa.

43. Galloway, *Choctaw Genesis,* 145.

44. Galloway's most recent analysis of the history, "Agustín Dávila Padilla's Fabulous History of the Luna Expedition: Ideology in Two Centuries," appears as ch. 5 of her *Practicing Ethnohistory,* 78–96.

45. For the debate, see Galloway, *Choctaw Genesis,* 143–60, and Hudson et al., "The Tristán De Luna Expedition," 31–45.

46. Priestley, *Luna Papers,* 2: 286–87.

47. I am indebted to John Worth, who graciously provided a translation of Dávila Padilla's work.

48. Hudson et al., "The Tristán De Luna Expedition," 34.

49. Hudson et al., "The Tristán De Luna Expedition," 34; Galloway, *Choctaw Genesis,* 149; Clayton, Knight, and Moore, *De Soto Chronicles,* 1: 236.

50. The exploration of the Escambia is plagued by varying interpretations as well. Galloway writes that the detachment under the command of Captains Álvaro Nieto and Gonzalo Sánchez de Aguilar "followed the bay's largest tributary river, the Escambia." This party traveled some twenty leagues, captured an Indian woman named Lacsohe, and returned to find the camp devastated by a hurricane. Hudson believes that this expedition was overland and that yet another explored the Escambia, both prior to the hurricane. Herbert Priestley timed the exploration of the Escambia at the same time the more famous party headed for Nanipacana (i.e., after the hurricane) and mentions two earlier expeditions that took place immediately upon landing at Achuse (prior to the hurricane), one of which explored the Escambia River. Since these divergent opinions are based on the same document, it should be clear that precision and clear details were not goals that Spanish testimony sought or achieved and that modern scholars frequently force details from extant documents that are not necessarily obvious to other readers. The document in question, the testimony of Cristóbal Velásquez, fails to actually note whether the expedition went by land or

water, but it does state that it left prior to the hurricane and arrived back at the base camp after the storm. See Galloway, *Choctaw Genesis,* 149; Hudson et al., "The Tristán De Luna Expedition," 34; Priestley, *Luna Papers,* 1: xxxv, and for the documents, 2: 303. See also *Luna Papers,* 1: 97, 2: 244.

51. Galloway, *Choctaw Genesis,* 149.

52. Priestley, *Luna Papers,* 1: 97.

53. Ibid., 2: 289, 305.

54. Ibid., 2: 291.

55. Hudson et al., "The Tristán De Luna Expedition," 36–37.

56. Priestley, *Luna Papers,* 1: 161.

57. Ibid., 1: 155.

58. Ibid.

59. Galloway, *Choctaw Genesis,* 151. Other descriptions of the route seem to confirm a delta location: "the land is so swampy, so full of canebrakes and brambles, and so full of obstructions." Priestley, *Luna Papers,* 1: 163.

60. Galloway, *Choctaw Genesis,* 150.

61. Hudson et al., "The Tristán De Luna Expedition," 36.

62. The source for the destruction of the village earlier by De Soto's expedition is Dávila Padilla. See Hudson et al., "The Tristán De Luna Expedition," 36.

63. DePratter, Hudson, and Smith, "The Hernando de Soto Expedition," 116.

64. Galloway, "Review of *The Juan Pardo Expeditions.*" See also Henige, "Proxy Data, Historical Method, and the de Soto Expedition," 162–65, for a critique of the "Chiaha" location proposed by Hudson and associates.

65. Hudson et al., "The Tristán De Luna Expedition," 40.

5
A Review of De Soto's Itinerary between Talisi and Apafalaya

Vernon James Knight Jr.

At this point it will be helpful to do a brief walk-through of an itinerary of De Soto's party as it approached and then departed from Mabila. In constructing this itinerary, decisions had to be made about what legitimately belongs on it. In this matter I have tried to be conservative, using the diary-based account of Rangel as the primary authority, with occasional corroboration from the anonymous gentleman from Elvas. The Biedma account is not of much use for travel segments on the route, except in giving directions—west and southwest in getting from Cosa to Talisi, south approaching the Gulf Coast in getting from Talisi to Mabila, and back north in getting from Mabila to Apafalaya. Although it is often overlooked, Biedma's brief description of Mabila itself (chapter 1, this volume) seems just as compelling as Rangel's or Elvas's, if not more so. Biedma's dispassionate, formal account was meant for the record, not for publication, so there is no literary embellishment or evident exaggeration, and his position as king's factor meant that he had no one's honor to defend but his own. Garcilaso's account is of no use in reconstructing the route for all the known reasons, and I have not depended on him here. Even in this short segment of the route, the Inca's tendencies to conflate separate scenes and to exaggerate numbers show through very plainly.[1] But he does include occasional descriptive details that are missing from the other narratives, and some such details are more likely to have come from the distant memory of his eyewitness source than from Garcilaso's own imagination. So these images are worth reporting too, with the appropriate caveats, and we can debate their merits, if need be, on a case-by-case basis. So, as long as Rangel provides the play-by-play, Garcilaso can be allowed to pipe in with color commentary.

The very nature of this chapter exposes a bias, one that is taken up as a special problem in chapter 12 (this volume). That bias, which amounts to a tacit assumption in previous route studies, is that a consensus itinerary is possible in the first place. To construct such an itinerary is to claim that the disagreements among three narratives, Rangel, Elvas, and Biedma, are sufficiently minor on matters of what was seen and done, that observations from all three can be merged into a single narrative, using the diary structure of the Rangel account as an armature. That is to say, even if we concur that these three accounts offer different visions of what really happened, as I think we must, we can still conclude that these witnesses' differences in perspective are only that, arising from experiences on the journey that were fundamentally the same.[2] A number of differences seem to be merely omissions within collapsed travel segments on the part of Elvas and Biedma, rather than conflicts per se.

I will begin, a bit arbitrarily, with the army's sojourn in Talisi and end with its arrival at the first village of Apafalaya province some days after departing Mabila.[3] This brackets Mabila on both sides and puts the whole segment within the present state of Alabama, according to all prior attempts at a route reconstruction. The period to be covered is two months' time, September 18 through November 18, 1540, starting from warm, dry, late summer days, and ending with the crisp days and chilly evenings of mid-November. It is worth remembering that according to Biedma's official transcript, it was not the soldiers' potential mutiny but the onset of winter and the potential shortage of food that prompted the Adelantado to move his army inland to more agriculturally productive lands.

Backing up a bit, De Soto's troop left the memorable town of Cosa on August 20, heading for a planned summer rendezvous with Captain Maldonado at the coastal port and native province of Achuse. They worked their way southwest over the next month, in no particular hurry, spending more than one day in the larger towns such as Itaba, Ulibahali, and Tuasi. Two days after leaving Tuasi, sleeping in the open, they came to the first towns of a long string of inhabited places. Ignoring for a moment their stay in Talisi, for the next eight travel days they were in sight of Indian towns every day, some large and some small. Thereafter they traveled two more days, camping in the open until reaching Piachi. Beyond Piachi was yet another gap of two days' travel time before reaching the very populous district of Mabila. Later, departing Mabila to the north, there were no settlements seen in five full days of continuous march. This rhythm of inhabited versus uninhabited territory is essential in matching the route to known clusters of appropriate archaeological sites and known gaps between those clusters.[4] In getting this route segment correctly placed on a modern map, it seems especially critical to identify that long, continuous eight-day stretch of river towns constituting two adjoining native provinces, in which Talisi was the third town and Atahachi the last. It seems plausible to me that most, if not all, of these towns are already recorded in the state archaeological site file, although, of course, we do not know which is which.[5]

All of our chroniclers agree that Talisi was a native province consisting of several towns, distinct from the provinces of both Cosa and Tascalusa. Elvas records that the large town of Talisi was the provincial capital, set among other subject towns and abundant cornfields on both sides of a copious river. For some two and a half weeks, from September 18 through October 4, De Soto took advantage of this abundance and stayed put in Talisi while he gauged the difficulty in passing the next obstacle, a province governed by a feared and therefore dangerous chief named Tascalusa. Garcilaso is the only one to give the distance between Talisi and Tascalusa's principal town, twelve to thirteen leagues, and to note that Tascalusa's town was approachable by two routes, of which the best was chosen.

After making contact with Tascalusa by way of messengers and emissaries, the army was back on the move on Tuesday, October 5. Of all the accounts, only the untrustworthy Garcilaso has them crossing the swollen River of Talisi upon their departure. Garcilaso may be conflating this event with the swollen river that impeded the army somewhat earlier at Itaba, according to the Elvas account. The first night out from Talisi they came to the small town of Casiste; Elvas agrees with Rangel on this point. It would still be two weeks on the march before they got to Mabila.

The next day, October 6, they came to a shabby river town named Caxa, said to be on the boundary line between the provinces of Talisi and Tascalusa. Caxa is probably the unnamed village referred to by Elvas as the first of those belonging to the province of Tascalusa. It is noteworthy that both Rangel and Elvas, in different ways, recognized that a boundary existed among these river towns between two abutting Indian provinces. This was an unusual circumstance since any political boundaries were ordinarily less obvious between more distantly separated polities.

De Soto's party spent the next three days in their approach toward Tascalusa's town of Atahachi. On the first night they camped in the open on the river bank opposite a town named Humati. The next day they came to Uxapita, said to be a new village. On Saturday, October 9, rather than entering Atahachi, they slept in the open one league short of it. Garcilaso claims that they were in sight of Tascalusa's town at this point. The following day they entered Atahachi, a new town, where they stayed two days. Concerning this town Garcilaso adds some uncorroborated details, saying that it was in a peninsula formed by the river, that it was not large enough to accommodate the entire army, and moreover that it was not really Tascalusa's capital but just one of his subject towns, on the latter point contradicting all three of the other main chroniclers. In these passages, though, Garcilaso conflates Atahachi with Piachi farther downstream, so it is difficult to sort out to which town each of his comments is meant to apply.

De Soto left Atahachi on Tuesday, October 12, with Chief Tascalusa and his principal men in tow. Their destination was Mabila, because Chief Tascalusa had told De Soto that additional burden bearers could be had there to meet the heavy demands of the Spaniards. Tascalusa seems to have convinced De Soto that Mabila was subject to him, but there are several reasons to doubt this claim. One of these reasons is the considerable distance of sparsely inhabited territory between the named provinces of Tascalusa and Mabila.[6] Between these two provinces, the river town of Piachi stood alone. Leaving Atahachi and sleeping in the open, it took two days to reach Piachi, and beyond Piachi, two more days to reach the densely populated district in which Mabila seems to have been the principal town.

Piachi was reached on Wednesday, October 13, with corroboration from Elvas that it was the second day out from Atahachi. A rate of march, given by Garcilaso as four leagues per day, probably applies to this leg of the journey, but then again it is hard to tell. Rangel, our most reliable source, gives us an image of Piachi so vivid that in my opinion, accurately identifying it on the ground could be a vital precondition to narrowing the search for Mabila. Piachi was said to lie atop a high, craggy river bluff.

If Piachi was on the Alabama River, as is alleged by all route proponents ancient and modern, it is disconcerting that none of the chroniclers tells us which side of the river the town was on. The Rangel and Elvas accounts can be read either way. If it was on the near side of the army's approach, it seems odd that the bellicose chief of Piachi would have contested that crossing, as Rangel's account alleges. But in one of the few emphatic contradictions in this segment of the journey, Elvas says that they crossed uneventfully and in safety. For what it is worth, the "De Soto map" shows the town symbol for Piachi on the east/south margin of the river.[7] Garcilaso alone tells us that this River of Piachi (Elvas's term) was the same one they had previously lived upon for some time in Talisi but that here at Piachi it was larger and fuller in current; according to the more reliable witness Biedma, they believed that this same river descended to the province of Achuse on the Gulf Coast, where Maldonado awaited in the army's brigantines to resupply them.

After crossing the river during an unspecified day, the army departed Piachi on October 16 and made camp in the bush. The following day they reached the first town of a thickly populated district, called the province of

Mabila by our best source, Rangel. At the unnamed palisaded town, they were brought a gift of chestnut bread by messengers from the next town, Mabila, chestnuts being plentiful in that district.

Our chroniclers agree that the town of Mabila was reached the morning of St. Luke's Day, October 18, a Monday. The vanguard that day consisted of a contingent of cavalry, including De Soto, Biedma, Moscoso, Gallegos, Rangel, the captain of the guard Espíndola, and others on foot including most or all of the captive burden bearers (with all their gear) and two priests. Everyone else (formally speaking, the battle line and rear guard) was strung along behind that morning, ransacking the populous countryside they had suddenly entered, "enjoying themselves" according to Garcilaso. Biedma, who was in that vanguard, says that they arrived at Mabila at about 9:00 in the morning; Garcilaso's informant remembered it as 8:00. The others got there later in the morning. This timing is a key bit of information, because the distance between Mabila and the palisaded town in which the army had spent the previous evening could not have been more than about five miles, and perhaps as few as three. It is now possible to calculate sunrise for any position on the globe at any date in history. Thus according to the government's National Oceanic and Atmospheric Administration, sunrise on October 18, 1540, in central Alabama occurred at 6:03 in the morning.[8] Assuming that it took at least an hour after sunrise to roust the troops, get them fed, gear up, pack up, and get moving (the most efficient of armies could hardly have done better than that), they could have been on the road for no more than two hours before reaching Mabila. The burden bearers, of course, were heavily laden and on foot.[9]

Because the purpose of this itinerary is to highlight events on the Spanish approach to Mabila and their departure from it, with a view toward using these data to narrow the search area, I will pass over most of the descriptive details of the town of Mabila itself.[10] Biedma's sketch will do. Mabila was a small, strongly palisaded town located on a plain (*llano*), and certain houses located outside this palisade had been removed. The terrain was such that the Spaniards could divide into squads and attack the town from four sides simultaneously. That could not happen if the town were tangent to any sizable body of water. It is the "Gentleman from Elvas" who tells the tale of the nearby pond (Portuguese *lagoa*) tinged with blood.

One thing that seems critical to identifying the location is the Spaniards' description of the area *surrounding* Mabila. While the other chroniclers use the more generic *campo* to describe these surroundings (field, countryside, terrain, open country), I think it is significant that Biedma's word choice is *llano,* or plain. This is not a word to be applied to a cleared patch of forest, to agricultural fields, or to terrain that is merely flat. It connotes something naturally open *and* flat. These features are not to be had just anywhere on the Coastal Plain and, contrary to some reconstructions, are not to be had at all in an alluvial delta. General Land Office surveys made prior to deforestation might be of use in narrowing down the possibilities.

Perhaps more important than all of this is the archaeological constraint that Mabila is to be found in the midst of a district that is heavily populated with other settlements, some palisaded like Mabila and others smaller, probably household farmsteads. The itinerary has already revealed that two palisaded towns were within only five miles or so of each other and that there were so many smaller settlements in between that looting them delayed the arrival of the main body of the army on the day of the battle. It is the Portuguese gentleman who gives us the most vivid picture. In Robertson's translation, "It was a very populous and fertile land. There were some large enclosed towns and a considerable population scattered about over the field (*campo*), the houses being separated from one another one or two crossbow flights." The phrasing indicates that there may have been more than just the two palisaded towns, and scattered farmsteads in between. For what it is worth, Garcilaso's account concurs. All of these settlements, large and small alike, will have left archaeological traces that ought to be readily identifiable, especially because, as Rangel relates, the Spaniards set a torch to them in the days following the battle, within a four-league radius according to Garcilaso. As a bit of negative evidence, the River of Piachi is nowhere mentioned in any of this. So here is our situation: We are actually looking for a tight *cluster* of archaeological sites of the correct period, *one of which* is Mabila. Any legitimate candidate for Mabila must be surrounded by the remains of other settlements, which will superficially look alike because they have all been burned.

As we have now strayed a bit from our itinerary, let us get back on track by relating that after an all-day battle, the army stayed at or near Mabila for a little less than a month, between October 19 and November 13. Elvas and Biedma are more or less in agreement about that length of time, about which Elvas says that the army camped *sempre no cãpo,* which in English we should probably read as "continually in the field" as opposed to within a town. It was Biedma who provided the graphic detail that the Spaniards harvested the bodies of the dead Indians for their fat to use as dressings for their wounds. This implies that the Spaniards did not simply leave the corpses where they lay but took more active measures to dispose of the bodies of the Indian combatants. For their part the Spanish dead, numbering some twenty, would have been accorded Christian burial, but not necessarily in the former town. Garcilaso, as is his custom, paints us a fuller picture. According to him, the Spaniards patched up what they could of the standing architecture of the town, building new roofs and creating temporary shelter there for eight days, while others dispersed into undamaged houses outside the town. Garcilaso concurs with Biedma on using the fat of dead Indians to dress their wounds. When they were physically able, they vacated the town's unpleasant ruins entirely, removing themselves to the immediate countryside while they gradually regained their health.

At this point the Spaniards learned through Indian informants that the coastal province of Achuse, their point of rendezvous with Maldonado toward which they had been steadily moving since leaving Cosa three months earlier, was within close reach to their south. As already noted, the Spaniards believed that the River of Piachi emptied into the port of Achuse. Biedma gives the distance to the Gulf as "up to 40 leagues," whereas Elvas gives the reported travel time to Achuse as six days, which is more or less in agreement. Given this apparent corroboration there is no reason to credit Garcilaso's contrary statement that the distance was a little less than thirty leagues. I find it intriguing that our best source, the Rangel narrative, is silent on the whole subject of the supply ships, the order that the soldiers not be told, the rumors of mutiny, and the decision to reverse direction.

The army stayed at Mabila for twenty-six days while the wounded recovered their strength, living in abandoned Indian lodges outside the town according to Garcilaso. Finally ready to march, they left Mabila on Sunday, November 13, heading into uninhabited country. According to Biedma the direction of travel was north. After four days they reached a fine river and followed it without crossing for another day through bad places and swamps before reaching Talicpacana.[11] Talicpacana was the first of five named towns of the province of Apafalaya, whose main town and chief were on the opposite side of the river.

Here is where our detailed itinerary ends. The narratives thus require another cluster of river towns for Apafalaya and, beyond that, yet another river crossing before reaching Chicasa where the army would overwinter for two months.

A smart way to use this itinerary, it seems to me, is to make not one but a series of trial fits with existing geographic and archaeological data. These trial fits can be phrased as competing hypotheses, and additional evidence for each of them can be sought in the field. In the end, with field testing, one such trial fit should emerge as superior to all others. That one should lead us to Mabila.

Notes

1. See George Lankford's discussion of Garcilaso's account in chapter 3, this volume.

2. On discrepancies between the Elvas, Rangel, and Biedma accounts, see Elbl and Elbl, "The Gentleman of Elvas and His Publisher." See also chapters 12 and 13, this volume.

3. In preparing this itinerary I have worked from the following sources: Oviedo y Valdés, *Historia General y Natural de las Indias,* book 17 (for Rangel); Elvas, *Relaçam Verdadeira;* reprinted in facsimile in Robertson, *True Relation;* Biedma, "Relación de la Isla de La Florida"; and Garcilaso de la Vega, *La Florida del Inca.* The most literal English translations of these four accounts may be found in Clayton, Knight, and Moore, *De Soto Chronicles.*

4. See my discussion of this approach in chapter 11, this volume.

5. See Craig Sheldon's discussion of the Alabama State Site File data in chapter 9, this volume.

6. See my related comments in chapter 11, this volume.

7. For the De Soto map, see Kathryn Braund's discussion in chapter 4, this volume.

8. I have converted the date from the Old Style Julian to the Gregorian calendar by adding ten days. Data from NOAA Surface Radiation Research Branch, sunrise/sunset calculator, available at http://www.srrb.noaa.gov/highlights/sunrise/sunrise.html.

9. Gregory Waselkov notes that there is light considerably before sunrise: "the vanguard may have set the pace by typically doing most of their travel before noon, scouting a good campsite, then allowing the rest to catch up throughout the rest of the day" (personal communication with the author, April 2007). If they departed at dawn, the vanguard could have made as much as three hours that morning, that is to say, seven to eight miles at the outside before reaching Mabila.

10. For the expected archaeological correlates of the town of Mabila, see the discussions by Jenkins, Regnier, Waselkov, and Sheldon in chapters 6–9, this volume.

11. Oviedo's spelling is possibly a mistranscription for Taliepacana.

6
The Village of Mabila

Archaeological Expectations

Ned J. Jenkins

For four years following their landing on the Florida Gulf Coast in May 1539, the De Soto *entrada* traveled through the land they called La Florida. This *entrada* was an incredible odyssey, as it witnessed and recorded aboriginal societies and lands that had never before been seen by Europeans. The Spaniards' descriptions of southeastern native provinces and chiefdoms are truly amazing, as most Europeans would never again encounter such societies free of some form of European contact. For many indigenous southeastern societies, the De Soto chronicles were their first and last descriptions, as this expedition helped initiate their decimation through military force and introduced diseases.[1]

After being on the march for over a year, De Soto arrived in central Alabama. The chronicles as well as the archaeology indicate that here he encountered three provinces or chiefdoms; Talisi, Tascalusa, and Mabila. The only principal chief mentioned by name in association with all these provinces was Chief Tascalusa. Tascalusa's emissaries met De Soto at Talisi while the chief of Talisi was initially "hiding in the woods." After a march of 12–13 leagues, De Soto stopped at Tascalusa's primary town of Atahachi. From Atahachi, Tascalusa was held hostage during a two-day journey across an unoccupied frontier. At a river crossing, the *entrada* reached Piachi on a Wednesday and the village of Mabila, according to Tascalusa "a town of one of his principal Indians, his vassal," the following Monday.[2]

Although much has been written about the De Soto *entrada* through the southeastern United States, the route through central Alabama has not been well understood up to the present, primarily because the *entrada* left few material remains to mark its course. In addition, the chronicles' locational descriptions are often brief or vague, and sometimes conflicting. Further, the Protohistoric ceramic chronologies of these three central Alabama native provinces have not been well understood; consequently the identification of De Soto–period sites in the absence of European artifacts has been problematic until recently. Previous reconstructions of his route have been based, therefore, on vague and sometimes conflicting locational descriptions, murky estimates of distance traveled per day, a slim trail of Spanish artifacts, and poorly understood Late Mississippian ceramic chronologies. Only recently has our understanding of indigenous ceramic complexes of the period and region improved to the point where we can accurately plot sites that would have been in existence during the mid-sixteenth century.[3]

At the time of the De Soto *entrada* there were three indigenous pottery complexes in use in the central Alabama area. First, the shell-tempered Big Eddy phase ceramic complex (Moundville-related) was utilized along the upper Alabama River, from a point just south of Montgomery, north to the junction of the Coosa and Tallapoosa rivers. Second, the coarse sand-tempered Shine II complex (Lamar-related) was utilized along the Tallapoosa River from the modern town of Tallassee westward to a point near the junction of the Coosa and Tallapoosa rivers. Third, the shell-tempered Furman phase complex (Late Pensacola-related), as described by Regnier, occurs along the Alabama River.[4] In each region, minority amounts of pottery from adjacent complexes can be found in association with the others at the spatial periphery of each phase.[5]

Mississippian Village Characteristics

My primary task is to address the probable archaeological appearance of Mabila. This should include understanding (1) the general characteristics of a Mississippian village, and (2) site characteristics of Mabila as described in the chronicles, and how these characteristics compare with archaeologically examined Mississippian villages elsewhere. This information will provide basic village attributes and thus important clues to what we should expect archaeologically at the village site of Mabila.

In order to better address the above questions, I examine the chronicles of Luys Hernández de Biedma, Garcilaso de la Vega, Rodrigo Rangel, and the "Fidalgo de Elvas" as translated in *The De Soto Chronicles*.[6] In an edited volume by Patricia Galloway, several authors discuss supposed variation in degree of accuracy, consistency, and content of these sixteenth-century authors.[7] The details provided by each chronicler, in distances and direction of travel, as well as in who and what was encountered, differ in quantity and quality of information. Garcilaso de la Vega comes across as the most suspect, since he tends to exaggerate, and his distances often do not agree with those of the other chronicles.[8] However, he often provides details not present in the other narratives.

What did Mississippian villages of the Southeast look like? Through links and interactions among chiefdoms, the structure of towns or villages came to resemble one another in many ways. All villages probably had a plaza, with wattle and daub houses situated around it. Some villages had one or more mounds aligned with the plaza. And many villages had a palisade that enclosed the complex. However, it is usually necessary to conduct archaeological excavation to conclusively identify houses, palisades, and the plaza.[9]

Some Mississippian and later Historic period villages also exhibited borrow pits, which were formed by digging dirt for mound fill or clay to be used for daub, a plaster employed in house walls and palisades. Borrow pits often formed small ponds or lakes, such as those at Moundville and the one adjacent to the mound and village at Fort Toulouse/Jackson Park near Wetumpka, Alabama. From excavations at the Historic period site of Fusihatchee, on the lower Tallapoosa River, it is known that such borrow pits could, through time, serve several functions. Although their initial purpose was as a source of clay for daub, they were secondarily used as ponds for watering livestock and as plantations for cultivating *Iris versicolor,* a powerful cathartic. Lastly, they often served as garbage receptacles.[10]

The first Mississippian villages appeared in the Mobile Bay Watershed in approximately A.D. 1050 or A.D. 1100. The people of these villages based their subsistence on corn, beans, squash, and deer. Plant domesticates provided a storable, fairly predictable food supply, in contrast to previous inhabitants of the region who were hunters and foragers, having almost no domesticates.

In the Black Belt of the nearby middle Tombigbee River valley, village sites were located on the highest ground of the upper terrace, near fresh water. Larger sites were always located on relatively high, loamy, well-drained soil, at least twenty to twenty-five feet above the level of the river or creek.[11] Above the Coastal Lowlands of the Southeast, Mississippian villages were often built within a sharp river bend of the active floodplain, or less often within the loop of an oxbow lake. Occasionally, villages were built at the junction of a large creek and a river. Natural barriers like creeks, rivers, and oxbow lakes in such localities could provide a more effective defense than elsewhere. Often such localities were palisaded, incorporating features of natural terrain in their defense. Palisades were built of closely spaced vertical poles set in the ground, strengthened with smaller horizontal poles. Palisade walls sometimes featured river cane lathwork, daubed over with a mixture of mud and grass, the grass holding the mud in place. Sometimes the outer palisade perimeter was scooped out, forming a ditch or dry moat, with the dirt piled as a ridge on the inside, into which the palisade ditch was dug. The earliest General Land Office plat for Cahawba (1817) seems to illustrate such a constructed ditch or moat, labeled as an "Ancient Indian Work." Archaeological investigations indicate that this was a Late Pensacola, Furman phase village of the approximate age of the De Soto *entrada,* although no Spanish artifacts were recovered.[12] Both archaeological excavations and early European drawings indicate that villages may have had an entrance protected by overlapping walls. Frequently the palisade was further enhanced by towers or bastions placed at intervals.[13]

Late Mississippian villages that are located on creeks, miles from the nearest river, are rare within the Mobile Bay Watershed but they do occur. Early Mississippian villages, by contrast, occur with greater frequency on creeks far from the river.

Descriptions of Mabila

The four chronicles offer some reasonably good clues to the general appearance of Mabila. These descriptions can be compared to what we know of excavated Mississippian villages in order to determine what Mabila might look like when encountered archaeologically.

Garcilaso de la Vega and Biedma time the arrival of De Soto and a vanguard of soldiers at the village of Mabila early on Monday, October 18, at eight or nine o'clock in the morning. These sources indicate that Mabila was close enough to the previous night's encampment that it took only a few hours to reach it early the next day. Garcilaso de la Vega also indicates that Mabila was located only a league and a half from the previous night's encampment.[14] Rangel indicates that the previous night was spent at an unnamed, palisaded village where De Soto and his army were fed much chestnut bread brought from Mabila, "for there are many and good chestnuts in his land."[15]

Even though there is probably more space in the chronicles devoted to the encounter with Chief Tascalusa (a period of about eight days leading up to the battle) and the battle of Mabila than to other episodes of the De Soto *entrada,* the information seems brief when one considers that this battle could have terminated the expedition and potentially altered Spain's future plans for conquest and colonization of the Southeast. The descriptions of the battle by Biedma, factor to the Crown, and Rangel, De Soto's private secretary, are brief. Elvas offers information mostly substantiating Rangel and Biedma, while Garcilaso seems to offer more detail as well as some blatant exaggeration.

According to Biedma, Mabila "was a very small and very strongly palisaded town. . . . There were some Indian houses on the outside of the palisade, but we found that the Indians had demolished them all to the ground in order to have the field more clear." He indicates that the town had gates that could be opened and closed and, importantly, the town could be completely encircled by horsemen. Thus it seems clear there was no protective creek or river on any side. Biedma further states that some houses had loopholes from which to fire weapons, and that the houses together concealed approximately five thousand Indians.[16]

Rangel offers additional detail, stating that there was a large plaza, a common feature of Mississippian villages, located in front of the town at the main gate. In addition, Rangel indicates that there was more than one gate, but he differs from Biedma in saying that the village was attacked and entered on three sides, not four as stated by Biedma.[17]

Elvas says that after leaving Piachi, "[t]he governor marched three days, the third day through a continuously peopled region. He reached Mavilla on Monday the eighteenth of October, he going in the vanguard with fifteen horse and thirty foot." Elvas also relates that "[a]t the signal [an arquebus shot], all four companies, each in its own position, attacked with great fury and doing great damage entered the town from one side and the other."[18] This account corroborates Biedma in an important way: Biedma says that four squads attacked the town, from which we can conclude with some certainty that there were no natural boundaries preventing attack from all sides.

Elvas is the only chronicler who provides what may prove to be another important clue when he states that "[i]t took them so long to get back that many of the Christians, tired out and suffering great thirst, went to get a drink at a pond located near the stockade, but it was tinged with the blood and they returned to the fight."[19] Within the Gulf Coastal Plain, "ponds" most often occur as oxbow lakes or some product of river channel movement. Thus the mention of a pond may indicate that Mabila was located within the active floodplain of the Alabama River. Smaller tributaries entering the Alabama River are narrower and more deeply entrenched into the chalk of the Black Prairie and thus have fewer oxbows (thus "ponds") than the Alabama River. "Ponds" may also result as a product of soil excavation for mound building or for clay extraction to be used as daub in both house and palisade construction. Hence, a "pond" might not necessarily have been located within the active floodplain.

In further describing the area, Elvas indicates that "[t]here were some large enclosed towns and a considerable population scattered about over the field, the houses being separated by one or two crossbow flights." I take this to indicate that there were continuous farmsteads between the unnamed palisaded village and Mabila. And it is possible that De Soto's soldiers encountered additional palisaded villages in the army's twenty-eight-day recovery period at Mabila, as indicated by Elvas.[20]

In many respects Garcilaso de la Vega offers much more detail, perhaps because he drew on the memories of Silvestre, Coles, and Carmona, who were also on the expedition.[21] However, in many places Garcilaso seems prone to exaggeration since his numbers of Indians participating in the battle of Mabila and the sizes of various items do not agree with the other accounts. This is unfortunate, since he also provides details not seen in the other narratives.

Garcilaso provides several additional details concerning the appearance of Mabila. He states that "[i]t contained few houses, scarcely more than eighty, but they were all very large and some had a capacity of fifteen hundred persons, others of a thousand, and the smaller ones of more than five hundred. We call a house any building of only one room, like a church, for the Indians do not build their houses by connecting several rooms together. . . . Since those of this pueblo had been erected as a frontier and a strong place and for displaying the power of the lord, they were very handsome."[22] This passage is highly interesting in that Garcilaso is the only one of the chroniclers who notes that Mabila was situated near a frontier, that is, near a vacant area providing separation from a neighboring chiefdom. In addition, he is the only chronicler who defines what he means by a house. But when he states that the houses could hold as many as 1,500, 1,000, or even 500, they are being described as tremendously larger than any examples of houses yet excavated archaeologically in the Southeast. These numbers of people inhabiting the houses simply are not believable.

Garcilaso may give a good description of Mabila's palisade, except for his exaggeration concerning the diameter of its posts. He says that

> [t]he pueblo was situated on a very beautiful plain and had an enclosure three estados high, which was made of logs as thick as an oxen. They were driven in the ground so close together that they touched one another. Other beams, longer and not so thick, were placed crosswise on the outside and inside and attached with split canes and strong cords. On top they were daubed with a great deal of mud and packed down with long straw, a mixture that filled the cracks and open spaces between the logs and their fastenings in such a manner that it really looked like

> a wall finished with a mason's trowel. At intervals of fifty paces around this enclosure were towers capable of holding seven or eight men who could fight in them. The lower part of the enclosure, to a height of an estado, was full of loopholes for shooting arrows at those on the outside. The pueblo had only two gates, one on the east and the other on the west. In the middle was a spacious plaza, around which were the largest and most important houses.

Elsewhere he says that the attacking Spaniards "made vigorous strokes at the wall with their axes and knocked off the mixture of mud and straw that was on top of it, uncovering the transverse logs and the fastenings by which they were attached."[23]

Except for the diameter of the posts—said to be the size of oxen—this palisade description is highly compatible with archaeologically known palisades. The excavated palisade nearest Mabila is that at the site of Moundville, to the northwest in the Black Warrior River valley. Postholes in the curtain walls of one excavated section were 10–15 inches in diameter, spaced 8–16 inches apart, and set in a palisade trench 12–20 inches wide and up to 51 inches deep. The bastions excavated at Moundville were spaced approximately 35–40 yards apart, fairly close to the fifty paces specified by Garcilaso.[24]

Garcilaso's palisade description is also potentially significant in that it is the only one to indicate that the palisade was coated with a mixture of mud and grass. Once this palisade burned, a brick-like daub would have formed, which should be highly visible to an archaeological survey, constituting an important on-the-ground signature for the village of Mabila.

Garcilaso's account of Mabila's village plan does differ from that of Rangel, who locates a plaza in front of the principal gate. This discrepancy can only make sense if the account was in error or if there were two plazas. One "plaza" may have actually been a chunkee yard or ball court. We know from archaeological and historical accounts that when no mound was present, the plaza was likely to be at the center of the village, as was the chunkee yard.[25] In addition, Garcilaso mentions "streets" numerous times, whereas the other chroniclers do so only rarely. Curiously, Garcilaso describes "fighting from the flat roofs or terraces."[26] At first I was inclined to dismiss this as Garcilaso's imagination at work, but it is possible that he was referring to a feature such as earth lodges, with broad rounded domes. When seen as more than one, these might be described as terraces, which could indicate that they were earthen. Alternatively, the terraces might refer to the terraced margins of a chunkee court as described by Bartram.[27]

Summary

So, what should the archaeologist expect to see when the village of Mabila is found in survey and/or excavated? It seems evident from the Spanish descriptions that the village was located on a broad plain. Whether this was an alluvial terrace or an upland prairie is a pivotal question that may guide our scope of search. It seems clear from the chronicles that there is no river or intersecting creek associated with the village site. The chronicles agree that the movement of men and cavalry was not impeded by bodies of water. The river was not mentioned again after the crossing at Piachi, three days before reaching Mabila.

It is fairly clear from the chronicles that Mabila was located within a continuously peopled area. Such an extensively populated region should have access to nearby floodplain soils necessary for intensive corn agriculture. Elvas describes it as "a very populous and fertile land."[28] However, it is interesting that Biedma refers to the Mabila region as a "land of little food," whereas in December of the previous year near Apalache, crops were still being gathered from the fields. Had the Indians denuded the Mabila region of food, or had this been a bad growing season, as possibly indicated by the mention of a very cold November?[29]

All of the chronicles indicate that there were houses within the village of Mabila. Mississippian houses of the period were constructed by digging individual holes for wall posts, then weaving split cane between the posts. A mixture of mud and grass was then plastered over the split cane. Roofs were made from a framework covered with cypress bark, palmetto fronds, or cane. When such buildings burned, the roof material would act as tinder, burning and firing the daub in the walls to a hard, brick-like orange material. These burned houses, and in particular the masses of fired daub, should provide a clear signature for the village for Mabila. It is true that houses occasionally burned in other circumstances, but rarely did an entire village burn, as did Mabila. In addition, the chronicles agree that hundreds, if not thousands, of Indians burned to death in these houses; hence burned human bones should be abundant. The chronicles also indicate that these houses had weapons of war stored in them. Thus we might expect to find quantities of small triangular chert arrow points in many houses.

The Spanish army is said to have lost all of its baggage and some weapons in the fire that consumed Mabila.[30] As stated by Rangel, "the fire traveled so that the nine arrobas of pearls that they brought were burned, and all the clothes and ornaments and chalices and moulds for wafers, and the wine for saying mass, and they were left like Arabs, empty-handed and with great hardship."[31] Many of the items left within the village during the fire would have been charred and/or melted. It is difficult to determine just how much of the baggage may have been recovered after the battle; nonetheless, there must have been Spanish artifacts lost as a result of the battle and fire, much of it in houses. This material should be archaeologically evident.

Another characteristic described by the chronicles was the palisade, with two principal gates and probably towers. A palisade represents a considerable communal labor investment in Mississippian villages in which they were present. As noted, Garcilaso seems to have exaggerated the size of the posts in the palisade as "thick as an oxen," as the palisade posts at the nearby Moundville site were only 10–15 inches in diameter. An important attribute of the Mabila palisade as described by Garcilaso is that it was mudded or daubed. When burned, this daub would turn to brick-like fired clay, augmenting the daub signature of the houses. Hence, an archaeological survey should look for large quantities of orange-colored daub. This is an important village attribute to look for, whether or not the palisade was daubed. One wonders how the Mabila palisade would compare with the one described by Rangel, two days south of Tuasi, as follows: "[O]n Wednesday they went to an old town that had double walls [*cercas*] and good towers. And those ramparts [*muros*] are built in this manner: they sink many thick poles, tall and straight, next to one another; they weave them with some long sticks, and daub them within and without, and they make their loopholes at intervals, and they make their towers and turrets [*cubos*] spread out along the curtain and parts of the rampart as suits them; and at a distance, they appear to be one very excellent wall [*muralla*] and such walls are very strong."[32] Except for the double wall, this compares very well with Garcilaso's description of the Mabila palisade and it could in fact be the source of Garcilaso's descriptive embellishment.

As referred to only by Elvas, there may have been a pond just outside the palisade. This pond may not have been a natural feature. Excavated examples of such "ponds" have been found at the historic Creek site of Fusihatchee.[33] These features were the product of the native excavation of clay, which was mixed with grass to form the daub used to chink the woven cane walls of houses or palisades.

Conclusion

The documentary clues are not bountiful, but the archaeological correlates should be sufficient to identify the site. The most prominent signature should be a dense scatter of daub. To date the daub scatter, the archaeologist should look for the distinctive shell-tempered ceramics of the Furman phase as described by Regnier. Smaller quantities of the shell-tempered Big Eddy phase ceramic complex, as well as the coarse sand-tempered Shine II phase ceramics (Lamar Complicated Stamped) may also occur. The site will probably be located at least twenty feet above the original level of the nearest flowing water, on a fine sand or fine sandy loam soil. The remnants of some sort of natural or excavated pond may or may not be visible. No mound is mentioned by any of the chroniclers. Upon excavation, the burned palisade and houses should be notable. Burned human bone and triangular arrow points should be numerous. Although many Spanish artifacts were no doubt ultimately removed by Spaniards and natives from Mabila, they should, nonetheless, be more numerous here than at any other Late Mississippian site in Alabama. Horse bones, with butcher marks, may also be found. The fire and its ashes should have preserved some number of perishable artifacts not normally recovered archaeologically.

Notes

1. Milanich, "The European Entrada into La Florida," 4.
2. Clayton, Knight, and Moore, *De Soto Chronicles,* 1: 99, 292–93.
3. See chapters 7 and 9, this volume.
4. See chapter 7, this volume.
5. Jenkins, "Tracing the Origins of the Early Creeks."
6. Clayton, Knight, and Moore, *De Soto Chronicles.*
7. Galloway, "Incestuous Soto Narratives."
8. Ibid., 27.
9. Lafferty, "Fortifications"; Lewis, Stout, and Wesson, "The Design of Mississippian Towns"; Schroedl, "Mississippian Towns in the Eastern Tennessee Valley"; Wesson, "Mississippian Sacred Landscapes."
10. Sheldon, "Where Bartram Sat"; Bartram, *The Travels of William Bartram, Naturalist Edition,* 454.
11. Jenkins, Curren, and DeLeon, *Archaeological Site Survey,* 69–75. Copy on file at Office of Archaeological Research, The University of Alabama, Tuscaloosa.
12. Knight, *Archaeological Test Excavations at the Site of Old Cahawba;* Martin, "Archaeological Investigations of an Aboriginal Defensive Ditch."
13. Fundaburk, *Southeastern Indians, Life Portraits,* 105; Lafferty, "Fortifications."
14. Clayton, Knight, and Moore, *De Soto Chronicles,* 1: 233, 2: 330.
15. Ibid., 1: 292.
16. Ibid., 1: 233–35.
17. Ibid., 1: 293.
18. Ibid., 1: 98, 101.
19. Ibid., 1: 101.
20. Ibid., 1: 104, 105.

21. Galloway, "Incestuous Soto Narratives," 34.

22. Clayton, Knight, and Moore, *De Soto Chronicles,* 2: 330–31.

23. Ibid., 2: 331, 339.

24. Lafferty, "Fortifications"; Scarry, *Excavations on the Northwest Riverbank at Moundville,* 181; Allan, "Moundville's Fortifications," 8.

25. Nabokov and Easton, *Native American Architecture,* 92–121.

26. Clayton, Knight, and Moore, *De Soto Chronicles,* 2: 340.

27. Waselkov and Braund, *William Bartram and the Southeastern Indians,* 154.

28. Clayton, Knight, and Moore, *De Soto Chronicles,* 1: 105.

29. Ibid., 1: 72–73, 236.

30. Waselkov, this volume.

31. Clayton, Knight, and Moore, *De Soto Chronicles,* 1: 294.

32. Ibid., 1: 285–88.

33. Sheldon, "Where Bartram Sat."

7
What Indian Pottery of Sixteenth-Century Central Alabama Looks Like and Why It Matters

Amanda L. Regnier

In order to establish a possible location for the battle of Mabila, one must not only estimate the distances traveled by the expedition party and match the details in the narratives to the geographic landscape but also correlate the Indian towns mentioned with known archaeological sites. This correlation is more complicated than it sounds. An archaeological site on the landscape that agrees well with the geographic setting and travel times mentioned in the narratives was not necessarily occupied by native peoples during the sixteenth century. Archaeologists determine the age of indigenous settlements primarily through the detailed study of changes in native pottery. Until very recently, assigning an archaeological site to the mid-sixteenth century was difficult, since archaeologists did not have a firm grasp of the ceramic assemblages typical of this period in central Alabama.

Fortunately, research in recent years by several archaeologists has provided a much clearer picture of native pottery in the region during this period. This research is crucial to the reconstruction of the route of the Hernando de Soto expedition, because it has allowed archaeologists to more easily differentiate ceramic assemblages of the sixteenth century from those that postdate European contact. Beyond this important development, there is a second, more subtle reason why the understanding of sixteenth-century ceramic assemblages is essential. My own recent research has focused on how the composition of sixteenth-century ceramic assemblages reflects the social and political organization of the towns under the leadership of Chief Tascalusa. The results of this investigation have been able to provide a better characterization of Tascalusa's political domain in the decades leading up to the events of 1540.

The Use of Pottery in Dating Archaeological Sites

The dating of archaeological sites can be accomplished by several means. Absolute methods, such as radiocarbon dating, provide dates for a site in calendar years. In contrast are relative methods, such as stratigraphy and seriation, which allow archaeologists to know which artifact types are older or younger than other artifact types, but not how much older or younger. Sites within our study area are also dated by reference to certain diagnostic types of European goods that occur in post-Contact native settlements in small quantities.[1]

The artifact category most frequently used to establish relative dates for sites from roughly the last three millennia of prehistory in central Alabama is pottery, usually found in broken form as potsherds. Pottery is not the only class of artifacts routinely recovered from sixteenth-century sites, but potsherds are plentiful, and their patterned changes provide good diagnostics for very narrow time periods. As a result of the scarcity of absolute dates and European goods from sixteenth-century sites in central Alabama, for the most part sites of this era have been relatively dated by comparing their pottery assemblages with well-defined pottery chronologies from neighboring regions, particularly the Black Warrior River valley and the Mobile-Tensaw Delta.

Archaeologists interested in building chronologies focus on three aspects of pottery production, each of which tends to change regularly with the passage of time. These aspects consist of the type of clay paste, the form of the vessel, and the manner in which the vessel is decorated.

Clay pastes are differentiated mainly by the type of temper added to the clay to strengthen the vessel. Tempering agents associated with ceramics from the sixteenth century in central Alabama consist of fine sand, coarse sand or crushed rock known as grit, and crushed shell. Shell tempering can be further subdivided based on the size of the shell particles, since vessels tempered with fine and coarse crushed shell are easily differentiated from one another. It is also useful to distinguish the type of shell used, whether from live river mussels or from fossilized marine shells abundant in local geological deposits.

The form that a vessel takes also provides clues concerning the dating of the artifact. The broad category of vessel form encompasses not only the basic vessel shape, whether a bowl, jar, bottle, or otherwise, but also includes secondary shape features, such as different rim forms. Vessel forms associated with assemblages from the area and time period of concern here consist of globular jars and three bowl shapes including the casuela, the flaring rim bowl, and the simple bowl. Secondary shape features associated with sixteenth-century pottery differ depending on the vessel form. On jars, these secondary

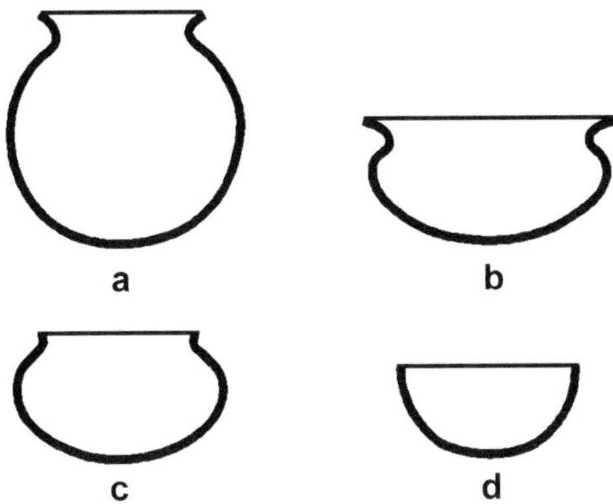

Figure 7.1. Vessel forms present in sixteenth-century ceramic assemblages from central Alabama: (a) globular jar, (b) flaring-rim bowl, (c) casuela, and (d) simple bowl.

shape features include handles and applied pieces of clay including nodes, appliqué ridges, and fillets. Secondary shape features that occur on casuela bowls and simple bowls are diverse but easily recognizable, consisting of a variety of choices of rim form. Rims typically exhibit a combination of attributes: profiles that are folded, straight, or curving, lips that are flattened and/or everted, rims that may be demarcated by an incised line, and lip exteriors that may be decorated with fine or wide notching.

Finally, archaeologists frequently use aspects of vessel decoration to distinguish ceramics from different time periods. Types of decoration observed on sixteenth-century pottery in central Alabama include complicated stamping, which is executed by pressing elaborately carved wooden paddles onto the exterior vessel surface; incising, in which a stylus is used to draw designs on the still-moist clay of the vessel body; engraving, in which the design is scratched into the surface after the vessel is allowed to dry to a leather-hard state; and punctation, in which an object is used to create multiple impressions in the clay surface. The manner in which each type of decoration is executed and the specific decorative motifs employed also provide clues concerning the date of an assemblage.

Mississippian Pottery Traditions

Ned Jenkins was the first archaeologist to note that pottery assemblages from sites in the upper Alabama River drainage occupied during the early sixteenth century exhibit a mixture of pottery associated with two major Mississippian traditions, termed Moundville and Lamar, which are easily distinguished from one another through differing combinations of the attributes described above.[2] My own research has shown that in addition to Mound-

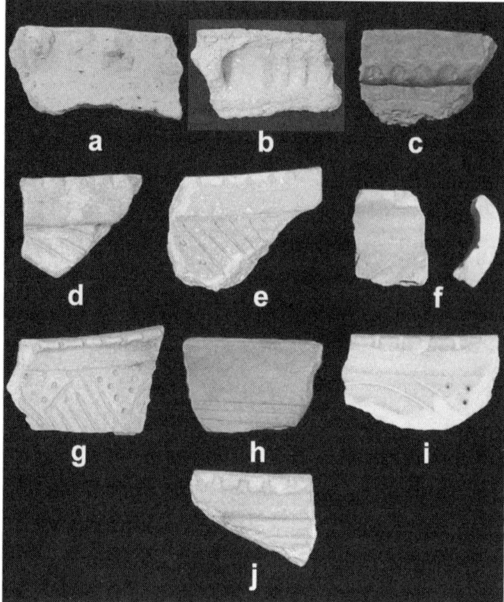

Figure 7.2. Ceramic attributes: (a) jar rim with attached nodes, (b) appliqué ridges on a jar rim, (c) fillet applied just below the lip of a jar, (d) folded rim on a casuela, (e) straight rim on a casuela, (f) curved rim on a casuela, (g) everted lip on a casuela, (h) incised line demarcating the rim of a simple bowl, (i) fine notching on the exterior of a bowl lip, and (j) wide notching on the exterior of a bowl lip.

ville and Lamar ceramics, assemblages from sites farther downriver also include ceramics associated with the Pensacola cultural tradition. The presence of pottery associated with these three cultural traditions is a direct result of the manner in which towns in the Alabama River valley were settled by Mississippian populations. The Mississippian cultural pattern, characterized by cultural traits such as intensive corn agriculture, settlement in the floodplain of major drainages, social stratification, politically centralized chiefdoms, and monumental architecture, first arose in the American Bottom of the Mississippi River valley near present-day St. Louis. This cultural pattern then spread across much of the southeastern United States. Between approximately A.D. 1100 and 1450, several different expressions of this cultural pattern arose as politically organized chiefdoms in most of the river drainages in what is now the state of Alabama. However, Mississippian occupation of the Alabama River valley during this period was only sporadic. These consisted primarily of intrusions of people from adjacent Mississippian chiefdoms, who appear to have attempted to establish new chiefdoms in the region. The short occupation spans observed at these sites suggest that these Mississippian intrusions met with little success until some time during the mid- to late fifteenth century. During this time, a series of new towns was established along the lower Tallapoosa and Alabama River valleys, between present-day Elmore and Wilcox counties. Several archaeologists have studied the fragile political structure of Mississippian chiefdoms, as they cycled through periods of fluorescence and decline.[3] Based on the evidence of ceramic assemblages from the Alabama River valley, it is no coincidence that the drainage was successfully settled during approximately the same era that three Mississippian polities in nearby regions went into political decline.

The origins of each of the three Mississippian ceramic complexes found at sixteenth-century sites in the Alabama River valley are closely tied to the political histories of three chiefdoms. Archaeologists have established that Lamar pottery styles in the area of our concern are directly descended from those associated with the chiefdom centered at the Etowah site in northwest Georgia. A Lamar ceramic assemblage consists of sand/grit-tempered complicated stamped and plain jars with applied rim fillets. Bowls in a Lamar assemblage are fine-sand tempered casuelas decorated with a series of incised motifs, including parallel lines with festoons, rectilinear designs, scrolls, triangles, and concentric rounded rectangles. These incised motifs are typically executed with multiple bold lines; evidence from Lamar sites suggests that the number of lines increases and the space between those lines decreases through time such that incised sherds from the fifteenth and sixteenth centuries have numerous, closely spaced incised lines.[4] Recent archaeological work based on collections found near the present-day city of Troy in southeast Alabama indicates that a population migrated from the Etowah chiefdom in northwest Georgia and settled in this area, likely because of internal political stresses.[5] It is possible that Lamar peoples of the Alabama River valley are descended from those migrants.

At sixteenth-century sites of the upper Alabama and lower Tallapoosa rivers, pottery associated with the Moundville tradition is found alongside Lamar pottery in the same communities. These two ceramic complexes are easily distinguished from one another, since Moundville-related ceramics are tempered with crushed shell. Pottery jars of the Moundville ceramic tradition tend to have a wider body than their Lamar counterparts, and they often exhibit handles, appliqué strips, or nodes near the rim of the vessel.[6] Moundville bowls come in three forms: flaring-rim, casuela, and simple. Rims on casuela bowls are typically folded and curved in profile. Lips are occasionally everted and are rarely flattened and decorated with notching. The exterior surfaces of these vessels are frequently burnished and may exhibit a black-filmed surface, which is achieved by firing the pot in an oxygen-reduced environment. Ceramics of the Moundville tradition are often decorated by in-

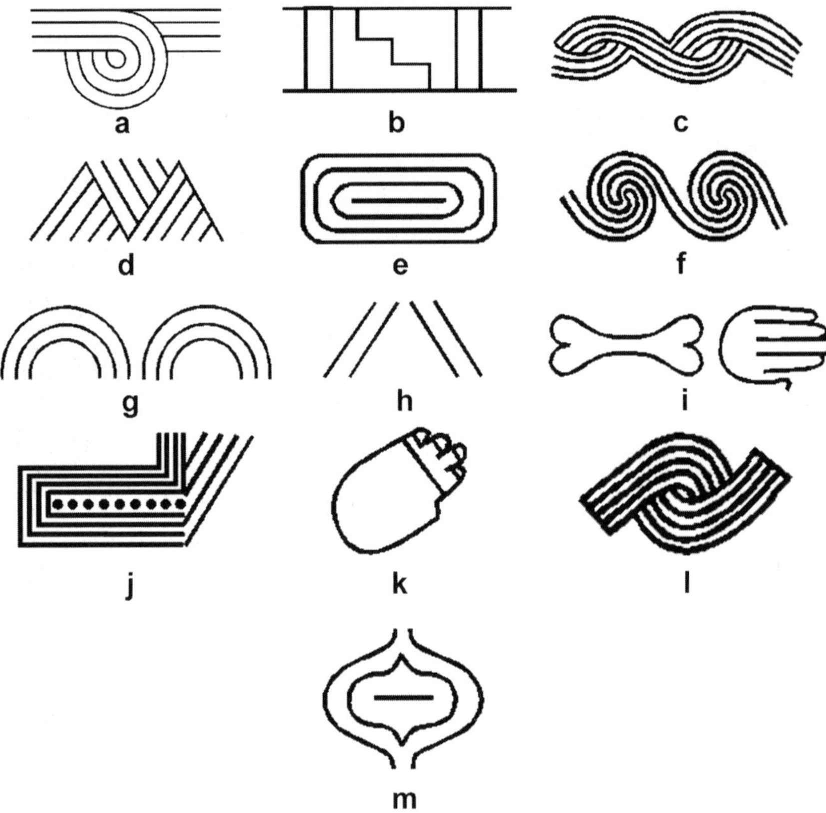

Figure 7.3. Incised motifs found on sixteenth-century ceramics. Lamar motifs: (a) festoons, (b) rectilinear motifs, (c) scrolls, (d) triangular motifs, (e) concentric rectangles; Moundville motifs: (f) scrolling guilloches, (g) semicircles, (h) chevrons, (i) hand and long bone; Pensacola motifs: (j) stylized skull, (k) stylized hands, (l) separate guilloche, (m) ogees.

cising, which occurs in a few specific motifs, including scrolls, semicircles, chevrons, and hands with long bones (see figure 7.3). The incising is executed in two or three bold lines, usually greater than 2 millimeters wide.

Where pottery associated with the Moundville ceramic tradition is found at sites in the Alabama River valley, it can be dated to the sixteenth century, based on comparison of traits with the well-defined ceramic chronology from the Moundville site. Chronologically, the appearance of Moundville ceramics at sites in the Alabama River valley corresponds to a decline in the political centralization of the Moundville chiefdom in the Black Warrior

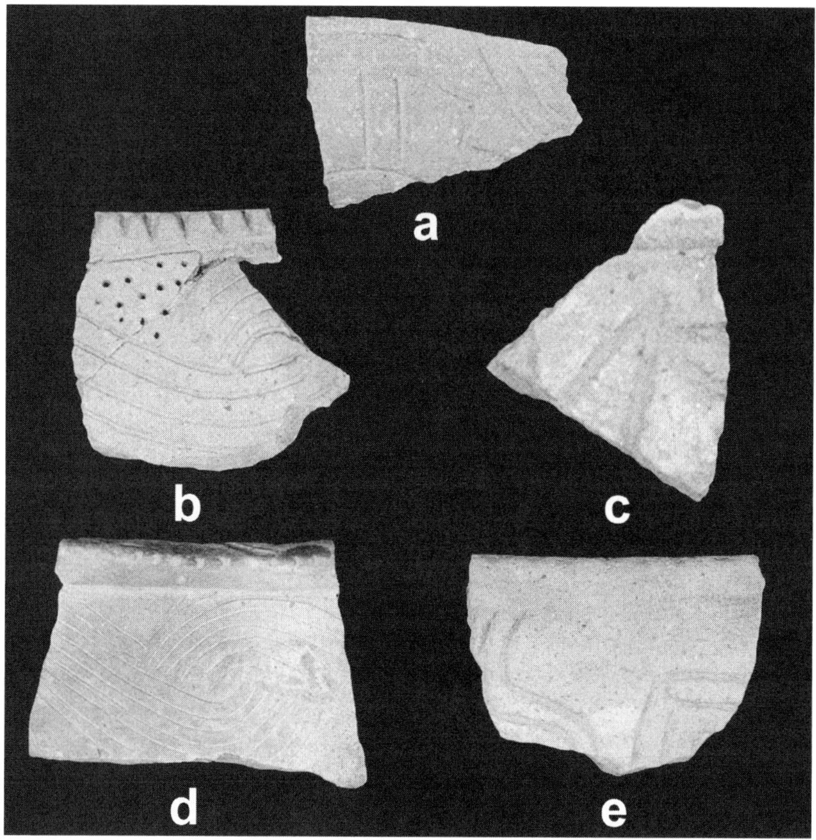

Figure 7.4. Incising styles and types of filler present on sixteenth-century pottery from central Alabama: (a) wide-line incising associated with Moundville tradition, (b) punctated design filler found on Pensacola-related ceramics, (c) engraved filler found on Pensacola-related ceramics, (d) fine incised, finely spaced lines derived from Pensacola tradition, (e) wide-line incising associated with Pensacola ceramics.

Valley.[7] During this period of decentralization in the late fifteenth and early sixteenth centuries, sites with Moundville-related ceramics also appear in the Cahaba River drainage, suggesting that groups of people moved eastward from the political center, perhaps as a result of internal political turmoil.

Pottery associated with a third cultural tradition, Pensacola, is also found at sixteenth-century sites in central Alabama. The political center of Pensacola culture was the Bottle Creek site, located in the Mobile-Tensaw Delta in southwest Alabama. The earliest pottery found at Pensacola culture sites dates to the thirteenth century and shows clear cultural ties to Moundville.[8]

Although Pensacola potters developed their own distinct styles over time, some Moundville traits survived in their pottery as late as the sixteenth century. Thus, globular utilitarian jars associated with Pensacola ceramics are very similar to those associated with Moundville. However, while incised globular jars had long since disappeared from the Moundville assemblage by the sixteenth century, they continued to occur in Pensacola assemblages. Such incised jars are readily differentiated from earlier Moundville examples because the incised lines are wider and have a row of punctations above them, and because these decorations occur on a slightly different paste than their Moundville counterparts. Pensacola bowls fall into the casuela and simple bowl categories, and are incised with motifs that include stylized skulls and hands, separated guilloches, and ogees (see figure 7.3). These motifs are frequently accompanied by punctation and engraved lines that serve as filler in the designs. Incising on Pensacola pottery in the Alabama River valley is executed in two distinct manners. The first occurs on paste with very finely crushed shell and heavy mica inclusions, and consists of numerous fine, closely spaced lines incised on a burnished surface; the other occurs on a paste tempered with larger shell particles, and consists of a maximum of three wider lines, spaced farther apart, incised on an unburnished surface (see figure 7.4). Pensacola bowl rims are typically folded, with flattened lips decorated with fine notching, or they may be unfolded, demarcated by an incised line, and decorated with wide notching at the lip. As is true for Moundville ceramics, the appearance of Pensacola ceramics at sites in the Alabama River valley during the fifteenth and sixteenth centuries also coincides with a period of decline at the Bottle Creek political center to the south.

Pottery associated with each of these three cultural traditions, Lamar, Moundville, and Pensacola, is not uniformly distributed across sites in the Alabama River drainage. Rather, an analysis of pottery assemblages from four Late Mississippian towns has shown that each individual town site exhibits a complex and varied assortment of pottery from each tradition. At downstream sites, such as Matthew's Landing in Wilcox County, the assemblage is made up primarily of Pensacola ceramics. Farther upriver, in Dallas County, the ceramic assemblage at the Durant Bend site includes both Pensacola and Moundville pottery. At the Bear Creek site, ceramics from all three traditions are represented, while sites just above the Coosa-Tallapoosa River junction show a combination of Moundville and Lamar ceramics. The composite nature of these assemblages is one of the reasons why pottery from these sites has been so poorly understood up through the present. Moreover, the nature of these assemblages has made it difficult for archaeologists to group sites into the named political provinces mentioned in the narratives of the De Soto expedition.

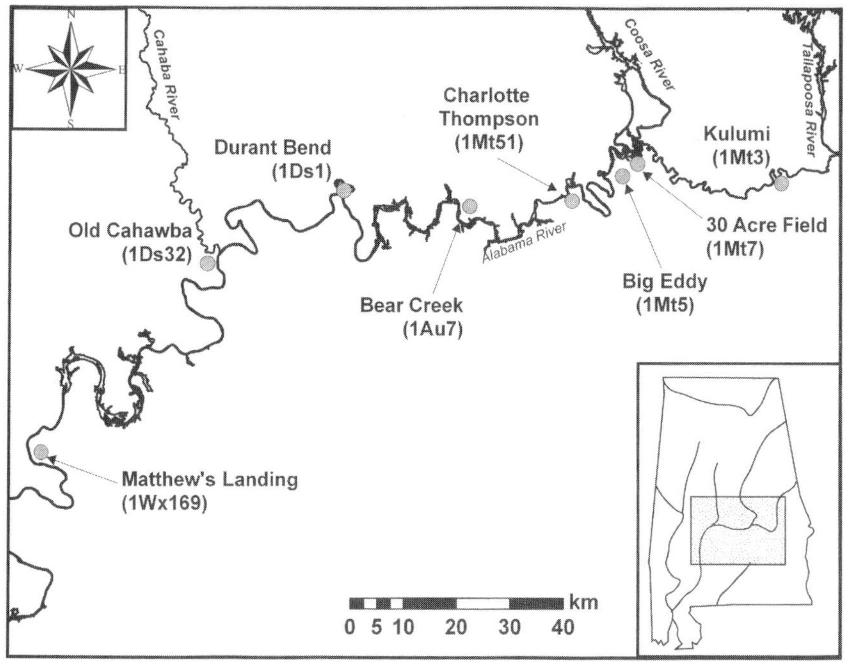

Figure 7.5. Locations of Late Mississippian towns in the upper Alabama River valley.

The variable mix of pottery at the four sites studied suggests that within each native community resided a distinct combination of potters trained in the ceramic arts of three very different cultural traditions. The presence of a series of recently settled towns housing a variable mix of peoples of different cultural backgrounds within the geographic area associated with the polity of Chief Tascalusa is especially interesting. The diversity in pottery assemblages from these towns suggests that Tascalusa's polity had a population that was multiethnic and had been established there for only a few generations. Because of this, it seems inaccurate to cast the political organization of the polity of Tascalusa in the same light as Mississippian chiefdoms with more ethnically uniform populations, such as those centered at Moundville, Etowah, and Bottle Creek. Instead, it appears that the group of towns united under the leadership of Chief Tascalusa were originally made up of culturally different peoples who coalesced as a political entity in the wake of turmoil that forced them to migrate from their homelands.

It is likely that these towns were only loosely consolidated into some form of confederacy. The towns of the Alabama River valley were so socially distinct that they probably functioned politically as a single unit only during

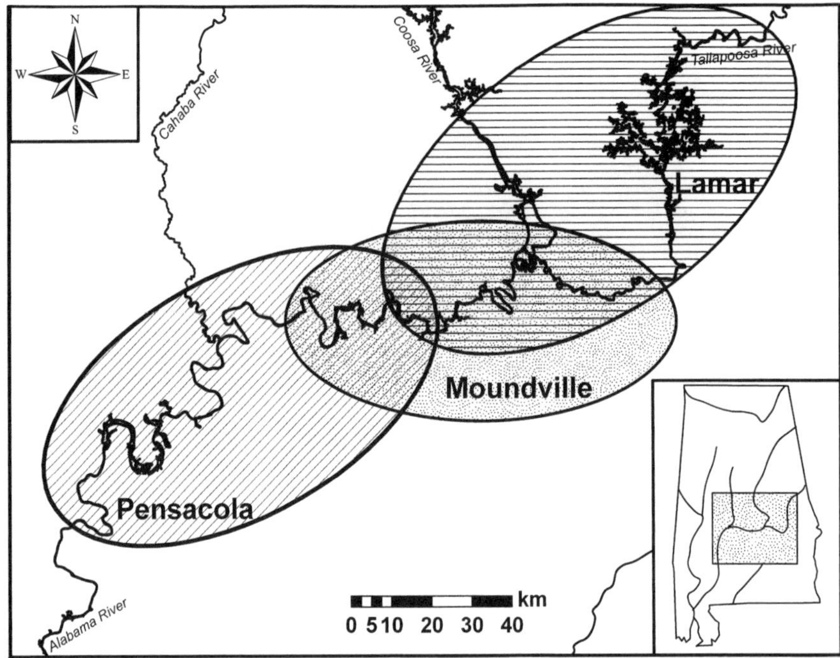

Figure 7.6. Overlap of Late Mississippian cultural traditions in the upper Alabama River valley.

times of threat, such as the appearance of an expedition led by a hostile soldier from an alien society. This loose form of political consolidation may explain why, when the De Soto expedition reached the Alabama River town of Piachi, Rangel reported that its "malicious" chief "took a position to resist the crossing" of the Alabama River.[9] This event suggests that within the territory governed by Chief Tascalusa, leaders of individual communities retained some degree of political autonomy.

In studies of De Soto's passage through what is now Alabama, native pottery assemblages of the time period must be understood for two reasons. First, such an understanding allows researchers to determine whether proposed site locations for towns identified in the chronicles were actually occupied at the time of the expedition. Any plausible location for towns mentioned in the narratives must yield artifacts dating to the sixteenth century, and native pottery is by far the most abundant datable artifact form found at all such town sites. Second, the nature of sixteenth-century pottery assemblages also reflects the social composition of the towns that made up the polity of Chief Tascalusa. Because ceramic assemblages from native sixteenth-century towns of the Alabama River valley indicate that each town had a distinct social composition, it is difficult to associate clusters of town sites with specific political entities. This fact complicates the usual method of correlating named provinces with tight clusters of archaeological sites having similar pottery, but on the positive side it helps researchers make better sense of the native political scene and the chroniclers' attempts to describe and interpret what they were seeing.

Notes

1. See chapter 8, this volume.
2. Jenkins, "Early Creek Origins."
3. Anderson, "Stability and Change in Chiefdom-Level Societies"; Anderson, *The Savannah River Chiefdoms;* Blitz, "Mississippian Chiefdoms and the Fission-Fusion Process."
4. Hally, "An Overview of Lamar Culture."
5. Jenkins, "Early Creek Origins."
6. Steponaitis, *Ceramics, Chronology, and Community Patterns.*
7. Knight and Steponaitis, "A New History of Moundville."
8. Fuller, "Out of the Moundville Shadow."
9. Rangel, "Account of the Northern Conquest and Discovery of Hernando de Soto," 1: 291–92.

8
What Do Spanish Expeditionary Artifacts of Circa 1540 Look Like and How Often Are They Preserved?

Gregory A. Waselkov

Information on the material culture of the De Soto expedition comes from two sources: (1) the documentary record of that and other sixteenth-century Spanish expeditions to the interior of North America; and (2) archaeological sites that have been attributed to that era. These sources coincide to a limited extent, but there remains considerable disagreement about the relevance of some archaeological artifact categories to the 1540 dateline.

The Documentary Record

De Soto expedition accounts mention many items of material culture, ranging from weaponry to clothing to subsistence items (see appendix).[1] As one might expect from the reminiscences and reports of conquistadors, their accounts are particularly rich in references to weaponry and armor, and much less forthcoming on more mundane artifacts. For instance, helmets are mentioned in several contexts, as are coats of chain mail and shields. Garcilaso, thought to be our least reliable chronicler, describes plate armor twice in his Mabila battle account. An arrow struck De Soto "in the small unprotected space . . . between the saddlebow and the breastplate" and entered his left hip after penetrating his underlying "coat of mail." Don Carlos Enríquez, a gentleman married to De Soto's niece, died from an arrow to the throat, the only part of his body not "well armored." Interestingly, Enríquez's horse was protected by leather, not plate armor.

Horsemen's lances are noted repeatedly. Foot soldiers carried swords and daggers, and particular companies were armed with arquebuses (a type of matchlock firearm), halberds, or crossbows. Arquebuses disappear from the accounts about a year into the *entrada,* perhaps because their gunpowder supply ran out, but the other weaponry remained in use throughout the expedition. Again according to Garcilaso, the army hauled a piece of light artillery—probably a wrought-iron, breech-loading hand cannon—by pack mule for the first year, until it was buried at Cofaqui (in Ocute) when its impracticality became apparent to De Soto.[2] Iron shot mentioned late in the expedition may have been intended for this cannon. According to Garcilaso, most of the Spaniards carried axes, probably of the hatchet-like Biscayan type that the army dug up at Cofitachequi. Ayllón's colonists had traded those particular axes to the Indians in 1526; the style remained in use by Spaniards in the Southeast throughout the sixteenth century.[3]

Nearly half of the six hundred troops in De Soto's army were mounted, and horses were key to the Spaniards' military successes in North America. Consequently horse gear figures prominently in the accounts. Early in the expedition horses were shod with iron horseshoes and equipped with iron stirrups and wooden saddles constructed on iron frames; Garcilaso specifically mentions supplies of iron for saddlebows. As the *entrada* proceeded for years without resupply, however, wooden stirrups eventually replaced ones of iron, horses went unshod (after the spring of 1541, according to Elvas), and saddle frames for the dwindling number of horses were repaired at makeshift forges. Dead horses were skinned and butchered for their hides and meat when necessary. Horses were only one of the animal species introduced by the Spaniards to the interior Southeast. De Soto's army introduced (famously) hogs to the region; a herd numbering in the hundreds accompanied the *entrada*. While the southeastern Indians kept dogs, they were unfamiliar with and terrorized by the Spaniards' very large mastiffs and De Soto's greyhound, Bruto. And of course the European invaders and their livestock carried within them infectious Old World disease organisms, which more or less devastated Indian populations along the army's route of march.

Measured by sheer volume, probably the most abundant artifacts carried by the expedition were their clothes, blankets, and other items of cloth. Rangel's account specifies buskins (tall, laced leather boots), "a cloak of scarlet cloth," "a hat of yellow satin, a shirt," and his own "quilted tunic of thick cotton," which he used in place of metal armor. Garcilaso specifies some linen clothing, which the Spaniards tore up to dress wounds after the debacle at Mabila. Clothes made from skins, furs, and mulberry bark cloth obtained from the Indians gradually replaced European clothing worn out or lost during the long *entrada*.

All of the chronicles agree that vast amounts of clothing, trunks, and other baggage (including swords, lances, halberds, saddles, shields, and the pearls stolen from Cofitachequi) were lost to fire at Mabila. Their entire camp equipage was carried on the backs of *tamemes,* human bearers enslaved by the hundreds and held in captivity by iron collars and chains ("joined with some S-hooks," according to Rangel). The bearers at Mabila were freed during the initial attack on De Soto's advance party; relieved of their shackles, they fought alongside Tascalusa's warriors to the death.

Other items of material culture appear sporadically in the *entrada* accounts. De Soto camped in a tent at Chiaha; whether other conquistadors had similar accommodations is unknown, although the chronicles mention the army billeting in native houses on several occasions.[4] The Spaniards sounded trumpets to coordinate maneuvers in battle. At Aquixo, they employed nails to build pirogues and later made new nails needed to construct their escape craft. The two caulkers working on those brigantines must have used some sort of chisel. De Soto purchased a variety of small goods to dispense to Indians in trade and as gifts. Feathers, glass beads (*margaritas* and *margaridetas*), knives, and mirrors are mentioned specifically in this regard. The conquistadors' discovery at Cofitachequi of glass and jet rosaries ("with their crosses") and Biscayan axes—objects presumably obtained by the Indians from Ayllón—suggests that those, too, may have been present among De Soto's trade packs. We know from several accounts of the battle of Mabila that the expedition's priests lost all of their paraphernalia needed to celebrate mass, including "chalices, altars, and ornaments," "wine for saying mass," and "a little wheat flour" and the "moulds for wafers." Finally, Garcilaso mentions the loss of olive oil, which had been reserved for medicinal use, and printed-paper playing cards in the fires at Mabila.

Though far from a comprehensive inventory, this listing of material goods carried by De Soto and his army into the interior Southeast between 1539 and 1543 provides a useful summary of the major categories of artifacts that might be found archaeologically at Mabila and other sites on and near the expedition's route. Since the route of De Soto's army has been actively debated, and evidence for that route actively sought for about a century now, one would correctly surmise that translating this list of broad artifact categories into precisely defined artifact types dating to the late 1530s has proven challenging. Nevertheless, substantial progress has been made along those lines, primarily by archaeologists, within the last three decades or so. One further proviso—the following discussion of artifact finds is undoubtedly incomplete; additional information is welcome.

The Archaeological Evidence

Archaeological evidence has come from many sources. So far, just one camp site of De Soto's army has been discovered (and widely accepted as such), the Governor Martin site in downtown Tallahassee, Florida, where the conquistadors spent the winter of 1539–40 among the Apalaches.[5] Two major efforts to trace the *entrada* route—one headed by John R. Swanton and the 1939 De Soto Expedition Commission, and the other led by Charles Hudson in the 1980s (as unfunded independent research, which was shared with the National Park Service and several state De Soto commissions)—generated a lot of related research by dozens of scholars. The latter research collectively uncovered many sites that have yielded artifacts of sixteenth-century Spanish origin. Because these artifacts were easily portable, their find spots may turn out to have been far from the expedition's precise route, but they still contribute to our growing understanding of the introduced Spanish material culture of that era and of the extent of effects of that army's march on the native peoples of the Southeast.[6] A third category of archaeological evidence derives from other sixteenth-century Spanish colonial sites, including sites in Mexico and Peru; the 1554 shipwrecks off Padre Island, Texas, and a 1559 Luna shipwreck in Pensacola Bay, Florida; and the early Atlantic coastal settlements at Santa Elena and St. Augustine.[7] Most recently, discoveries of artifacts apparently from the contemporaneous Coronado expedition across the American Southwest and the much later first permanent English settlement at Jamestown, Virginia, have contributed important new information.[8]

Before reviewing the archaeological record of the De Soto expedition in the Southeast, it is important to note that few if any of these artifact types are so precisely dated that we can distinguish with certainty the artifacts of De Soto (1539–43) from those of the earlier Ayllón (1526) or Narváez (1528), and the later Luna (1559–61) or Pardo (1566–68). Certain artifact types (particularly varieties of beads and bells) have attracted considerable attention, analysis, and debate, while others have received almost none. Precision in dating is highly desirable and may be achievable for some categories, but we are not there yet and much remains to be learned.

Let us first consider armor and weaponry. Despite claims of plate armor discoveries over the last two centuries, only two certain sixteenth-century Spanish examples have been recovered archaeologically in the Southeast: a breastplate from a 1559 shipwreck in Pensacola Bay attributed to Luna and two fragments from Santa Elena (1566–87) on the South Carolina coast.[9] While plate helmets probably saw wide use in De Soto's army, the cost of full plate armor for humans and horses limited its use to the wealthiest conquistadors. Coats and shirts of mail, however, were widely available to Spanish foot soldiers and cavalry in the sixteenth century. Bits and pieces have been found at several archaeological sites in the Southeast, including over two thousand links from the Governor Martin site, De Soto's 1539–40 winter campsite, and some from the Tatham Mound, both in Florida, as well as the Pardo-era Berry site in western North Carolina, and Etowah, Little Egypt, and Poarch Farm in Georgia.[10] At each of these sites archaeologists initially failed to recognize the centimeter-long, fragmentary links of rusted iron as mail, a condition not unexpected in the moist, acidic soils common to much of the Southeast. In contrast, an exceptionally well-preserved mail gauntlet, probably lost by Coronado's army in 1541, turned up in the 1950s in an arid area of northwest Texas.[11] The quilted cotton armor worn by Rangel may have incorporated iron or brass plates or jacks (*escaupiles*), dome-shaped round or octagonal disks with a central perforation that were sewn between layers of cloth. Examples have been recognized at Santa Elena and late sixteenth-century Indian sites in Tennessee and Georgia but may have been misidentified elsewhere as native-made or European trade ornaments.[12] All types of armor would have required fasteners, whether laces, buckles, or hinges. Santa Elena has yielded a wide range of buckle and hinge types from reliable late sixteenth-century contexts.[13]

In contrast to its abundance in the expedition's material culture, cloth seldom preserves archaeologically and little should be expected to be found at Mabila. However, more durable clothing accessories do tend to remain behind long after the wearing apparel has disintegrated. Once again, the excavations at Santa Elena and St. Augustine have given us many examples of mid-sixteenth-century clothing accessories, including brass and iron buckles; iron hooks and eyes; brass and white metal ball buttons; copper aglets (lace tips); and copper, gold, and silver wire *bordado,* sewn appliqué-style onto clothing.[14]

Spanish weapon parts have been recovered in small numbers across the Southeast. An iron lance head was found at the Pine Log Creek site in southwest Alabama, presumably a Luna-period contact site. Mid-sixteenth-century swords have turned up at several locations, including a spectacular basket-hilt type from the King site and a blade fragment from the Poarch Farm site, both in northwest Georgia, and blade fragments from Pine Log Creek and the Ledford Island and Brakebill sites in Tennessee.[15] Iron and brass crossbow bolt (or quarrel) tips, one of the most reliable indicators of sixteenth-century Spanish military contact, have been found at the Governor Martin and Poarch Farm sites, on the 1559 Luna shipwreck, and at Santa Elena.[16] Iron elements of crossbow triggers and the "goat's-foot" lever used to draw the bow have been identified thus far only at Santa Elena and from the 1554 shipwrecks off Padre Island, Texas.[17] Arquebus parts have been limited thus far to the Santa Elena site and are not anticipated from the western portions of De Soto's route.[18] Hatchets or axes, on the other hand, are known from several mid-sixteenth-century sites in Tennessee and Alabama. Smaller celt-like axes without eyes, wedges, or chisels were carried by at least the De Soto and Pardo expeditions for trade and gifts to the Indians. Indicative of their intended wide distribution, they are known from a great many southeastern sites dating to the mid-sixteenth to mid-seventeenth centuries.[19]

Hand-wrought iron objects are notoriously difficult to identify chronologically; it can also be difficult to identify their function. Fortunately, a recent comparative metallurgical analysis of Spanish colonial, French colonial, and early American wrought iron has detected chemical differences that distinguish De Soto–period iron artifacts from their similar-looking, but infinitely more abundant, later counterparts.[20] One important iron artifact category that ought to be found in abundance at Mabila is iron chain.[21] Judging from the appearance of some well-documented examples from the 1544 Padre Island shipwrecks, chain links and shackles from the mid-sixteenth century are not likely to look very different from eighteenth- and early nineteenth-century specimens, so archaeological context and chemical makeup will be particularly important in their recognition.

The most direct evidence for horses, of course, would be the skeletal remains of that invasive species, as is the case for hogs. De Soto's army first introduced those Old World animals deep into the Southeast. Numerous horses and hogs were killed at Mabila, leaving behind abundant archaeological evidence—evidence, however, that might not be immediately recognized as sixteenth-century in date. One easily recognized Spanish horse accoutrement is the sixteenth-century iron horseshoe, examples of which have been noted at sites in eastern Tennessee and from Hightower Village and Pine Log Creek in Alabama.[22] Archaeologists studying the Zuni site of Hawikku in west-central New Mexico, attacked by Coronado in 1540, found nineteen "caret-head" nails thought to have been used in cavalry horseshoes.[23] Similar, large-headed nails have been reported at Santa Elena and Pine Log Creek.[24] Iron stirrups, bits, spurs, harnesses, and saddle frame parts have so far eluded archaeologists working in the Southeast, although all would be stylistically distinctive of the mid-sixteenth century.[25]

Two categories of Spanish trade items—sheet brass bells and glass beads—have attracted the most sustained interest of archaeologists searching for the De Soto route and associated sites. The Spanish practice of handing out beads and small bells to Indians began with Columbus and continued throughout the fifteenth, sixteenth, and seventeenth centuries. Because we know little about the European sources of these trade goods, archaeologists have depended on the appearance of particular styles at sites of known occupation date limited to the sixteenth century. For beads, preeminent among those is the site of Nueva Cadiz, an important Spanish port on an island off the coast of Venezuela that was established in 1515 and destroyed by an earthquake in 1541. That early site gave its name to a class of long drawn beads, multilayered (usually three-layered, with clear, blue, and white glass), navy blue or turquoise in surface appearance, square in cross section, and sometimes twisted. A similar-looking red variety occurs on early seventeenth-century sites in the Northeast, but Marvin Smith has argued strongly for an early to mid-sixteenth-century (pre-1560) date for the turquoise and navy blue varieties in the Southeast.[26]

The recent discovery of turquoise Nueva Cadiz beads in early seventeenth-century contexts at Jamestown, Virginia, however, has raised new doubts about this artifact's chronological placement.[27] Smith suggests that the English at Jamestown may have pilfered Nueva Cadiz beads from chiefly graves of the Powhatans, who had had contact with the Spanish, particularly at their short-lived mission of Ajacan, located somewhere in the Chesapeake Bay area between 1565 and 1572.[28] However, the archaeological find-spots of Nueva Cadiz beads at Jamestown—from fill redeposited above an early grave and in the original 1607 palisade trench—suggest that these beads may derive from a slightly earlier, mid- to late sixteenth-century Algonquian Indian occupation of Jamestown Island.[29] This Virginia discovery at least points out the danger of basing a chronological conclusion on small, easily portable items that may have been used or reused over many years.

Chevron beads have also been found on sixteenth-century sites, although they have long been recognized as occurring over an extended time span. These distinctive beads have multiple layers of colored glass that form a "toothed, star pattern" when viewed on end.[30] Marvin Smith has pointed out that sixteenth-century chevrons commonly have seven layers of glass, usually including a thin layer of green, while seventeenth-century varieties have five layers, and eighteenth-century types have four. Furthermore, chevron beads of the early sixteenth century generally have ground facets, while later forms are usually tumbled, with a smooth surface achieved by heat alteration.[31]

Clarksdale bells are another category of small, distinctive artifact that has been closely associated with De Soto and other early conquistadors in the Southeast. These bells are made of sheet brass (rather than the sheet copper or cast brass of later bells), a bit more than an inch in diameter, with two hemispheres carefully joined "by an equatorial seam that was folded, crimped, and soldered," and a wide strap brass loop (a quarter inch wide) attached through the top and soldered on the inside.[32] The type has been widely reported, but it is known to have remained in use well into the first third of the seventeenth century.[33]

The destruction of the expedition's religious and culinary paraphernalia in the burning of Mabila suggests several other types of evidence that might be recoverable archaeologically. While wheat flour and wine would not be expected to survive in recognizable form, containers for wine might, as would containers for olive oil. Spanish olive jars of the early sixteenth century have a distinctive shape, and even small fragments of those ceramic vessels are distinguishable from other forms of European and native pottery.[34] The recovery of two brass items from a burial mound at Pine Log Creek, in southwest Alabama, has provoked speculation that they might have been a communion set from the De Soto or Luna expedition. The candlestick is a Spanish capstan form with a rectangular candle clean-out hole, a type attributable generally to the mid-sixteenth century. Unfortunately, candlestick typologies are not well understood and it does not seem possible currently to be more precise about the date of this piece. Interestingly, a similar brass capstan candlestick was excavated by a collector from a grave at the Durant Bend site on the Alabama River.[35]

The brass bucket from the Pine Log Creek assemblage, which has been proffered as a "holy water container," is even less well understood. While no comparative examples have been located in the archaeological or material culture literature, it does not resemble known holy water receptacles.[36] A sickle from Pine Log Creek and another one (though of a different style) from Hightower Village site have led some scholars to relate both sites to the Luna colonizing expedition rather than to the De Soto *entrada* on the assumption that sickles imply farming—a priority for Luna and definitely not for De Soto. However, sickles could have proven useful in gathering fodder for horses, clearing campsites, and other daily tasks of both expeditions.

Finally, we end with coins, which often carry a great deal of information on date and origin stamped into their surfaces. So far, just five coins have been associated with De Soto's expedition, three Portuguese *ceitils* and two Spanish *maravedis,* all found at the 1539–40 Governor Martin site in Tallahassee, Florida.[37] A four-reales coin minted about 1554 has been found in Henry County, southeast Alabama, that may derive from the Luna expedition.[38] Silver two-reales coins minted at Mexico City between 1536 and 1572, late in the reign of Charles and Johanna, have been found at four sites near the Alabama coast and on the lower Alabama River. Such a wide date range leaves us unable to attribute these coins to De Soto, Luna, or perhaps some undocumented coastal contacts by Spaniards.[39] With all of the baggage lost at Mabila, surely some coins are among the De Soto expeditionary artifacts awaiting discovery.

If we contemplate the possible appearance of these sorts of mid-sixteenth-century Spanish artifacts in archaeological context at the site of Mabila, we should note that many of the examples known thus far from the Southeast have come from Indian graves. In other words, most of these artifacts fell into native hands in one way or another—some as gifts, some probably stolen, some lost or discarded by Spaniards and found by Indians, and others perhaps taken as trophies in battle. A few may have been lost by Spaniards and directly entered the archaeological record without recycling, reuse, or reinterpretation by Indians, but the native contexts of most discoveries suggest that this must have been a rare occurrence. Mabila may be one site where we can expect to find some De Soto expedition artifacts in primary contexts of loss. Even there, however, the Spaniards certainly must have made efforts to retrieve otherwise irreplaceable weapons and armor and other goods. And upon their departure, surviving Mabilians (or their successors in that location) may well have scavenged objects from the ruins, sending diagnostic De Soto–related artifacts off on a native trajectory of use and loss or discard elsewhere, perhaps far from the scene of the crime.

APPENDIX: SOME MATERIAL CULTURE REFERENCES IN THE DE SOTO ACCOUNTS

[All page references are to Clayton, Knight, and Moore, *De Soto Chronicles.*]

Gentleman of Elvas

In Florida, there were horsemen, foot soldiers with swords and shields, arquebusiers, crossbowmen. Arquebuses, crossbows, armor, links of mail (1:59).

Captives put in chains (1:68).

Halberdiers, lance, javelin (1:69).

Stirrups, hounds (1:80).

Dagger and some beads of Ayllón (1:84).

De Soto's tent at Chiaha (1:91).

At Mabila, clothes, swords, and halberds lost in packs; chains removed from captive bearers (1: 100).

Arquebus fired (1: 101).

Clothing, ornaments for saying mass, pearls all burned (1:104).

Nails for piraguas near Aquixo (1: 114).
Horses now unshod for a year, in March 1542, for lack of iron (1: 130).
At Nilco, an Indian given some *margaridetas*—a kind of bead much esteemed in Peru (1: 131).
At Aminoya, chains and iron shot and all iron in camp collected to make brigantines. A forge was set up, nails made, and timber cut. Basque carpenters hewed planks, two caulkers calked them with tow; a cooper made two quarter casks (hogsheads) for each (1: 151).
They made anchors out of iron stirrups (1: 152).

Biedma

While digging in the temple at Cofitachequi, De Soto's men found two Castilian axes, rosary beads of jet, and glass beads, all believed to have been obtained in trade with Ayllón (1: 231).
At Tascalusa, the Indians showed the Spaniards a dagger that Don Teodoro, who had been with Narváez, had owned (1: 233).
At Mabila the Spaniards sounded a trumpet and used swords; they lost trunks, wooden saddles, lances, and shields to fire (1: 235, 237).
Hogs and horses mentioned throughout.

Rangel

"Light artillery" (hand cannon) mentioned in Florida (1: 257).
"Crossbowman" (1: 261).
A greyhound from Ireland seized an Indian (1: 262).
Lost a sword in Apalache (1: 266).
Chains, joined with some S-hooks of iron, to restrain Indian captives (1: 269).
Chief of Ocute was given a hat of yellow satin, a shirt, and a feather (1: 272).
On the way to Cofitachequi, they crossed a river broader than a long shot of an arquebus (1: 274).
At Cofitachequi, found "beads of glass and rosaries with their crosses . . . Biscayan axes of iron," from Ayllón (1: 279).
At Itaba, they bartered for some Indian women in exchange for mirrors and knives (1: 285).
Trumpets at Talisi (1: 288).
At Atahachi, De Soto gave Tascalusa "a horse, some buskins, and a cloak of scarlet cloth" (1: 291).

At Mabila, De Soto placed his helmet on his head (1: 292).
Rangel's armor was "a quilted tunic of thick cotton" (1: 293).
At Mabila, lances and axes used, clothes burned, "chalices and moulds for wafers" and "wine for saying mass" destroyed; "a sword without a scabbard" (1: 294).
"Coats of mail;" De Soto's "coat of armor;" iron saddle frames, lances (1: 298).
Crossbow (1: 300).

Garcilaso de la Vega

"much iron, steel, irons for saddlebows, spades, mattocks, panniers, ropes, and baskets—things very necessary for settlements" (2: 72).
Piece of artillery, transported by pack mules, left at Cofaqui (2: 264–65).
Spaniards used axes to break in the gates at Mabila ("most of them carried axes with them"). Don Carlos Enríquez, a gentleman, had a horse protected by "breast-leather" and wore full body armor (2: 339).
At Mabila, three crossbowmen and five halberdiers of the governor's guard (2: 340).
An arrow struck De Soto "in the small unprotected space . . . between the saddlebow and the breastplate" and entered his left hip after penetrating his underlying "coat of mail" (2: 341).
Olive oil reserved for medicinal use lost at Mabila (2: 348).
Linen clothing torn up for dressing the wounded. Dead horses skinned and butchered (2: 349).
"A little wheat flour, amounting to about three fanegas, and four arrobas of wine," carried in the governor's equipage to celebrate mass, "along with the chalices, altars, and ornaments they were carrying for divine worship," all lost to fire at Mabila (2: 353).
De Soto's helmet at Alibamo (2: 381).
Playing cards burned at Mabila (2: 431).
Still had mastiffs at Auche (2: 459).

Notes

1. All De Soto accounts cited here refer to translations found in Clayton, Knight, and Moore, *De Soto Chronicles.*

2. See Arnold and Weddle, *Nautical Archeology,* 190.

3. DePratter and Smith, "Sixteenth-Century European Trade," 71.

4. According to several veterans of the expedition, De Soto had "a fine Peru-

vian tent made of wool and cotton from the Andes." Avellaneda, *Los Sobrevivientes De La Florida,* entries for Pedro Carrion, Gonzalo Martin, Alvaro Nieto, Alvaro de San Jorge, Juan Sayago, and Juan de Vega.

5. Ewen and Hann, *Hernando de Soto among the Apalachees.*

6. Brain, "Artifacts of the Adelantado"; M. Smith, *Archaeology of Aboriginal Culture Change in the Interior Southeast;* Blakely, *King Site.*

7. Arnold and Weddle, *Nautical Archeology;* Deagan, *Artifacts of the Spanish Colonies of Florida and the Caribbean,* vol. 1: *Ceramics, Glassware, and Beads,* and vol. 2: *Portable Personal Possessions;* Smith and Good, *Early Sixteenth-Century Glass Beads in the Spanish Colonial Trade;* South, Skowronek, and Johnson, *Spanish Artifacts.*

8. Flint and Flint, *The Coronado Expedition;* Hartman, "Where Coronado Camped," 13; Kelso, *Jamestown Rediscovery I.*

9. Bratten, "Buried Secrets," 31–34; South, Skowronek, and Johnson, *Spanish Artifacts,* 109–11.

10. Ewen and Hann, *Hernando de Soto among the Apalachees,* 78–79; M. Smith, *Historic Period Indian Archaeology of Northern Georgia,* 25–26, 100–101; Beck, Moore, and Rodning, "Identifying Fort San Juan," 73–74.

11. Hartmann, "Where Coronado Camped."

12. South, Skowronek, and Johnson, *Spanish Artifacts,* 115–17. Similar objects have been identified, perhaps correctly, as musical tambourine jingles; see Deagan, *Artifacts of the Spanish Colonies,* 2: 303–04.

13. South, Skowronek, and Johnson, *Spanish Artifacts,* 109–15. Aglets have also been found at the Pardo-era Berry site; Beck, Moore, and Rodning, "Identifying Fort San Juan," 71–72.

14. South, Skowronek, and Johnson, *Spanish Artifacts,* 122–42; Deagan, *Artifacts of the Spanish Colonies,* 2:161–65, 174–83.

15. Blakely, *King Site,* 7; M. Smith, *Archaeology of Aboriginal Culture Change,* 48–50.

16. M. Smith, *Archaeology of Aboriginal Culture Change,* 48; Ewen and Hann, *Hernando de Soto among the Apalachees,* 80; Smith et al., *The Emanuel Point Ship Archaeological Investigations.*

17. South, Skowronek, and Johnson, *Spanish Artifacts,* 100–108; Arnold and Weddle, *Nautical Archeology,* 252–53; Arnold, Watson, and Keith, "The Padre Island Crossbows"; cf. Payne-Gallwey, *The Book of the Crossbow.*

18. South, Skowronek, and Johnson, *Spanish Artifacts,* 95–99; cf. M. Brown, *Firearms in Colonial America,* 42–62.

19. DePratter and Smith, "Sixteenth-Century European Trade"; M. Smith, *Archaeology of Aboriginal Culture Change,* 48–50.

20. Holmes and Bates, "A Comparison of Trace Elements."

21. M. Smith, *Archaeology of Aboriginal Culture Change,* 45.

22. Ibid., 50–51.

23. Damp, "The Summer of 1540," 4–5.

24. South, Skowronek, and Johnson, *Spanish Artifacts,* 33–47.

25. Deagan, *Artifacts of the Spanish Colonies,* 2: 187–92.

26. Smith and Good, *Early Sixteenth-Century Glass Beads;* M. Smith, *Archaeology of Aboriginal Culture Change,* 30–33; Deagan, *Artifacts of the Spanish Colonies,* 1: 9, 162–64.

27. Kelso, *Jamestown Rediscovery I,* 18.

28. Mallios, *The Deadly Politics of Giving.*

29. Kelso, *Jamestown: The Buried Truth,* 14, 57–58, 126, 179.

30. Deagan, *Artifacts of the Spanish Colonies,* 1: 164.

31. Smith and Good, *Early Sixteenth-Century Glass Beads;* M. Smith, *Archaeology of Aboriginal Culture Change,* 30–33; Deagan, *Artifacts of the Spanish Colonies,* 1: 164–67. A dissenting view is expressed in Little and Harrelson, *Pine Log Creek,* 36–37, 46. Little and Harrelson posit that certain types of chevron beads derive exclusively from the first half of the sixteenth century, and consequently that the presence of two of those early types at the Pine Log Creek site indicates a De Soto (not Luna) origin to the Spanish artifacts found there.

32. Brain, "Artifacts of the Adelantado," 131–34.

33. Brain, *Tunica Treasure,* 204; M. Smith, *Archaeology of Aboriginal Culture Change,* 42–43; South, Skowronek, and Johnson, *Spanish Artifacts,* 142–44; Deagan, *Artifacts of the Spanish Colonies,* 2: 144–46, 149.

34. Deagan, *Artifacts of the Spanish Colonies,* 1: 31.

35. Ned J. Jenkins, personal communication, September 2006.

36. Schiffer, Schiffer, and Schiffer, *The Brass Book,* 154–55; Michaelis, *Old Domestic Base-Metal Candlesticks,* 57–60; Deagan, *Artifacts of the Spanish Colonies,* 1: 153.

37. Ewen and Hann, *Hernando de Soto among the Apalachees,* 80–81.

38. M. Smith, "A Sixteenth-Century Coin from Southeast Alabama."

39. Sheldon, *The Southern and Central Alabama Expeditions of Clarence Bloomfield Moore,* 35–36; Vogt, *Standard Catalog of Mexican Coins, Paper Money and Medals,* 19–20.

9
The Present State of Archaeological Survey and Site File Data for the Alabama River and Adjacent Regions

Craig T. Sheldon Jr.

On October 18, 1540, a Spanish expedition under Hernando de Soto fought a bitter battle with the inhabitants of the Indian community of Mabila, somewhere in the interior of the southeastern United States. Four weeks later, after the expedition left the battlefield, knowledge of the location of Mabila was lost. The search for the archaeological site of Mabila is over 120 years old. This hunt for a single site, along the mostly unknown route of a 450-year-old Spanish *entrada,* has proven extraordinarily difficult, and over time it has taken on an identity all its own.

The *Final Report* of the 1939 United States De Soto Commission's attempt to retrace the expedition's route was a classic document of historical, linguistic, and geographical scholarship. The commission, under the leadership of John R. Swanton, postulated that Mabila was on the Coastal Plain somewhere along the Alabama River. However, archaeology had not progressed as a discipline to the level that it could identify the specific archaeological correlates of the aboriginal towns described in the Spanish accounts. Fifty years later, the Alabama De Soto Commission had better historical translations and much more archaeological information on the architecture, material culture, and settlement pattern of the Mississippian cultures encountered by the Spanish. Even so, the new information was not at an adequate level for the geographical pinpointing of any of the Indian communities along the expedition's route.[1]

The 2006 "Search for Mabila" conference stressed the value of a multidisciplinary approach. Past research has contracted the probable area in which Mabila may be found to the Coastal Plain in the vicinity of the Alabama River, and to sites occupied during the Late Mississippian cultural period of A.D. 1400–1550. This chapter presents an overview of the present status of archaeological survey data of sixteenth-century Mississippian sites in the Alabama River valley and adjacent portions of the Coosa and Tallapoosa river valleys. Using the Alabama State Site Files, the study plots the overall distribution of individual sites, clusters of sites, and the equally important vacant or "buffer" zones between such clusters. A similar macro-scale survey using the Georgia Archaeological Site Files was fairly successful in plotting the distribution of Mississippian mound sites along the Coosa River and its tributaries in north Georgia and northeast Alabama. In that study, David Hally was able to reconstruct clusters of mound sites and intervening vacant areas that he correlated with possible chiefdoms or provinces. The present study is not an attempt to trace the specific route of the expedition or to correlate specific site clusters with aboriginal provinces, or chiefdoms described in the De Soto chronicles. Such endeavors are reserved for the summary chapter on archaeology.[2]

Archaeological Surveys

One of the first steps in uncovering the prehistory or history of a region is archaeological field survey or reconnaissance, which attempts to discover locations with evidence of past human activities. In the Alabama River valley and surrounding parts of central Alabama, there have been three different types of archaeological surveys, dependent on their goals and scope.

1. Cultural resource assessments (sometimes called Phase I surveys) are legally mandated intensive surveys of areas that may be affected by construction or other ground-disturbing activities. They rely on pedestrian reconnaissance, shovel testing, and, occasionally, mechanical and electronic techniques. Such Phase I surveys are restricted to project areas of possible disturbance and can range in scale up to several square miles, although most are much smaller, frequently less than one acre.
2. Extensive surveys, mostly by the U.S. Army Corps of Engineers (USCE), have concentrated on immediate river banks, areas of potential flooding, and public access areas such as boat ramps. The earliest surveys, prior to the flooding by the USCE dams on the Alabama River, were largely based on information from local informants and pedestrian examination of likely areas. Later post-flooding inventory surveys were more systematic, relying not only on informants but also on shovel testing and metal detectors. Unfortunately, dams constructed prior to the 1960s were not required to have archaeology surveys. As a result, the areas flooded by the Jordan, Mitchell,

and Lay dams on the lower Coosa River and by Martin Dam on the lower Tallapoosa were not surveyed.

3. Intuitive or opportunistic type reconnaissance surveys focus the search on the most favorable parts of the terrain for archaeological sites. Such prior selection results from consulting with local landowners and artifact collectors, by examining topographic maps for locales with favorable environmental conditions, or, finally, by returning to previously discovered sites. Most such surveys have specific research goals such as locating sites to construct a local cultural chronology, or the discovery of Spanish contact sites.

This mixture of different types of surveys makes it difficult to determine what percentage of the Alabama River and lower Coosa and Tallapoosa river valleys has been actually covered. Often researchers report on what sites were found, but not on the extent or location of intervening vacant areas, or even the geographical limits of the area that was searched.

The most common archaeological survey technique is pedestrian reconnaissance, consisting of systematically walking back and forth across plowed fields, river floodplains, and terraces in search of surface artifacts such as pottery sherds and lithic debris. Small shovel test excavations or mechanically excavated test pits are often employed at sites with vegetative cover or shallow alluvial deposits. To locate sites buried beneath deep floodplain deposits, larger mechanical equipment can be used. Electromagnetic detectors can locate historical metal artifacts. These techniques can be used to explore all of a bounded area, often including much terrain with no sites. Alternatively they can be employed at selected locales in a river valley. Unfortunately, many forms of remote sensing, such as aerial photography, have not proven very effective in detecting unknown sites, mostly because of the disruptive and pervasive extent of agricultural plowing and the more recent planting of pastures and commercial forests in central Alabama.

Once located, an archaeological site is further examined to determine its size and depth, to recover more artifacts to determine its period of occupation, and sometimes to check for subsurface features. Small test excavations, removal of selected portions of the plow zone using machinery, and various types of remote sensing such as ground penetrating radar or magnetometry can indicate the presence of subsurface features such as houses, pits, or palisade walls. Critical information from discovered sites is recorded on site forms and United States Geological Survey topographic quadrangle maps, which are the backbone of the archaeological site recording system in Alabama. These standardized site forms are submitted to the Alabama State Site File (ASSF) maintained by the Office of Archaeological Research of the Alabama Museum of Natural History, a unit of The University of Alabama at Moundville, Alabama. This is the official state repository and centralized database for such archaeological information. The ASSF was begun by Professor David L. DeJarnette and Dr. Walter B. Jones in 1931 at The University of Alabama. Since then, many archaeologists have contributed to the file, which has been greatly expanded and refined, mostly because of the efforts of Eugene Futato and the Office of Archaeological Research, which have managed the system since 1976. In 1988, the ASSF paper records were encoded into a computer database, and in 1990 the database went on-line as the Alabama Online Cultural Resources Database (AOCRD), so that professional researchers can record new sites or research existing site records remotely. Presently, there are over 25,000 archaeological sites in the file.[3]

The ASSF uses a standardized format with data on site location, terrain, size, nature of deposits, features, types of artifacts, and estimations of the age of the site. Each site is assigned an official state site number:

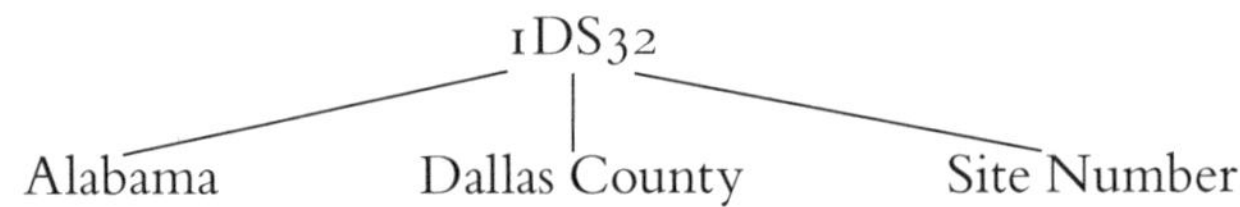

There are two parts to the online Web site. First is the actual site file, which can be searched for individual sites by site number or for the sites in a particular township, range, and section. Second, there is the Area Surveyed database of Phase I surveys, which shows how much of a county or region has been examined.

In a broad-scale search for sites of any period, including that of De Soto, the ASSF is highly valuable as a single database containing data on many thousands of archaeological sites. The site file has several limitations, however. Eugene Futato and his staff at the ASSF can only enter the data submitted to them. A number of sites are listed as "unknown aboriginal," with no indication of the period of occupancy because the locations yielded no diagnostic artifacts or because the archaeologist presented little or no analysis. Simply stating that a location was occupied during the Mississippian period of A.D. 1000–1550 is not sufficiently precise to include or exclude it in the search for Spanish contact sites. Shell-tempered pottery, the hallmark of many archaeological Mississippian cultures in much of Alabama, lasted for over five hundred years. In such cases there was not sufficient time to revisit these locations to gain additional diagnostic artifact collections. In addition, the ASSF does not contain detailed information about subsequent excavations, although it frequently refers to them. Finally, researchers do not often send updates to the files. We must therefore abandon the notion that we can simply program an inquiry into the database for Mississippian period sites with Spanish artifacts and magically produce a precise location for Mabila.

It sounds simple: we could walk along the river's edge in search of artifacts that would indicate a Spanish contact site. Alternatively, we could comb through the ASSF of known sites and examine topographic maps for likely locations. In reality, there are many problems. First, there is the sheer scale of the Alabama River valley alone, which has 634 miles of river banks, has 600–800 square miles of floodplain, and spans nine Alabama counties. The critical adjacent areas of the lower Coosa and Tallapoosa river valleys encompass parts of an additional nine counties. Access to portions of the floodplain is often difficult, requiring boats and much slogging across muddy terrain. A historic shift to pasture and managed forests has obscured many archaeological sites that were once visible in plowed fields. These "green" and "brown" fogs of vegetation and ground litter are the principal problems of surveying in south and central Alabama. Alluvial or flood-borne deposits may have buried many sites. Many Mississippian sites were one- or two-house farmsteads—small in area and difficult to detect. There are a number of known and unknown Mississippian sites that could be Mabila, leading us to a problem that will reverberate throughout this project. Where in the middle of a four- to ten-acre site do we find the very limited number of European artifacts or features that would identify a Spanish contact site, and, more important, how do we find those particular types of artifacts that clearly identify the Mabila site?[4]

Brief History of Archaeological Investigations

References to named aboriginal communities visited by De Soto appeared on numerous European maps from the late sixteenth century onward, but none was of sufficient accuracy to be of use in relocating Mabila. Ironically, the earliest known historic reference to a potential De Soto site on the Alabama River is the name Vieux Mobiliens ("Old Mobilians") on the 1733 Baron De Crenay map, placed somewhere in the vicinity of the archaeologically excavated Liddell site (1WX1) in Wilcox County. Most scholars agree that this is not the site of sixteenth-century Mabila, but it is a tantalizing clue.[5]

Literary speculations about the actual location of the great battle at Mabila began with Albert Pickett in 1851, when he suggested Choctaw Bluff in Clarke County as a likely candidate. Interest in the battle's location continued throughout the remainder of the nineteenth century. In 1882, Timothy Ball described "[t]he old burying ground and mound on the site of old Mauvilla (the latter now obliterated) 4 1/2 miles east of Gainestown on the Alabama River." This same location, later known as French's Landing, was further investigated by representatives of the Smithsonian Institution in the 1880s under the direction of Cyrus Thomas. They reported that "[n]ot a vestige of the old fort now remains and the mound that once stood here has nearly all disappeared, a strip only about 20 feet wide remaining." They found three "deposits" of "skeletons in compact bundles" and fragments of pottery. This location is now known as site 1CK162. The Smithsonian expedition also briefly investigated Mississippian mound sites in Elmore and Montgomery counties but found no Spanish items.[6]

In 1899, the first systematic archaeological survey and excavations along the Alabama River were made by Clarence Moore in his private steamboat, the Gopher. L. D. Cutting, the engineer aboard the Gopher, traveled upriver by commercial steamer, stopping at landings and wood yards, to make preliminary inquiries of local inhabitants and landowners about mounds and burying grounds. Moore, who was interested in burial mounds and their rich associations, investigated nineteen sites, of which at least ten were clearly of the Mississippian or Protohistoric periods. They included important mound and non-mound sites at Little River, Matthew's Landing, Durant Bend, Charlotte Thompson, Big Eddy, and Thirty Acre Field. Both Charlotte Thompson and Durant Bend (in later excavations) yielded sixteenth-century Spanish artifacts.[7]

In 1901, Thomas Owen assembled a catalogue that contained thirty brief reports of "prehistoric works" in eight of the nine counties that border the Alabama River. Ten years later, an expanded version listed fifty-eight sites. Between 1909 and about 1943, the Alabama Anthropological Society industriously sought and dug many prehistoric and historic sites in Montgomery and Elmore counties, with occasional forays to Macon, Lowndes, and Dallas counties. Over seventy-one sites in the Montgomery area and along the upper Alabama River were largely located through inquiries to landowners and agricultural laborers. Many of the archaeological sites located by the Alabama Anthropological Society were tentatively identified by names of historic Indian towns from the sixteenth through the nineteenth centuries. Although the primary focus of most members was to accumulate artifacts for their personal collections, several wrote on a variety of topics, including Historic

Creek and early American history and culture, and the route of the De Soto expedition.[8]

The first serious, modern archaeological surveys of the Alabama River came in the 1960s and 1970s with the construction of the locks and dams at Claiborne, Miller's Ferry, and Jones Bluff. Informant and pedestrian surveys were limited to the areas of potential flooding, which were widest immediately above the dams and much narrower at the head of the reservoirs. This pattern accounted in part for the clusters of sites frequently found just above the dams. Just below the dams, at the head of the downstream reservoir, the surveyed areas were restricted to the existing river course, leaving most of the floodplain unsurveyed. The limited pedestrian and informant surveys, not adequate by today's standards, located numerous sites, of which a small percentage were excavated prior to reservoir flooding. Most of the excavations yielded artifacts and features of the Late Woodland or Protohistoric periods but comparatively few of the Mississippian era.[9]

In the late 1970s and 1980s, the U.S. Army Corps of Engineers contracted with The University of Alabama and Auburn University to resurvey the entire length of the Alabama River, but restricted their coverage to the immediate water's edge, flood easement zones, and public access areas. Many high terraces with potential for Mississippian sites were visible to the survey parties but were not explored since they fell outside the contracted survey area. Auburn University surveyed from the mouth of the river to Jones Bluff Lock and Dam, while The University of Alabama covered the river from there to Wetumpka. The surveys, relying on pedestrian reconnaissance and shovel tests, made no major excavations but managed to find seventy-nine Mississippian sites along the river.[10]

Several smaller surveys with more specific research goals are worth noting. In 1973, Marvin Jeter surveyed a 6 × 40-mile, north-to-south transect across the Alabama River floodplain in Autauga, Dallas, and Lowndes counties. He located 85 sites, of which only three were occupied during the Mississippian period. In 1987, Robert Atchison surveyed 1,105 acres of the Cahaba River drainage in Bibb, Perry, and Dallas counties. He found six sites with Mississippian components, and postulated that Mabila could be located in the Black Belt physiographic provenience.

In 1990, Paul Patterson's informant-aided and intensive pedestrian survey of 5,350 acres of Black Belt in Perry, Marengo, and Dallas counties was a search for Mississippian sites occupied during the Spanish entrada. He found 63 aboriginal sites, of which 31 had Mississippian or Protohistoric components. Many of these small sites were located well to the west of the river, in the vicinity of the modern communities of Faunsdale and Uniontown. This is one of the few surveys conducted away from the immediate Alabama River valley and in the region of the prairies. The discovery of Mississippian occupations in what was once regarded as an aboriginally remote region is an indication that the overall bounds of the Mabila search area should be expanded.[11]

Caleb Curren and Janet Lloyd conducted an informant-aided and pedestrian survey of the lower Alabama River region in a specific search for Spanish contact sites in 1987. Ned Jenkins and Teresa Paglione explored four counties along the lower river, finding seventy sites, of which six were Mississippian. Both of the latter projects relied on information from local informants and collectors, as well as investigations of likely terrain visible on topographic maps. These projects may have located the bulk of larger-sized, accessible Mississippian sites in the lower region.[12]

In the uplands north of the Coastal Plain, the lower Coosa and Tallapoosa river valleys were flooded by hydroelectric dams before archaeological surveys were required. Only the archaeological survey of the Harris Reservoir, constructed in 1983 on the middle reaches of the Tallapoosa, serves as an indication of what was lost. Modern surveys by The University of Alabama and Auburn University across the Piedmont and Valley and Ridge regions adjacent to the two rivers found numerous sites occupied during the Woodland and Historic Creek Indian periods, but many fewer of the Mississippian period.[13]

In the past twenty years, most of the archaeological survey activity in the Alabama River valley has been cultural resource assessments (Phase I) of proposed roads, bridges, power lines, and other areas of potential disturbance. The location and scale of most of these surveys are shown on the Area Surveyed part of the Alabama State Site File Web site.

The Central Alabama Region

Before reviewing the data in the site file, we should briefly look at some critical physical characteristics of the Alabama, Coosa, and Tallapoosa river valleys that have, and will, affect surveys and attempts to reconstruct the route of the De Soto expedition and determine the location of Mabila.

The Alabama River originally ran 317 miles from its origin at the junction of the Coosa and Tallapoosa rivers, near Montgomery, to its terminus with the Tombigbee River in the Mobile Delta. Throughout its entire course, it is a Coastal Plain river with low-gradient, extensive meandering bends and a well-developed floodplain of alluvial soils, backswamps, levees, and terraces (see chapter 14, this volume). It contrasts sharply with the entrenched tributary Coosa and Tallapoosa rivers in the Valley and Ridge, Piedmont, and Fall Line Hills to the north of the Coastal Plain. Above Wetumpka and Tallassee, the rivers were deeply engorged into the rocky terrain. In this area, the narrow width of the floodplains and restricted agricultural land tended to force aboriginal settlements to locate along smaller tributary streams away from the rivers. Along the Alabama River, in contrast, aboriginal settlements could be situated within the broad meander belt, which was up to four miles wide.

Flowing across the Coastal Plain, the Alabama River crosses six major east-west trending physiographic provinces. The effects of such zones, with their potential variations in natural resources, on aboriginal settlement in the adjacent floodplains are not presently well understood. In places, such as at the Claiborne Dam in Monroe County, the local physiography may significantly constrict the width of the river floodplain. Where many of the hills are eroded by river bends, high bluffs stand as the most distinctive landmarks along the river. Most of the local physiographic characteristics on the Coastal Plain are greatly subdued in scale when compared to the more rugged hills and ridges of the Piedmont, Valley and Ridge, and Fall Line Hills regions to the north. In other words, mention of hills, ravines, and similar landmarks in the Spanish chronicles may have different meanings here than in the northern regions.

A unique characteristic of the Alabama River is its general course. Most southeastern rivers flow directly across the Coastal Plain to the Gulf of Mexico or the Atlantic. The upper third of the Alabama River, however, flows directly west to the vicinity of Selma, before turning to a southwesterly course. This one-hundred-mile stretch of the river is entrenched between the Fall Line Hills to the north and the Black Belt zone to the south. The significance of this unusual course to aboriginal settlement and the route of the Spanish expedition after the battle of Mabila is not well understood.

The meandering of the river is well developed. There are 317 river miles from start to finish, but only 156 miles if traced along the center line of the river floodplain. Reconstructions of the De Soto route must consider these deep, frequently miles-long bends. Shifts in the river channel since the sixteenth century do not appear to have been major. While there has been localized cutting or collapse of banks on outer bends, comparison of the present channel with those depicted on the 1733 Crenay map, the 1813 survey by Howell Tatum, or the 1884 Army Corps of Engineers map suggest few important changes. A greater problem for archaeological surveys is the extensive deposition of alluvial soils by floods along the river—in places, up to five feet deep over known Mississippian period sites. Detection of such buried sites, particularly in the southern stretches of the river, is difficult.[14]

Prior to the installation of the three locks and dams on the Alabama River and the hydroelectric dams on the lower Coosa and Tallapoosa rivers, water levels varied considerably, often exposing sand bars and large portions of the riverbed. In the nineteenth century, there were a number of places along the rivers fordable by wagons. Such fords are important, given the importance of river crossings in tracing the De Soto route. During the expedition, fording streams, even major rivers, may have become routine to the point of being unrecorded.

Present Overview

Even with the aforementioned limitations, the AOCRD allows for an examination of general archaeological site distribution across central Alabama during the Mississippian and Protohistoric periods. The present search was conducted in two adjacent but distinctive geographical areas. The primary area was a 30- to 66-mile-wide corridor centered on the Alabama River from its beginning above Montgomery to its end in the Mobile Delta. The second was a 42- to 60-mile-wide area extending across the lower Coosa and Tallapoosa river valleys extending north from Wetumpka in Elmore County to Childersburg in Talladega County.

Using the AOCRD, 316 townships of 36 square miles each were systematically inspected. A total of 4,361 site forms were examined, 311 of which were of the Mississippian and/or Protohistoric periods. The existing ceramic typological information in the ASSF was not sufficiently precise to pinpoint only Late Mississippian occupations of the De Soto time line, so all sites with diagnostic shell-tempered or Lamar-paste pottery sherds were recorded. These included sherds of the Moundville, Pensacola, and Lamar series, and the Bottle Creek, Bear Point, Furman, Alabama River, Big Eddy, Bull Creek, Shine II, Nelson's Bend, and Kymulga phases. The post–De Soto period Protohistoric sites were included in the study because they are often confused with Late Mississippian site components, particularly in the case of small samples of surface ceramic sherds.[15]

Within the 11,376 square miles of central Alabama inspected in the AOCRD, it is difficult to estimate how much territory was actually examined by archaeologists. Site frequencies within individual 36-square-mile townships ranged from 0 to 149. The absence of sites in a township does not mean that there were no sites, only that no sites were reported. Modern cultural resource (Phase I) assessments are very specific as to their boundaries, but as already noted, most of the earlier and informal surveys record only the location of sites, not the extent of areas where no sites were found. Most of these informant-based surveys tended to concentrate on the higher terraces and other likely areas, but not all such "hot spots" were adequately examined because of ground cover, landowner refusal, or difficulty of access.

Although there is considerable disagreement, most scholars would locate the sixteenth-century province of Cosa somewhere on the Coosa River in northeast Alabama or northwest Georgia. Between Rome, Georgia, and Riverside, Alabama, the river is slow-flowing with relatively broad floodplains and a large number of Barnett phase (circa A.D. 1500–1650) sites.[16] Conventional interpretation places the Spanish expedition on a southerly track after leaving Cosa, but is inconclusive about whether the Coosa or Tallapoosa River valleys or the crest of the intervening drainage divide were followed toward the Coastal Plain. The lower Coosa River in the Piedmont region between Riverside and Wetumpka was in a narrow, entrenched valley, containing some of the "worst" rapids in the eastern United States. Floodplains suitable for prehistoric agriculture or habitation were very narrow within this gorge. Travel along the river's edge, or on the bluffs above, would have been very difficult due to the rugged terrain. Construction of Jordan Dam (1929), Mitchell Dam (1923), and Lay Dam (1929) flooded the floor of the gorge before any archaeological surveys were conducted. Although we do not know what Mississippian sites may have been inundated in the main gorge, it is interesting to note the larger number of such sites along the major tributaries such as Tallaseehatchee and Talladega creeks.[17]

The presence of a larger number of Late Woodland and Historic Creek sites in the lower Coosa area, particularly along the tributary streams, indicates that the area was inhabitable but not intensely occupied during the Late Mississippian period. Examination of the AOCRD in a 30- to 36-mile-wide transect across the river valley between Wetumpka and Childersburg yielded only 23 Mississippian and/or Protohistoric sites of 1,107 total sites (Table 9.1). Some produced ceramic collections attributable to the Kymulga phase of A.D. 1500–1650. Most of the sites were small and none had earthen mounds. Near Sylacauga were the Hightower (1TA150) and Sylacauga Water Works (1TA115) sites, where iron chisels, horseshoes, glass beads, and other sixteenth-century artifacts were found.[18]

The southern portion of the Tallapoosa River in the Piedmont part of Elmore and Tallapoosa counties was flooded in 1925 by Lake Martin, prior to any archaeological survey. Numerous eighteenth- and nineteenth-century Historic Creek settlements are known to have existed in the inundated area,

Table 9.1 Mississippian and Protohistoric Sites in Central Alabama

Area	Number of Townships	Square Miles	Number of Sites	Number of Mississippian Sites
Lower Coosa River	51	1,836	1,107	23 (2.0 %)
Piedmont Tallapoosa River	53	1,908	365	9 (2.4 %)
Lower Tallapoosa River	29	1,044	477	44 (9.2%)
Alabama River	183	6,588	2,412	235 (9.7%)
Total	316	11,376	4,361	311 (7.1%)

but no major Mississippian mound or other sites are exposed during periods of low water. Further upstream, the Rother B. Harris Reservoir on the Middle Tallapoosa River valley was systematically surveyed in the 1970s, revealing a number of Late Mississippian sites, mostly of the Nelson's Bend phase of the Lamar cultural tradition. Most were small and appear to have been specialized for exploiting local resources such as fish and game. Within the 1,908 square miles of the Piedmont portion of the Tallapoosa River drainage that were examined in the AOCRD, 9 of a total of 365 sites were utilized during the Mississippian and/or Protohistoric periods. Again, most of these sites were small in extent, and none appears to have had earthen mounds.[19]

Whatever route was taken south across the Piedmont region, the expedition probably found it to be devoid of large settlements or clusters of smaller sites. Once they reached the upper Coastal Plain, south of the Fall Line at Tallassee and Wetumpka, the settlement pattern changed radically. Extending from the Fall Line on the Coosa and Tallapoosa rivers to just below Montgomery is one of the largest and densest concentrations of Late Mississippian, Protohistoric, and Historic period aboriginal sites in Alabama. Much of this intensive usage is attributable to the concentrated fertile soils and natural resources of the floodplain. Occupied almost continuously from the early Archaic period to the time of Indian Removal in 1836, the region has a complex culture history that is poorly understood.[20]

Two distinct, archaeologically defined subregions are present in the lower Tallapoosa River valley and the upper Alabama River valley, respectively (Figure 9.1). One hundred years of archaeological surveys of the lower Tal-

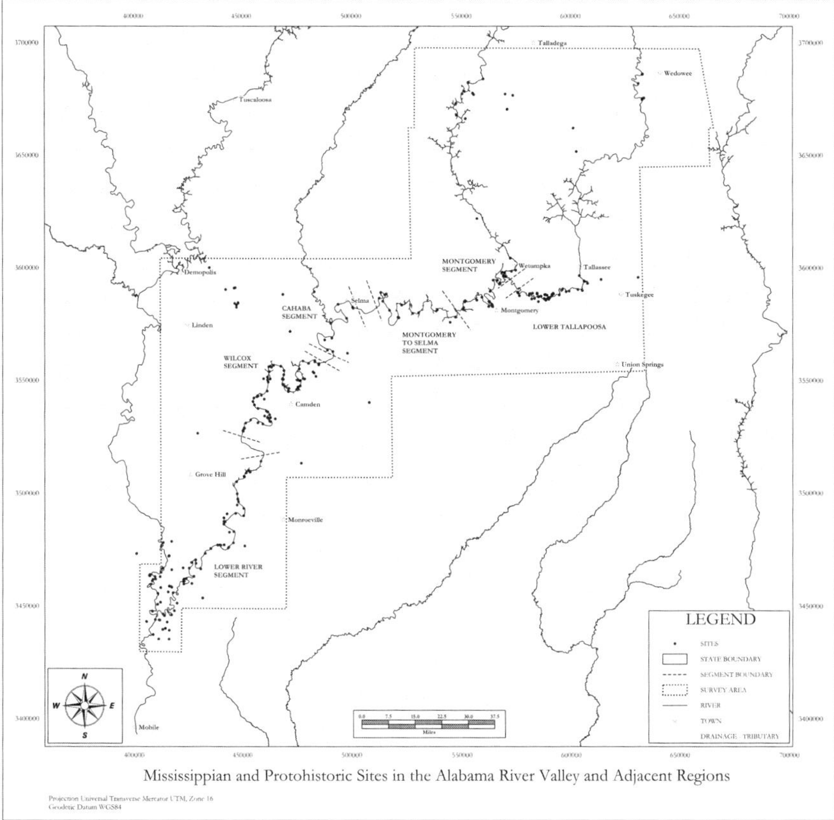

Figure 9.1. Archaeologically defined subregions, Alabama and lower Tallapoosa river valleys, showing sites currently on record in the Alabama State Site File. GIS map by Terance L. Winemiller, Auburn University Montgomery.

lapoosa River valley between the modern town of Tallassee and the junction with the Coosa River, in Montgomery, Elmore, and Macon counties, have revealed six major Mississippian sites with one to four mounds each, situated at about six-mile intervals along the river. Interspersed among these mound sites is an unknown but apparently high number of contemporaneous domestic sites of widely varying sizes. In this subregion the AOCRD revealed 477 sites, of which 44 were of the Mississippian and/or Protohistoric period. This is probably a serious underrepresentation of the actual number of sites from these periods. De Soto period sites in the lower Tallapoosa River valley appear to be of the Shine II phase (circa A.D. 1400–1550), which is ancestral to Protohistoric and Historic Creek Indian phases. Many of the sites, including most of those with mounds, were continuously occupied throughout the entire era. A limited number of sixteenth-century brass bells and glass beads with no provenience have been recovered from the general lower Tallapoosa River area. Three sixteenth-century-style iron chisels were found on the surface of the mound site of Atasi (1MC6).[21]

Moving west to the second subregion in the upper Alabama River valley, 235 of 2,412 sites in the AOCRD were Mississippian or Protohistoric. It is possible to adopt a slightly more sophisticated approach to measuring site density along the Alabama River. The locations of 175 sites with shell-tempered ceramics within a 12-mile-wide, 156-mile-long corridor were determined using the nearest river miles recorded on U.S. topographic quadrangle maps. Distances in river miles between adjacent sites were calculated. Major gaps in site distribution were used to define cultural segments along the river. The average intrasite distance was then calculated for each segment. This is a rudimentary, preliminary approach, but it provides a tentative basis for discussing discontinuities in site distribution along the river. Using this procedure, five distinctive segments were found along the Alabama River (Table 9.2). Four such segments are clusters of sites separated from each other by barren areas of five to twelve river miles in length. The fifth segment is actually an almost vacant zone between Montgomery and Selma.

The Montgomery segment extends along the Alabama River from just south of the city of Montgomery to the junction of the Coosa and Tallapoosa rivers. It is separated from the cluster of contemporaneous sites in the lower Tallapoosa River valley by a six-mile-long segment of usable but unoccupied floodplain. The Montgomery cluster includes eighteen known sites with shell-tempered ceramics, of which seven have one to four mounds. Many small, undetected farmstead sites probably exist within the meander belt of this segment. Other than excavations by Clarence Moore in 1899, very few of these sites have been systematically investigated. Ned Jenkins has assigned most of the sixteenth-century sites in this area to the undefined Big Eddy phase. The Charlotte Thompson site near Montgomery yielded the largest number of sixteenth-century Spanish artifacts found in central Alabama. Six of the mound sites were abandoned at the end of the Late Mississippian around the time of the De Soto expedition. Only Pakana or Taskigi (1EE1) at the junction of the Coosa and Tallapoosa continued to be occupied throughout the Protohistoric and Historic periods.[22]

In the thirty-seven miles (fifty-six river miles) between the Charlotte Thompson mound site west of Montgomery to Selma, the river valley has few Mississippian settlements and no mounds (Table 9.2). Only eighteen sites with shell-tempered ceramics are recorded in the state site file. Jenkins has

Table 9.2 Mississippian and Protohistoric Cultural Segments of the Alabama River

Segment Number	Segment Name	River Miles from Terminus of Alabama River	Total Sites	Mississippian Sites	Mound Sites	Average Distance between Sites (Miles)	Distance to the Next Upstream Site Cluster (Miles)
1	Montgomery	276-311.3	215	18	7	1.9	6.0 (to Shine II sites on Tallapoosa River)
2	Montgomery to Selma	220-276	665	18	1	3.3	3.7
3	Cahaba	172.3-207.8	241	9	2	4.6	12.2
4	Wilcox	101.2-165.9	190	66	3	1.0	5.5
5	Lower River	0-88.5	202	64	3	1.6	12.7
	Total		1,728	175	18		

identified most of the Late Mississippian ceramics from these sites as a mixture of types from the downstream Pensacola series and the upstream Big Eddy and Shine II series. The reasons for the near vacancy of this segment during the Late Mississippian are unknown, but they appear to be political or social rather than environmental, because in the preceding Late Woodland period and in the succeeding post–De Soto Protohistoric period there were a fair number of sites here. While archaeological survey coverage is certainly not total, there have been at least three major surveys within the region, which found only eighteen Mississippian sites. I believe that the low frequency of such sites in the surveyed areas indicates that this was a true archaeological buffer zone at various times. The only Mississippian occupation of any size was isolated near the center of the zone, at Durant Bend (1DS1) where a possible mound, sherds of the pottery type Moundville Incised, a diagnostic spatulate ax of ground stone, and a sixteenth-century brass capstan-style candlestick were found. Most of the occupation actually belongs to the seventeenth-century protohistoric Alabama River phase, a terminal Moundville manifestation.[23]

The Cahaba segment, centered on the historic nineteenth-century town of Old Cahawba, would appear to be a nearly vacant zone similar to the region just upstream. I have chosen to designate it as a separate segment because it contains two mound sites and a scattering of small domestic sites along thirty-five river miles. There has been very little archaeological survey in this part of the river valley. The Cedar Creek Mound (1DS172), south of Old Cahawba, appears to have been used during the preceding Middle Mississippian period. The Mississippian mound site at the junction of the Cahaba and Alabama rivers (1DS32) was seriously disturbed by the nineteenth-century town of Cahawba. The presence of prehistoric earthworks at Cahawba was first noted on an 1817 map and in Albert Pickett's *History of Alabama* in 1851. Excavations on the terrace adjacent to the river have revealed an aboriginal component with Pensacola ceramics overlain by artifacts from the nineteenth-century town. A possible aboriginal ditch running in an arc to and from the river bank yielded a mixture of Pensacola ceramics and historic objects. Obviously, additional excavations are necessary at this site.[24]

Additional reasons that the general Cahaba area deserves more attention are the thirty-one Mississippian and/or Protohistoric sites found by Paul Patterson in the vicinity of the modern communities of Uniontown and Faunsdale some twenty-six to thirty miles west of Cahawba. Most are small in extent, perhaps farmsteads, and the majority appear to date to the Protohistoric period. These sites are located on or near the divide between the Cahaba and Tombigbee rivers, within the drainages of the tributary Bogue Chitto, Chilatchee, and Chickasaw Bogue creeks. As previously stated, this would be considerably outside the traditional search area for Mabila, but the Black Belt zone or similar areas away from a major river cannot be ruled out.[25]

The Wilcox segment is the largest and densest concentration of sites on the middle part of the river. Beginning at Pine Barren Creek and extending 64.7 river miles to the town of Coy, near the southern boundary of Wilcox County, are sixty-six Mississippian and Protohistoric sites. The level of archaeological survey here ranges from limited intensive examination of the areas immediately adjacent to the river banks to nonexistent on many of the higher terraces and tributary streams. Many of these sites with shell-tempered pottery will ultimately prove to be of the post–De Soto Alabama River phase, but there is clearly a greater concentration of Late Mississippian sites here than upstream and downstream. Mounds have been identified at the Phillippi, Furman, and Dale sites. Excavations by Clarence Moore (1899), Caleb Curren (1982), and Amanda Regnier (2005) at the Furman site (1WX169) near Matthew's Landing in Wilcox County have yielded ceramics of the Furman phase, clearly related to the Pensacola series. The cultural and temporal relationships of the Furman, Alabama River, Moundville, Bottle Creek, and Bear Point phases are very complex and as yet not well understood, but it is clear that the Wilcox segment was extensively occupied during both the Mississippian and Protohistoric periods.[26]

Beginning twelve miles below the Wilcox segment, the eighty-eight miles of the Lower River segment possesses sixty-four sites. Small sites are scattered along the river in Monroe and Clarke counties, many yielding only a few shell-tempered sherds. Some sites are exposed in eroding river banks under one or more meters of flood-borne deposits. Without a doubt, much of this paucity of sites is due to the very limited number and scale of archaeological surveys in this area. Surveys were largely restricted to U.S. Army Corps of Engineers reconnaissance along the river bank and to intuitive surveys that concentrated on the most likely locations for sites. This is clearly the least well-known portion of the Alabama River valley. At Choctaw Bluff the river valley widens and merges with the Mobile Delta. Here, the majority of the numerous Mississippian and Protohistoric sites are of the Bottle Creek and Bear Point phases of the Pensacola culture.[27]

Only two Mississippian mound sites have been positively identified on this stretch of the river. The Little River mound (1MN227) is located on the southern border of Monroe County. This site, and most of the nearby smaller domestic sites where the ceramic collections have been adequately identified, belong to the Bottle Creek or Bear Point phase. Twenty-six miles downstream, on the lower part of Pine Log Creek, is Site 1BA462, which yielded an assemblage of Bear Point phase ceramics in association with the largest number of sixteenth-century Spanish artifacts found in south Alabama.[28]

Although the valleys of the lower Tombigbee and Black Warrior rivers lay outside the formal survey area, they must be briefly considered. With a paucity of Mississippian sites, the lower Tombigbee River stands in sharp contrast to the 130 sites found in the Lower River and Wilcox segments of the Alabama River. The Tombigbee River between Demopolis and the junction with the Alabama River was visited by Clarence B. Moore in 1905 and was surveyed by the University of South Alabama in 1983. The northernmost site with ceramics of the Pensacola series, so common in the Mobile Delta (1CK20), was located near the boundary between Washington and Choctaw counties. North to Demopolis, there were only fourteen small sites with shell-tempered ceramics. Most of the mounds in this area date to the Woodland period. None has been clearly identified as Mississippian. Although poorly surveyed at this time, there is sufficient information to indicate that Mississippian settlement patterns in the lower Tombigbee closely resemble those of the mostly uninhabited segment of the Alabama River between Montgomery and Selma.[29]

North of Demopolis, there are major clusters of Mississippian period sites on the central Tombigbee and the lower Black Warrior rivers. Along the central Tombigbee River from the vicinity of Columbus, Mississippi, to near Demopolis, Blitz identifies six sites with mounds and numerous smaller sites. Many of these locations are included by Jenkins and Krause as part of the Moundville variant, a Late Mississippian cultural complex with obvious but as yet imperfectly understood relationships to Moundville on the Black Warrior River. Whether these sites formed a single paramount chiefdom or a series of smaller chiefdoms is unknown, but it is clear that this would have been a densely occupied area in the sixteenth century.[30]

In the vicinity of the junction of the Tombigbee and Black Warrior rivers, near Demopolis, there are eleven small sites with Moundville-related or Protohistoric ceramics. Little is known about these scattered sites, except that the majority are fairly small. Archaeological survey coverage of this area is limited, and it is probable that there are a fair number of additional sites. This area is forty-six miles west of Old Cahawba on the Alabama River.[31]

Eighteen miles north of Demopolis on the Black Warrior River is the Stephen's Bluff mound site, the southernmost edge of a large cluster of Mississippian sites centered on the great site of Moundville in Hale and Tuscaloosa counties. From the Stephen's Bluff site north to Tuscaloosa on the Fall Line of the Black Warrior River, there are eleven single-mound sites surrounded by scattered homesteads along approximately thirty-seven miles of river floodplain. From approximately A.D. 1050 to 1600, these sites formed the densest and most cohesive Mississippian site cluster in Alabama. Moundville, with its twenty-nine mounds, enclosing wooden palisade, cemeteries, domestic houses, and elaborate material culture, not only was the largest Mississippian site in Alabama but also is the clearest example in the region of what some scholars reconstruct as a paramount chiefdom. Although past their peak, Moundville and some of its surrounding subsidiary sites continued to be occupied during the sixteenth century. The distance from Old Cahawba westward across the northern edge of the Black Belt to the Black Warrior River then turning north to Moundville is approximately seventy miles.[32]

Summary and Recommendations

1. In general, archaeological knowledge of the Alabama River valley and most of the adjacent parts of the Coosa and Tallapoosa rivers is at a rudimentary level. Levels of archaeological survey vary widely from intensively examined project areas to large stretches of archaeologically unexplored floodplain. Most of the past survey activity has concentrated on the immediate river floodplain. Areas adjacent to the floodplain and along the tributary streams have received little to no examination.

   Presently, the Alabama State Site File does not contain the types of specific information that would allow for other than general coverage of the search area. Until the existing survey data are refined and some of the gaps filled in by new reconnaissance, it will be difficult to use such information to pinpoint the location of Mabila.
2. The present review of the ASSF has demonstrated that there are clusters of sixteenth-century aboriginal sites separated by distinct vacant stretches of the lower Coosa, lower Tallapoosa, and Alabama river valleys. Broadly speaking, significant clusters exist along the upper Coosa, the lower Tallapoosa, the area near Montgomery, the central Alabama, the central Tombigbee, and the lower Black Warrior. There are a number of small intervening vacant zones, but the largest of these are those found along the lower Coosa, the Piedmont section of the Tallapoosa, the Montgomery-to-Selma segment, and the lower Tombigbee. This pattern of archaeological site clusters as "beads on a string" along the rivers may correlate with the provinces and intervening barren regions mentioned in the historic Spanish accounts. It closely resembles the settlement system described by David Hally for supposed chiefdoms along the upper Coosa River in north Georgia and northeast Alabama. Future surveys in Alabama and the subsequent culling of sites found not to be occupied during the mid-

sixteenth century might blur some of the geographic boundaries of these clusters and vacant zones, but probably not to any significant degree.

3. The ceramic chronology and typology for the Alabama River must be refined so that early sixteenth-century occupations can be identified. Earlier and later occupations can be removed from consideration, thus tightening the number of possible sites. The existing artifact collections from Alabama River sites curated at Moundville Archaeological Park and other institutions must be analyzed using these refined typologies. The more precise temporal and cultural identifications must be entered in the centralized database of the ASSF. A descriptive classification of early Spanish artifacts should be developed. Distribution maps of sites with the appropriate Mississippian assemblages and/or Spanish artifacts should be continually updated.
4. In order to identify Spanish contact sites in the ASSF or in future surveys, we need to develop necessary and sufficient conditions to focus on the most likely locations.

   Necessary conditions are those for a De Soto contact site generally:

location on the Alabama Coastal Plain
location within an archaeologically identifiable cluster of Mississippian sites
occupation during the early sixteenth century (as identified by diagnostic ceramic complexes)
archaeological remains of houses and palisades
evidence of burning
sixteenth-century Spanish artifacts

Sufficient conditions are those that would specifically identify or raise to a high probability that a site is Mabila:

Spanish artifacts with identifying marks of persons known to be killed at Mabila
horse gear
graves of sixteenth-century Europeans and Africans

Notes

1. Swanton, *Final Report;* Brain, "Introduction: Update of De Soto Studies," xi–lxxii; Curren, *The Route of the Soto Army through Alabama;* Little and Curren, "Con-

quest Archaeology of Alabama"; DePratter, Hudson, and Smith, "The Hernando de Soto Expedition from Chiaha to Mabila"; Knight, *A Summary of Alabama's De Soto Mapping Project and Project Bibliography.*

2. Hally, "The Settlement Patterns of Mississippian Chiefdoms in Northern Georgia"; Hally, "Archaeology and Settlement Plan of the King Site."

3. Eugene Futato, personal communication, August 2006.

4. Fuller and Brown, *The Mound Island Project.*

5. Swanton, *Early History of the Creek Indians and Their Neighbors;* Waselkov and Gums, *Plantation Archaeology at Rivière aux Chiens.*

6. Pickett, *History;* Ball, *A Glance into the Great South-East,* 672–74; Thomas, *Report on Mound Explorations of the Bureau of Ethnology,* 286–90.

7. C. Moore, "Alabama River"; Sheldon, introduction.

8. Owen, "Prehistoric Works"; Owen, *Handbook of the Alabama Anthropological Society;* Waselkov, "A History of the Alabama Anthropological Society"; Sheldon, "Anthropological Society Field Activities."

9. Graham, *A Preliminary Report of Salvage Archaeology;* Nielsen, *Archaeological Investigations of Three Additional Sites;* Cottier, *Archaeological Salvage Investigations;* Dickens, Prince, and Benthall, *Archaeological Investigations in the Jones Bluff Reservoir;* Dickens, "Archaeology in the Jones Bluff Reservoir."

10. Cottier and Sheldon, *Interim Report;* Oakley and Watson, *Cultural Resources Inventory.*

11. Jeter, *Archaeological Survey;* Atchison, *Archaeological Survey;* Patterson, "Archaeological Reconnaissance."

12. Curren and Lloyd, *Archaeological Survey;* Jenkins and Paglione, *Archaeological Reconnaissance.* See Curren, "Alabama River Phase"; and Curren, *Archaeology in the Mauvila Chiefdom.*

13. Knight and O'Hear, *Archaeological Investigations;* Waselkov, *Coosa Valley Archaeology;* Knight, *East Alabama Archaeological Survey;* Knight, Cole, and Walling, *Archaeological Reconnaissance.*

14. Waselkov and Gums, *Plantation Archaeology at Rivière aux Chiens,* 6; Hamilton and Owen, "Topographic Notes and Observations on the Alabama River"; United States Army Corps of Engineers, "Alabama River from Junction to Hurricane Bluff Bar, Sheet No. 1," and "Alabama River from Hurricane Bluff Bar to Wetumpka, Sheet No. 2."

15. See discussions of regional ceramic types in Knight, "Aboriginal Pottery of the Coosa and Tallapoosa River Valleys"; Chase, "Prehistoric Pottery"; Fuller, "The Bear Point Phase of the Pensacola Variant"; Stowe, "The Pensacola Variant and the Bottle Creek Phase"; Regnier, "A Stylistic Analysis of Burial Urns."

16. For discussions of Cosa and the De Soto expedition, see M. Smith, *Coosa;* Curren, *The Route of the Soto Army through Alabama;* Little and Curren, "Conquest Archaeology of Alabama"; DePratter, Hudson, and Smith, "The Hernando de Soto Expedition," 108–26.

17. Jackson, *Rivers of History;* United States Army Corps of Engineers, 144–45; "Map of the Coosa River from Wetumpka Ala. to Lock No 4 Ala.," and "Map of the Coosa River from Lock No 4 Ala. to Greensport Ala."

18. Waselkov, *Coosa Valley Archaeology;* Knight, Cole, and Walling, *Archaeological Reconnaissance;* Knight, *East Alabama Archaeological Survey;* Knight, introduction.

19. Knight and O'Hear, *Archaeological Investigations;* Knight, "Cultural Complexes of the Alabama Piedmont"; Hubbert and Wright, "Lalakala, the Fishing Place," 201.

20. Chase, "A Brief Synopsis of Central Alabama Prehistory"; Chase, "Prehistoric Pottery."

21. Knight, *Tukabatchee;* Waselkov, *Lower Tallapoosa River Cultural Resources Survey.*

22. C. Moore, "Alabama River," 319–47; Sheldon, introduction, 23–26; Ned J. Jenkins, personal communication with the author, 2004–6.

23. C. Moore, "Alabama River," 303–19; Sheldon, introduction, 19–20; Jeter, *Archaeological Survey;* Ned J. Jenkins, personal communication with the author, 2004–6; Oakley and Watson, *Cultural Resources Inventory;* Nance, *The Archaeological Sequence at Durant Bend.*

24. Ned J. Jenkins, personal communication with the author, September 2006; Cottier and Sheldon, *Interim Report;* Pickett, *History,* 154–55; Martin, "Archaeological Investigations," 60–74.

25. Patterson, "Archaeological Reconnaissance"; Atchison, *Archaeological Survey.*

26. C. Moore, "Alabama River," 297–303; Sheldon, introduction, 17–18; Cottier, *Archaeological Salvage Investigations;* Curren, "Alabama River Phase"; Curren, *Protohistoric Period;* Cottier and Sheldon, *Interim Report;* Regnier, "Stylistic Analysis."

27. C. Moore, "Alabama River," 290–97; Sheldon, introduction, 14–17; Curren, "Alabama River Phase"; Curren, *Protohistoric Period;* Cottier and Sheldon, *Interim Report;* Curren and Lloyd, *Archaeological Survey;* Jenkins and Paglione, *Archaeological Reconnaissance;* Brown, *Bottle Creek;* Brown and Fuller, "Bottle Creek Research"; Fuller and Brown, *The Mound Island Project;* Fuller, Silvia, and Stowe, *The Forks Project.*

28. C. Moore, "Alabama River," 291–96; Sheldon, introduction, 16–17; Curren, *Mauvila Chiefdom,* 96–115.

29. C. Moore, "Lower Tombigbee River"; Sheldon, introduction, 47–58; Brose, "Modeling Site Locations"; Jenkins, "Ceramic Summary Descriptions and Chronology."

30. Jenkins, *Archaeology of the Gainesville Lake Area;* Blitz, *Ancient Chiefdoms of the Tombigbee;* Jenkins and Krause, *The Tombigbee Watershed in Southeastern Prehistory;* Peebles, *Prehistoric Agricultural Communities in West Central Alabama.*

31. Sheldon et al., *Cultural Resource Assessment of the Demopolis Lake Reservoir.*

32. Knight and Steponaitis, "A New History of Moundville"; Welch, "Outlying Sites within the Moundville Chiefdom"; Hammerstedt, "Late Woodland and Mississippian Settlement of the Black Warrior Valley."

10
The United States and Alabama De Soto Commissions

Douglas E. Jones

The mystery of the first European penetration into the interior of the American Southeast by Hernando de Soto between 1539 and 1543 has challenged the attention of professionals and the public alike for nearly five hundred years. This chapter describes and compares two institutional attempts, during the twentieth century, to discover and commemorate the route taken by the famed Spanish conquistador through the southern states. Commissions were formed at the national level for the 400th anniversary and at the state level for the 450th to study this issue and make recommendations. The United States De Soto Expedition Commission was set up in 1935 with Smithsonian anthropologist John R. Swanton at its head. Among several state-level commissions formed for the 450th anniversary was the Alabama De Soto Commission, established in 1985 with the present author as its chairman.

The United States De Soto Expedition Commission, 1935–1938

The first governmental effort to solve the riddle of the route taken by De Soto was the creation of the United States De Soto Expedition Commission by the 74th Congress, August 26, 1935, to commemorate the 400th anniversary of Soto's arrival in La Florida—the Spaniards' name for the lands north and east of Mexico. Acting in accordance with this authority, President Roosevelt appointed the following people as members of the commission (Figure 10.1):

Hon. W. G. Brorein, Tampa, Florida
Miss Caroline Dorman, Chestnut, Louisiana
Col. John R. Fordyce, Hot Springs (later Little Rock), Arkansas

Figure 10.1. The United States De Soto Expedition Commission, 1935–1938. This photograph was taken on the steps of Smith Hall at The University of Alabama. John R. Swanton, commission chairman, is in the front row, second from right. Douglas E. Jones is in the front row at the far left. Photo courtesy of The University of Alabama Museums.

V. Birney Imes, Columbus, Mississippi
Andrew O. Holmes, Memphis, Tennessee
Dr. Walter B. Jones, The University of Alabama, Tuscaloosa
Dr. John R. Swanton, Smithsonian Institution, Washington, D.C.

In early March 1936, an organizational meeting of the commission was held in Washington in the Regents Room of the Smithsonian Institution. All members were present, and the following officers were elected:

Chairman: John R. Swanton
Vice chairman: John R. Fordyce
Secretary: Walter B. Jones

The group also elected Swanton to chair the "fact finding committee," along with Fordyce and Dorman, to establish where the trail route lay. In his *Final*

Report, Swanton wrote, "The interest of all of the members of the fact-finding committee in the expedition of De Soto antedated the appointment of the Commission by many years and considerable time and thought had been devoted by them to the problems connected with it. During the period in which the Commission has been in existence its members have added several weeks of their time every year, often at their own expense, to the sum total of their field investigations."[1]

In Swanton's case this was an understatement, in that prior to the commission's formation, he had already produced at least seven works, dating from 1911, that either discussed De Soto's route or attempted to correlate the Indian societies De Soto encountered with tribes documented in more recent times.[2] He had also made field investigations; according to William Sturtevant, between 1931 and 1934 Swanton made field trips to investigate the topography and archaeology of the route in Florida, Georgia, North Carolina, Arkansas, and Louisiana.[3] As early as 1932 Fordyce and Swanton had collaborated with James Y. Brame Jr. of Montgomery, Alabama, an amateur archaeologist with extensive De Soto trail experience in Georgia and Alabama, with whom Swanton made a number of field trips. From these early sources, it is clear that Swanton's conclusions on the contours of the route were already fully formed before the appointment of the U.S. commission. In 1932 he published a map of the route essentially identical to the one included in the commission's *Final Report* some seven years later.[4] During the life of the commission, Swanton corresponded frequently with Fordyce and Dorman but had little direct contact with the other members.[5] Within nine months of the organizational meeting at the Smithsonian, Swanton had already submitted the body of the *Final Report,* a manuscript of about five hundred pages.[6]

Soon after the Smithsonian meeting, Swanton hired Miss Irene A. Wright, an experienced archivist and linguist then living in Spain, to seek out, copy, and translate relevant documents from Spanish sources. She worked for several months until the shortage of funds and the outbreak of the Spanish Civil War curtailed her efforts in mid-July 1936. The commission also hired Dr. Charmion Shelby of Austin, Texas, to make an accurate English translation of the Garcilaso de la Vega document, *La Florida del Inca,* one of the four known De Soto chronicles.[7]

Two charges had been made to the group: first, to determine the travel route of the expedition, and second, to plan and encourage a broad array of public programs to celebrate the memorial event. The second charge was simple. The first, however, would set the stage for an almost continuous succession of formal, informal, and generally inconclusive investigations that have continued until the present day. In retrospect, the lesson that would be learned during the following half century was that the state of archaeological research and technological development in the 1930s was inadequate to support the task of determining the route.

The United States De Soto Expedition Commission preceded the era of standardized archaeological dating methods and the establishment of the physical characteristics of various indigenous cultural traditions throughout the region. Consequently, in the 1930s it was impossible to determine occupational chronologies of archaeological sites, a circumstance that would have a significant impact on the reconstruction of the trail route. Swanton was quite aware of these circumstances; nevertheless, he embarked on a voyage into the unknown with very few navigational aids.[8]

As a respected Smithsonian ethnologist and expert on Southeast Indians, Swanton knew that the De Soto trail route was critical to his understanding of its impact on native populations. For this reason, he began to reach conclusions about it as early as 1911. Swanton was thoroughly familiar with relevant American and European archives, particularly the four basic De Soto chronicles, three authored by expedition participants and one based on interviews with survivors. Listed in the order of priority that Swanton attributed to their accuracy and dependability, these documents are those of Rodrigo Rangel, De Soto's private secretary; the anonymous "Gentleman of Elvas"; Luis Hernández de Biedma, the king's factor; and the last, and least useful, the account by Garcilaso de La Vega, *La Florida del Inca.*[9]

Swanton correlated these sources with his personal knowledge of terrain and cultural features of the Southeast. Apparently overestimating their permanency, he transposed town names depicted on eighteenth- and nineteenth-century maps to those of the sixteenth century. In the eyes of modern-day investigators, who know that indigenous groups and their towns and names sometimes were quite mobile, this was a major error. More important, it is now accepted that much of the native population and many of the towns that De Soto encountered were wiped out within a short time by Spanish-borne viruses and bacteria. Nonetheless Swanton held firm to his opinions as published in the *Final Report,* many of which had been formed as early as 1911–12.[10]

Swanton had decided most of the De Soto trail route before the commission was established, and he expected that his plan would receive the federal stamp of approval. It did, but how much of it was correct? Despite the errors revealed by other scholars soon after the report was released, and since that time, the people whose communities lay along the published route considered the De Soto trail a matter of official fact and the source of considerable local pride. Many towns and historic associations across the Southeast erected, and fiercely defended, handsome highway marker signs and monuments. Until overwhelmed by the onset of World War II, public programs envisioned and encouraged by the commission on the topic of De Soto's march consisted of popularized articles and books, art exhibits, lectures, radio programs, and stage dramas throughout the country.

Having something to brag about was important for folks suffering through the final years of the Great Depression. Alabamians were particularly proud that Dr. Swanton had placed the site of the fabled Mabila battlefield in their state: near the forks of the Tombigbee and Alabama rivers in south Clarke County. This battle between De Soto's army and thousands of native Americans assembled by the equally fabled Chief Tascalusa on October 18, 1540, was the greatest conflict of its kind in the history of North America. Sadly, little archaeological justification exists for Swanton's placement of Mabila here.

However, as Charles Hudson writes, "Swanton did not claim finality for his route. He was quite aware of the discovery of new manuscripts, and most practically the expansion of Southeastern archaeology, which was in its infancy in the 1930s, could require the route to be redrawn. Time has proven him right on both counts."[11]

With one exception, and despite many years of professional and amateur effort to discover them, Hernando de Soto's footprints across the Southeast remain invisible. The only documented De Soto–related archaeological site in North America is the Governor Martin site in downtown Tallahassee, Florida.[12]

The Alabama De Soto Commission, 1985–1990

In an effort to ameliorate this historic stalemate by applying archaeological philosophies and technologies developed during the half century since the Swanton era, a small group of University of Alabama faculty proposed to President Joab L. Thomas in 1985 that a state commission be appointed by the governor to commemorate the 450th anniversary of De Soto's arrival in Alabama.

By an executive order in the fall of 1985, Governor George C. Wallace created the Alabama De Soto Commission (Figure 10.2). Its mission was to conduct archival and field investigations of interest to the reconstruction and marking of the De Soto trail route and to plan public programs celebrating the 450th anniversary of De Soto's arrival in the state as the first chapter of a significant Hispanic history in Alabama. Douglas E. Jones, then professor

Figure 10.2. The Alabama De Soto Commission, 1985–1990. In this photograph, also taken on the steps of Smith Hall at The University of Alabama, commission chairman Douglas E. Jones is in the front row at the far left.

of geology and director of the Alabama Museum of Natural History, was named chairman; Professor of Anthropology Vernon James Knight Jr. served as secretary. Over the five-year existence of the commission, twenty-four individuals, including five ex-officio members and the consul general of Spain in New Orleans, served at various times.

Richard Bailey, Gunter Air Force Base, Montgomery
Clifford Bibb, Alabama State University
Edwin Bridges, Alabama Department of Archives and History, Montgomery
Joe Caver, Maxwell Air Force Base, Montgomery
C. J. Coley, Alexander City
Caleb Curren, Camden
Margaret Sizemore Douglass, Birmingham
Kenneth Hannon, Mobile
Jay Higginbotham, Mobile
Nicholas Holmes, Mobile

Charles Hudson, University of Georgia
Bessie Jones, Alabama A & M College, Huntsville
Alfred Mitchell, Pike Road
Paul Mohr, Talladega College
James Oakley, Centerville
Lawrence Oaks, Alabama Historical Commission, Montgomery
Jean Pinkerton, Sylacauga
Joe Smitherman, Selma
Mabel Ward, Mobile
Dan Williams, Tuskegee Institute
Amos Wright, Alabama Archaeological Society, Huntsville
Juan Ramon Parellada, consul general of Spain, New Orleans (until his retirement when he was replaced by Sr. Joaquin Cervino)

Four committees were established to facilitate the goals set for the organization: Archaeological Research, Nicholas Holmes, chair; Historical Research, Edwin Bridges, chair; Public Outreach and Education, James Oakley, chair; Trail Marking, Amos Wright, chair. Administrative support staff was provided by the Alabama Museum of Natural History. All groups worked actively throughout their tenure and contributed significantly to the various projects undertaken during the life of the commission.

Formal commission meetings were held at a number of venues in Alabama, principally in Tuscaloosa but also in Birmingham, Montgomery, and Selma, among others, in an effort to encourage public participation and input.

One of the most successful projects the commission accomplished was publication of the De Soto Working Papers, a series of short papers to inform and seek professional and lay input regarding various route hypotheses under consideration, the results of archaeological field investigations, and other relevant topics. A mailing list of four hundred was considered adequate for this purpose; consequently, this number of each of the thirteen papers was distributed during the life of the commission. The De Soto Working Papers alone constitute a fairly comprehensive review of the commission's work.[13]

The "pre-archaeological" conditions suffered by Swanton had been ameliorated during the fifty-year interval preceding the creation of the 1985–90 Alabama commission. Dating technology had improved significantly, and great progress had been made by archaeologists in defining cultural phases based on ceramics, burial practices, foodstuffs, and construction characteristics. It was now possible to determine at what time and by whom a particular site was occupied.

Among the most significant and revealing examples of this enhanced capability was the "Alabama De Soto Mapping Project" described in Working Paper no. 9, by Vernon James Knight Jr., secretary of the commission. One computer-generated map included in that paper depicts known sites considered by the experts to correlate to the mid-sixteenth century. A second map depicts the known presence of De Soto–era Spanish artifacts, including Clarksdale-type brass bells and glass beads of the Nueva Cadiz type. The success of this particular project was broadened to other southern states, which was in large part a result of the establishment of the regional De Soto Trail Commission in 1988 (Figure 10.3). The mission of this wider group, made up primarily of archaeologists, was to promote research on the expedition and to coordinate state initiatives with federal efforts to study and plan a De Soto National Historic Trail. While this plan never materialized, the organization itself provided the forum for these experts to develop mutually agreed upon standards for sites across the region. Ultimately, digitized maps of known sixteenth-century sites were produced for Georgia, Tennessee, Alabama, Mississippi, and Arkansas.[14]

With these mapping data in hand, the Alabama commission decided early on to focus its attention on the Mabila site because it should have distinctive archaeological attributes beyond the ordinary criteria. If found, it could serve as the linchpin for the balance of the trail route. However, this locality remains a mystery.

After considering all the data collected during its tenure, the commission approved "The Highway Route of the De Soto Trail in Alabama," as described in De Soto Working Paper no. 8 by Douglas E. Jones. Like Swanton, the group could not prove that this route was correct, but, based on all available data, it was felt that the highway route selected fairly represented the principal corridor along which De Soto traveled, although the identity of no single town site could be confirmed.

To meet its obligations toward public education, the commission authorized the Alabama Museum of Natural History to design and install De Soto Trail road markers along Alabama highways. Instructive and attractive De Soto kiosks were installed at all major visitor centers and other points of special interest in the state. A colorful brochure advertising the Highway Route of the De Soto Trail was created and distributed by the thousands to visitor centers in the state for a number of years.

With the completion of these projects and the concurrence of commission members, Chairman Jones recommended to then-governor Guy Hunt in 1990 that the Alabama De Soto Commission be officially discharged; this was done. The data and conclusions assembled by the commission are now "grist for the mill" for subsequent generations of truth seekers whose tech-

Figure 10.3. The regional De Soto Trail Commission, 1988–1990. Commission chairman Douglas E. Jones is in the front row at the far left.

nical and archival resources will add to the De Soto saga in Alabama and the Southeast.[15]

Notes

1. Swanton, *Final Report,* ix.

2. Swanton, *Indian Tribes of the Lower Mississippi Valley and Adjacent Coast of the Gulf of Mexico;* Swanton, "De Soto's Line of March"; Swanton, *Early History of the Creek Indians and Their Neighbors;* Swanton, "Relation of the Southeast"; Swanton, "Ethnological Value of the De Soto Narratives"; Swanton, "The Landing Place of De Soto"; Swanton, "Tracing De Soto's Route."

3. Sturtevant, foreword.

4. Swanton, "Relation of the Southeast," appendix, figure 3; this 1932 map was drafted by archaeologist Frank M. Setzler of the Smithsonian. Swanton credits the research of Colonel John R. Fordyce and J. Y. Brame for assistance with its details for the Arkansas and Alabama segments, respectively.

5. Hudson, *Knights of Spain, Warriors of the Sun,* 460–61.

6. Sturtevant, foreword, v.

7. Swanton, *Final Report,* viii.

8. Hudson, *Knights of Spain, Warriors of the Sun,* 463.

9. Swanton, *Final Report,* 10; see chapter 3, this volume.

10. Hudson, *Knights of Spain, Warriors of the Sun,* 461.

11. Ibid.

12. Ewen and Hann, *Hernando de Soto among the Apalachee.*

13. The De Soto Working Papers series is currently available at http://www.as.ua.edu/ant/Mabila/index.htm.

14. Knight, *A Summary of Alabama's De Soto Working Paper Series and Project Bibliography;* Morgan, *The Mississippi De Soto Trail Mapping Project;* Morse, "Archaeology and the Population of Arkansas in 1541–1543."

15. The archives of the Alabama De Soto Commission and the regional De Soto Trail Commission were placed on deposit in the William Stanley Hoole Special Collections Library of The University of Alabama in Tuscaloosa. A finder's guide to these materials was prepared by Andrea Watson and is available to researchers at the library.

11
Seeking Methods That Work

Vernon James Knight Jr.

What is our rationale, at this particular moment, for making a new attempt at the search for Mabila? Part of the answer is that, in my view, a great deal has been learned about evaluating alternative methods of tracking conquistadors through the southern states. Much of this practical knowledge was hard-won from experiences during the late 1980s, with the 450th anniversary of the De Soto expedition, the Columbus Quincentenary, and the several years of scholarly activity surrounding those anniversaries. Lest we repeat the mistakes of the past, I would like to use this opportunity to outline what I believe are key features of a more enlightened approach than has often been applied. I will speak of matters of organization, of our use of historic documentation, and of our use of the known archaeological record.

Matters of Organization

As for matters of organization, I do not mean organizing the logistics of a field survey. That practical topic can be addressed by others. Instead I refer to a broader approach, what we conceive of as a multidisciplinary, team effort. Such a group approach, by a team of scholars working closely together, has many advantages over lone scholars working in isolation.

As Douglas E. Jones points out in chapter 10, the United States De Soto Expedition Commission of the 1930s was to a large extent a one-man show, dominated by John R. Swanton of the Smithsonian's Bureau of American Ethnology. Although Swanton gathered data from many others during the commission's tenure, and depended especially on the work of James Y. Brame Jr. of Montgomery for the Alabama portion of the route, nonetheless Swanton dominated the commission's fact-finding committee and was the sole author of the published *Final Report*. To that extent, the now classic

Final Report represents the unexamined reflections of a single scholar. After its publication, Swanton's reconstruction was challenged by a number of archaeologists whose data seemed to contradict Swanton's final route determinations.[1]

The subsequent Alabama De Soto Commission of the 1980s was a much more democratic enterprise, as is shown by the variety of voices heard in the commission's Working Paper series. In essence, this state commission found itself in the position of evaluating multiple working hypotheses. The overall effect was salutary, in that each of the three proponents of specific routes who presented their views to the state commission were asked to reflect on the challenges posed by the other two, and to address these challenges openly. Champions of specific routes were therefore moved to clarify and hone their arguments, in a timely way and in a common context. In this manner, potential flaws in each proposal were brought to the fore.[2]

What we seek at this point is a far less competitive setting, one in which the concept is to work toward a consensus among participants in a long-term working group, some trained in the disciplines of history, archaeology, geography, geology, and folklore, and others whose expertise lies primarily in their keen familiarity with the territory in question. As an initial agenda, we have begun not by seeking this consensus on our private notions of where Mabila might be on the landscape so that we might eliminate the competitive and argumentative tone that has too often surrounded these questions. Rather, our first business as I see it is to agree on fundamental matters of *method,* so we can productively talk to one another. Having the several disciplines represented in the working group is intended to provide checks and balances I think we need. It is sobering to learn that one's personal approach to date has been naïve in one or another respect. This is a feeling that I suspect most of us have experienced at one time or another, but it can be offset, I suspect, by the excitement of contributing to consensus-building in a group that can not only make progress but speak with much greater authority than any individual. In this setting, the idea of multiple working hypotheses is one to which I hope we can return.

Use of the Chronicles

During the Columbus Quincentenary and associated events, archaeologists and anthropologists were accused of using documentary materials naïvely, treating the content of problematic narratives in questionable English translations at face value as accurate history.[3] Such critics, unfortunately, were often correct. To be taken seriously, we must be sensitive to the fact that centuries-old historical documents do not give us anything like direct access to the realities of the past, and the De Soto chronicles are especially tricky in this regard. In the form that we have them, only one major account is first-hand (chapter 1, this volume), and none was composed at a time close to the events they describe. An important lesson is that no matter what our training, we must make every effort to behave with some measure of sophistication in the way we work with historical data.

First and foremost, we must recognize that the surviving Spanish and Portuguese chronicles of the era are very different from one another in their value as historical documents. As George Lankford reveals in chapter 3, the main accounts of the De Soto expedition are layered, their authorship is not straightforward, and they are not necessarily independent of one another. There is a long history of scholarship on these complex questions, and much is yet to be decided, but some things are clear.[4] For example, today historians do not consider the account of Garcilaso de la Vega as a trustworthy source for details, particularly in matters of narrative sequence and quantities of things, such as distances traveled or numbers of Indians. This is despite any value Garcilaso's history may have as a superb literary portrayal of a true story.[5]

In the late 1980s, some of us embarked on a project to republish the De Soto chronicles together in improved, more literal English translations.[6] It was disconcerting to hear from our detractors that our resources were being misspent. According to these critics, the existing published translations by Buckingham Smith, Edward G. Bourne, and John Varner and Jeannette Varner were perfectly serviceable, and any available resources would be much better spent in digging archaeological sites.[7] However, I am still convinced that our detractors were wrong. Even John Swanton recognized that the older translations needed to be emended in places, as the translators not only were insensitive to the realities of the native American world being described but were also mostly ignorant of the geography along the line of march.[8] An example pertinent to the Mabila problem will suffice. During the early twentieth century there were at least two attempts by members of the Alabama Anthropological Society to trace the route of De Soto through the State of Alabama. Both depended heavily on the translation by Edward G. Bourne of the Rangel account, as originally found in Oviedo's *Historia General y Natural de las Indias.*[9] In the Bourne translation from the Spanish, the Indian town of Piachi, near Mabila, is described as being "high above the gorge of a mountain stream," beyond which "they departed thence into a mountain." These passages must have caused some difficulty, as "gorges," "mountain streams," and "mountains" are hard to come by in the Gulf Coastal Plain. The first reconstruction in 1921, based on the research of Peter Brannon and

Major Daniel Marshall Andrews and claimed by the society as "definitive," decided that "we must turn to the stream, furnishing such a gorge, which is only found on the Black Warrior [River], and to which it is only logical to search." They therefore placed Piachi on a ridge overlooking the Black Warrior River near Old Erie in Hale County.[10] The second reconstruction, by James Y. Brame in 1928, used the same descriptive evidence to place Piachi some eighty-five miles to the south of the first location, at Claiborne on the Alabama River in Monroe County. Brame says,

> In my field investigations I have found no place that so well fits the chroniclers' description of Piachi as does the site of old Claiborne. . . . Here on a commanding bluff of level land high above the river was an extensive aboriginal village with a fine spring of water. . . .
>
> Across the river from Claiborne there is a mile or so of meadow lands to the foot of a high range of hills, mountainous in elevation. Ranjel says that after crossing the river "they departed thence into a mountain," and these hills were evidently the mountains to which Ranjel referred. Certainly no locality is to be found that would better answer the description of the place as recounted by the chroniclers.[11]

Unfortunately for both of these noble efforts, there is nothing in the original Spanish of Oviedo that mentions a gorge, a mountain stream, or a mountain beyond Piachi. It is doubly unfortunate that some years later John Swanton followed Brame's logic in placing Piachi on the bluffs at Claiborne based on the same mistranslated historical evidence.[12]

I am confident that the more literal translations found in *The De Soto Chronicles* have allowed English-speaking audiences a better appreciation of what the Spanish and Portuguese chroniclers were trying to convey. But I would go further than this. Some readers may not want to hear it, but serious scholarship demands that we work with the chronicles in their original languages. Here I am not just expressing the chauvinism of those who happen to know their Spanish and Portuguese (a category in which I freely admit my status as a novice). Many passages in the chronicles are straightforward in translation, but others demand a sensitivity not only to the original language but to usages peculiar to ordinary participants in the De Soto expedition, that is to say, largely men who acquired their linguistic habits in the arid province of Estremadura in Spain during the early sixteenth century, and who later picked up New World usages from the Greater Antilles prior to their entering the North American Southeast. For these reasons, our workshop group includes members with research expertise in southern Spain and in sixteenth-century Spanish, and whose professional networks provide us with access to additional Spanish scholars with specific expertise in the geographic terminology used in sixteenth-century Spain and adjacent Portugal. For our original workshop sessions, pertinent documents were made available to participants on-line in their original languages. Moreover, we have consulted with colleagues in Spain concerning appropriate English translations of key descriptive phrases in the chronicles that are pertinent to Mabila and surrounding indigenous towns.

Use of Archaeological Data

As described by Douglas E. Jones in chapter 10, John Swanton and the United States De Soto Commission of the 1930s were working largely in an archaeological vacuum. Route reconstructions of that era therefore depended almost entirely on matching historical records to geography. In contrast, we now live in an era of computerized state archaeological site files that maintain systematic, accurate data on many thousands of archaeological sites in our areas of interest. Decades of archaeological surveys and excavations, together with improved methods in the arsenal of the archaeologist, have revealed an increasingly clear picture of the cultural chronologies in each area and the artifact types diagnostic of each period. It could be argued that most archaeological sites corresponding to large Late Mississippian villages are already on record in these databases, as the discovery of new sites of this category has become increasingly uncommon with time. While there are still many gaps in this record, not to use this extraordinary data set in reconstructions of routes taken by Spanish expeditions is, to say the least, ill advised. It is no longer adequate to simply trust the minimal geographic data in the chronicles and estimates of directions and distances traveled to try and map routes on that basis alone. The distribution of appropriate archaeological sites narrows the field of play considerably. The only matter seemingly at issue is how best to use these archaeological data in conjunction with our other sources.

One obvious task is to plot the archaeological sites corresponding to the De Soto time line on digital maps at an appropriate scale. For the State of Alabama this was done in 1988 and published by the Alabama De Soto Commission, together with a second map of all European artifact finds of the expeditionary period then known (Figure 11.1).[13] For each site plotted, the original documentation was reviewed for accuracy based on the knowledge available at that time. Today, thanks to the archaeological work in central Alabama of workshop participants Amanda Regnier, Ned Jenkins, Craig Sheldon, Gregory Waselkov, and Linda Derry, among others, we know con-

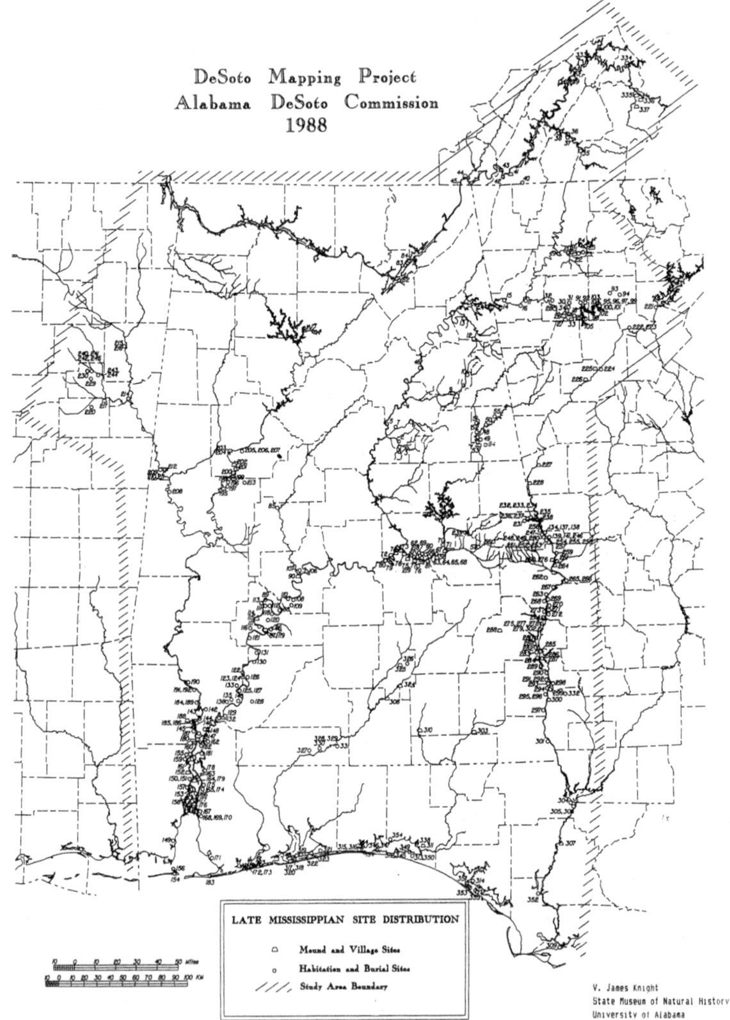

Figure 11.1. Map of Late Mississippian archaeological sites in Alabama and adjacent portions of Tennessee, Georgia, Florida, and Mississippi. Published by the Alabama De Soto Commission in 1988 as an item in the commission's Working Papers series.

siderably more than we did in 1988 about the dating and distribution of the indigenous settlements in our area of interest and the archaeological cultures they reflect.

Some recent attempts to reconstruct De Soto's route have proceeded by trying to match the towns and villages mentioned in the expedition chronicles to specific, known archaeological sites. But this very specific matching, which is difficult to prove, is not the only possible approach. In the early 1980s Jeffrey P. Brain, an archaeologist, took the archaeological data available at that time and constructed a route drawn as a broad swath on a map in order to incorporate several alternative possibilities (Figure 11.2).[14] Yet another less specific approach arises from observing that archaeological sites of the De Soto horizon are not uniformly distributed in space. Instead, they tend to form tight clusters conforming to different archaeological cultures, with sparsely inhabited territory in between. Since the towns mentioned in the De Soto chronicles are often described as belonging to named provinces, the archaeological site clusters should conform to these provinces. Also, the spaces between the archaeological site clusters have significance, as these should conform to the uninhabited areas (called *desiertos,* or *desplobados*) through which the Spaniards marched as they moved from province to province constantly seeking populated places where they could provision the army. Thus, where it may not be possible to match specific towns in the chronicles with specific sites, it may be entirely possible to archaeologically identify late prehistoric political provinces that should match the provinces named in the chronicles. As far as I know, the pioneers of this approach were Marvin Smith, who used it in 1976 to define portions of De Soto's route through eastern Tennessee, northern Georgia, and northeast Alabama, and George Lankford, who used it in his 1977 reappraisal of De Soto's route through Alabama.[15]

Some years ago, at a conference connected with the 450th anniversary of De Soto's *entrada,* I introduced a concept that I called the long-ribbon approach.[16] If we can imagine De Soto's day-to-day itinerary as plotted on a ribbon, it is easy to envision trying to pin that ribbon onto a modern map in such a way as to yield the best fit (Figure 11.3). Assuming that we can all agree on the items belonging on the itinerary itself, with its towns, rivers, deserted areas, and other geographic features, then in theory we could even objectively score alternative routes by ranking their relative degree of fit with the items entered on the ribbon. Thus a copious river in the chronicles requires a real river, not a creek, a large town requires a large archaeological site of precisely the right period, and so forth. So far this is pretty simple-minded, but what makes it the *long*-ribbon approach is this. A *short* segment of the itinerary can be fitted to a modern map literally just about anywhere. That is why,

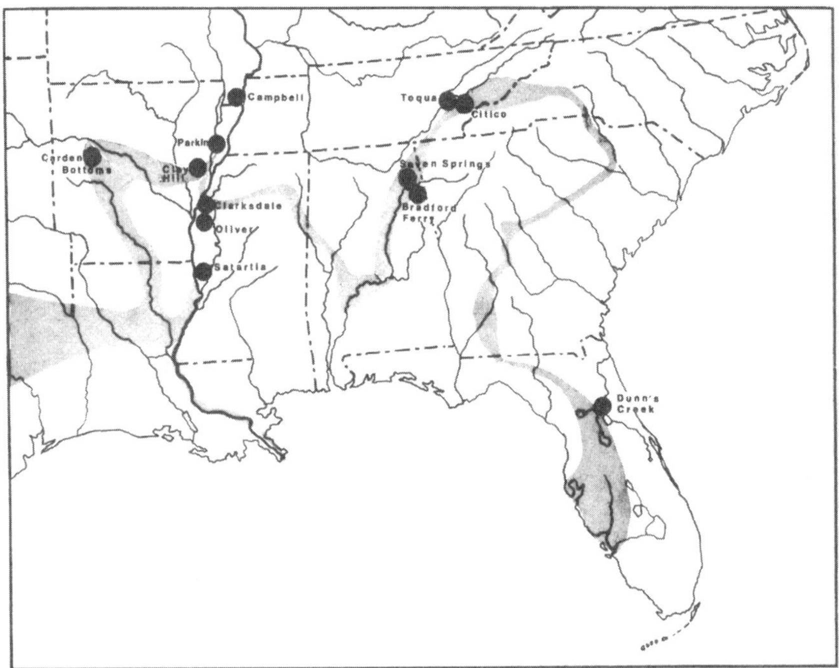

Figure 11.2. Map of De Soto's route through the southeast by archaeologist Jeffrey P. Brain, depicted as a broad swath of variable width to allow for alternative possibilities. From Brain, "The Archaeology of the De Soto Expedition," in R. Badger and L. Clayton, eds., *Alabama and the Borderlands: From Prehistory to Statehood* (University of Alabama Press, Tuscaloosa, 1985).

in the State of Florida, we can have three perfectly sober reconstructions of De Soto's march inland from a hypothesized landing at Tampa Bay, Charlotte Harbor far to the south of Tampa, or even Cape Canaveral on the Atlantic coast; any one of these can be made to fit the initial itinerary, but as soon as we lengthen the ribbon to include events as far away as the 1539 winter camp in Apalache, and insist on archaeological sites of the correct period along the way, some reconstructions immediately move ahead of others in their plausibility. Attempts to reconstruct shorter segments of the route are inherently less convincing than attempts to match longer segments (or, ultimately, the entire journey). The longer the ribbon, the tougher the requirements. A review of the history of De Soto route reconstructions in Alabama shows that in our case, where we choose to place distant Cosa on the one hand and the winter camp at Chicasa on the other has a great deal to do with our conclusions concerning where Mabila might be.[17] Conversely, anyone proposing a

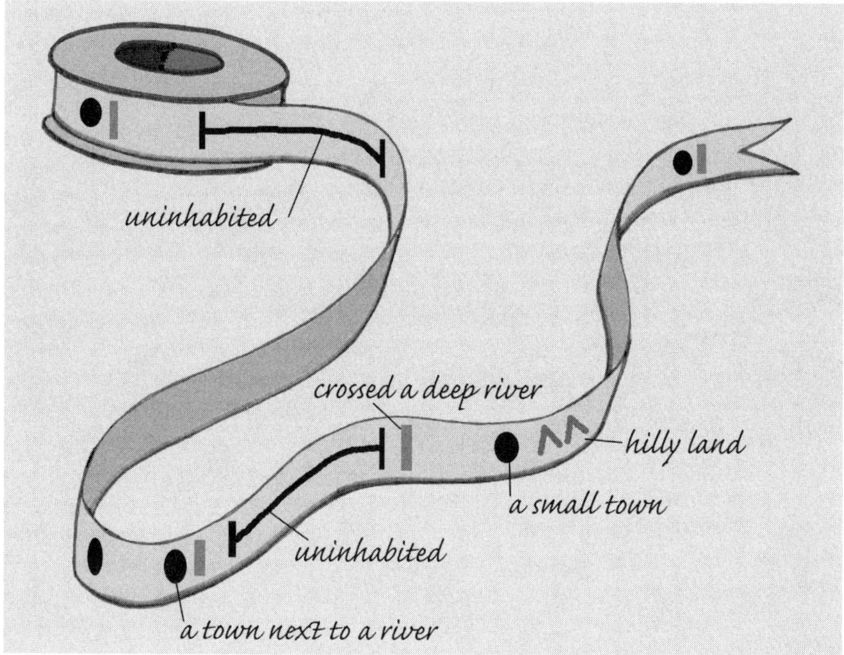

Figure 11.3. The "long-ribbon method." The longer the ribbon, the more difficult it becomes to match the itinerary to a modern map.

Mabila location needs to convince us of corresponding locations for Cosa and Chicasa with plausible archaeological sites, geography, and travel times in between, and, for that matter, beyond.

I believe it is also important to bear in mind what southeastern archaeologists have learned about the scale and structure of native societies of the Late Mississippian period, independently of what the chronicles tell us. In anthropological parlance, these societies were *chiefdoms,* agricultural societies governed by hereditary elites, unlike the later egalitarian tribes of the colonial period such as the Choctaws, Chickasaws, or Creeks. Late Mississippian chiefdoms were quite small in scale. Each chiefdom generally consisted of a small number of closely spaced towns with populations in the hundreds, politically unified under a chief. These chiefs usually, though not always, lived on artificial mounds raised by their followers at administrative centers.

Research by David Hally is especially pertinent to understanding the normal size and spacing of chiefdoms of this area and period. Using archaeological site data from north Georgia, Hally has found that the size of chiefdoms was limited to approximately 19 miles in diameter (30 kilometers), no more than one day's travel on foot. The distance between administrative centers averaged about 28 miles (45 kilometers), and chiefdoms tended to be separated from one another by lightly inhabited or uninhabited intermediate zones, commonly about 12–19 miles (20–30 kilometers) across. These intermediate areas probably functioned as military buffer zones against potentially hostile neighbors. These societies, in short, were very small and restricted in scale, and while it is clear from the Spanish documents that there were ties among some neighboring chiefdoms, these ties were on the order of temporary military alliances rather than consolidated political units. Hally argues that any larger political units would have been very difficult to govern, given the political control mechanisms available to these chiefs.[18] Thus, there are archaeological reasons to be skeptical of claims such as the one reportedly made by Chief Tascalusa that the chief of Mabila was his political subordinate, since Mabila was a named province apparently separated by four days' travel across sparsely inhabited terrain from Tascalusa's own.

Such a perspective offered by the archaeology allows us to make sense of certain passages in the chronicles. For example, if the chief of Mabila were really a vassal of Tascalusa, then one would presume that the chief of the intermediate town Piachi was as well. But we are told in the Rangel account that the malicious chief of Piachi resisted the Spaniards' crossing of the River of Piachi, despite the presence of Chief Tascalusa, who was there precisely to guarantee the Spaniards safe passage to Mabila, which lay beyond.

Conclusion

For this chapter I have selectively mentioned just a few things that I believe could be involved as we take stock of what to do next in our search for Mabila's location. Before closing, I must not neglect to mention that there are several other perspectives that are helpful to our task. We need the eyes of geographers and geologists on the problem to assist with matters of terrain, natural vegetative cover, potential trail locations, river crossings, and possible correlates of the geographic features mentioned in the chronicles. Neal Lineback of our workshop group has called attention to the potential use of records of the General Land Office. These records date to the early nineteenth century and they document the natural landscape at the time it was first surveyed, prior to its development in fields, farm roads, and towns. In our area of interest the surveyors noted trails, lakes, natural prairies, and even Indian earthworks that have long since vanished.

In short, we look forward to a fruitful collaboration involving multiple voices.

Notes

1. Phillips, Ford, and Griffin, *Archaeological Survey in the Lower Mississippi Alluvial Valley;* Bullen, "De Soto's Ucita and the Terra Ceia Site"; DeJarnette and Hansen, *Archaeology of the Childersburg Site, Alabama;* M. Smith, "Route of DeSoto"; Fleming, "Historic Aboriginal Occupation of the Guntersville Basin, Alabama."

2. Jones, *The Highway Route of the De Soto Trail in Alabama,* 1–4.

3. Galloway, "The Archaeology of Ethnohistorical Narrative."

4. E.g., Swanton, "Ethnological Value of the De Soto Narratives"; Hoffman, "Introduction: The De Soto Expedition"; Galloway, *The Hernando de Soto Expedition.*

5. E. Moore, foreword.

6. Clayton, Knight, and Moore, *De Soto Chronicles.*

7. B. Smith, *De Soto's Conquest of Florida;* Bourne, *Narratives;* Varner and Varner, *The Florida of the Inca.*

8. Swanton, *Final Report,* viii.

9. Bourne, *Narratives*; Oviedo y Valdés, *Historia General y Natural de las Indias.*

10. Brannon, "The Route of De Soto from Cosa to Mauvilla," 4.

11. Brame, "De Soto in Alabama," 65–66.

12. Swanton, *Final Report,* 217.

13. Knight, *A Summary of Alabama's De Soto Mapping Project and Project Bibliography.* See also Morgan, *The Mississippi De Soto Trail Mapping Project;* Morse, "Archaeology and the Population of Arkansas in 1541–1543."

14. Brain, "The Archaeology of the De Soto Expedition."

15. M. Smith, "The Route of DeSoto"; Lankford, "A New Look at DeSoto's Route through Alabama"; see also Smith and Kowalewski, "Tentative Identification of a Prehistoric 'Province' in Piedmont Georgia."

16. Vernon J. Knight Jr., informal remarks on a "long-ribbon" approach, presentation to the Mississippi De Soto Trail Commission Symposium, Mississippi University for Women, Columbus, December 8, 1989.

17. For bibliographies on De Soto route reconstructions in Florida and Alabama, see Brain, "Introduction: Update of De Soto Studies"; Brain and Ewen, "Introduction to Bibliography of De Soto Studies."

18. Hally, "The Territorial Size of Mississippian Chiefdoms."

II
Conference Results

12

A Comparative Analysis of the De Soto Accounts on the Route to, and Events at, Mabila

Robbie Ethridge, Kathryn E. Holland Braund, Lawrence A. Clayton, George E. Lankford, and Michael D. Murphy

Constructing a single narrative from multiple sources is the goal of history. To achieve this, historians have devised good methods for scrutinizing documents, for assessing their reliability, for corroborating evidence from any single document, and for resolving discrepancies between documents. However, these methods are most useful when used with ample documentary records. In the case of the American South, the amount of documentary evidence decreases as one goes back in time. There are relatively many documents for the twentieth and nineteenth centuries, fewer for the eighteenth century, even fewer for the seventeenth century, and fewest for the sixteenth century. Since the Indians had no system of writing, there are no documents for pre-Contact times.

It is essential that the historian's methods be applied to the documentary evidence of the sixteenth-century De Soto expedition and our search for Mabila. Documentary evidence from the expedition is sparse, to say the least. As discussed in chapter 3 of this volume, there are only four major narratives of varying reliability, which means that scholars may not be able to get the kind of corroboration between documents that they would like.

Of the four narratives, the Garcilaso account is especially problematic in that it cannot be used for any corroboration whatsoever. George Lankford, in chapter 3 of this volume, details the problems with the Garcilaso account, and we will not repeat those here except to say that given the unreliability of the narrative, we are in favor of disregarding Garcilaso as a reliable source for reconstructing the route and, hence, in our search for Mabila.[1] This is not to say one should dismiss Garcilaso altogether. Given that only four accounts exist, it would be foolhardy to dismiss one of them out of hand. Although Garcilaso is unreliable on specific details of chronology, places, town names, distances/days traveled, and so on, he provides anecdotes and details about life on the march that are missing in the others. His account is also a very good popular history, and one can read it in several ways other than as a verifiable reconstruction of the De Soto route. Finally, Garcilaso's narrative can also be used as an oral history, a story that provides interesting tales and legends about the expedition.

So, although we do not recommend dismissing Garcilaso altogether, we do contend that Garcilaso cannot be taken at face value, and given his confusion of dates, places, events, towns, distances, and so on, his narrative cannot be used to reconstruct the route. Instead, we recommend that De Soto route researchers exclude or, at the least, marginalize Garcilaso in their analyses because his account is not trustworthy on the route details. Furthermore, one should never use Garcilaso to corroborate testimony from Biedma, Rangel, and/or Elvas. And any route details taken from Garcilaso that are not already in one or more of the other narratives must be considered suspicious at best.

De Soto investigators reconstructing the route and the events of the *entrada* have concluded that full historiographic corroboration is not always possible with this particular set of documents. In the past few decades, they have added archaeological evidence to their historical tool kits, with much success (as many chapters in this volume attest; see especially chapter 15). They have also used supplementary documentation by Spaniards who later attempted to retrace parts of De Soto's expedition, in particular the expeditions by Tristán de Luna and Juan Pardo (see chapter 4, this volume).[2] In using the Biedma, Rangel, and Elvas narratives, however, some previous De Soto scholars have strayed somewhat from the usual rigors of historical methodology. Under the circumstances, they felt it justifiable to use the four chronicles to create a single narration by combining or ignoring contradictory details, by privileging one document over another, by alternately using or ignoring the omissions or ellipses across the narratives, and by occasionally "cherry picking" pieces of evidence. Let us briefly examine each of these practices in turn.

Using uncorroborated evidence in De Soto research is virtually impossible to avoid given the nature and proveniences of the four chronicles. In the case of Mabila, for example, there are only a few instances of agreement in the sections of the Biedma, Rangel, and Elvas narratives pertaining to Mabila and the trek through present-day Alabama. And Garcilaso cannot be used to corroborate any of these narratives for the reasons discussed above. In addition, any similarities between Rangel and Elvas are problematic since, given the possible borrowing between the two, one cannot always consider any agreements between Rangel and Elvas as corroboration. The modern scholar, then, is faced with the problem of what to do when one or more chroniclers describe an event slightly differently or when one or more offer a different set of details. In the past, scholars have usually combined the narratives to reconstruct a particular event such as the battle of Mabila without discussing the problems inherent in this approach. Combining variable evidence into a single narrative leaves the reconstruction always vulnerable to debate, especially over specific details. In addition, combining four different sets of details into a single narrative inevitably invites the hazard of masking disagreements among them.

In many, but not all, cases of narrative disagreements, scholars typically privilege the Rangel account, since it is generally considered the most reliable of the four. However, in some cases of disagreement, scholars have chosen to rely on Elvas over Rangel; in other cases scholars have chosen Biedma over Rangel. Clearly, given the nature of this evidence, "privileging" is one of the necessary tools that scholars must use. Even so, one should be explicit about whom one is privileging and why. The burden falls on scholars to explain in each instance why they have chosen one narrative over another, especially if they give precedence to one of the less reliable narratives over one that is generally regarded as more reliable.

There is also the matter of omissions and ellipses across the documents. Biedma, for example, clearly has omitted much in his account; but, as we will see, there are also several instances in which the other chroniclers are silent about various particulars. Given the uncorroborated nature of these documents, one should not let these gaps pass without remarking on them. For example, Biedma does not mention an advance guard entering Mabila, yet Rangel reports that an advance guard went ahead. If one's reconstruction of the events at Mabila includes an advance guard, one must account for Biedma's silence if only to remark that De Soto typically sent out an advance guard. Conversely, if Rangel, for instance, is silent on a detail, scholars will sometimes privilege a less reliable narrative simply because it provides more for them to work with. If one elects do this, then one must also address Rangel's omission.

Finally, when using documentary evidence, there is always the temptation to "cherry pick," or to take an uncorroborated detail or event and use it as a historical fact that serves to anchor a reconstruction. In other words, cherry picking is uncritically using details from any narrative to fit a preconceived conclusion. Building a reconstruction around an uncorroborated piece of the narrative can easily lead one to understand this detail as "true" and therefore disregard or dismiss any conflicts it may have with the other narratives. In the search for Mabila, especially, if one cherry picks, one risks abandoning the long-ribbon approach by favoring the details, regardless of provenience, that conform to a preconceived idea about the location of Mabila.[3]

Obviously, a good deal of evaluation and interpretive finesse is necessary when working with documents from the sixteenth-century South. However, it is our contention that we must not only be alert to the shortcomings of the evidence and the problem of corroboration but also be explicit about when and why we privilege one narrative over another. All relevant discrepancies, omissions, and ellipses among the narratives likewise must be revealed and explored. And scholars should be careful to avoid presenting as "fact" things that are mere conjecture.

In this chapter we compare and contrast the Biedma, Rangel, and Elvas narratives detail by detail in order to highlight the uncorroborated nature of the evidence. We include Garcilaso only minimally, not merely because his details about the route are minimal but mostly because these details are unreliable. Since we are only interested in locating Mabila, our workshop group carefully read only small segments of the three narratives, which enabled us to make fine-grained distinctions among the documents as well as among the routes depicted by each.[4] In our comparative analysis, we highlight both the similarities and differences among the accounts in order to pinpoint with specificity where the disagreements, agreements, and omissions occur among and within them. In what follows, then, we first offer a section on translation issues that are pertinent to establishing the route and locating Mabila. This is followed by a close comparison of the narratives regarding the route from Cosa to Chicasa that includes four schematic maps that depict the route as described by each of the four chroniclers. Inserted in its proper place chronologically is a detailed comparison of Biedma's, Rangel's, and Elvas's relation of the battle and the town of Mabila.

Issues of Translation in the Accounts of the Expedition's Route from Cosa to Chicasa

It goes without saying that any effort to locate what is now the archaeological site of Mabila must begin with the four accounts of the De Soto expedition presently known to us. In recent years, serious efforts have been made to better understand these narratives, both as literary texts and as historical documents, as George Lankford's chapter 3 in this volume attests.[5] As a result we now have a much better understanding of the circumstances under which these texts were produced as well as their possible relationships to each other. Keeping these issues in mind, it is clear that there is another important question: How can we best understand key passages in these essential accounts?

Vernon James Knight Jr. addresses this important issue in chapter 11 of this volume, arguing that contemporary scholars ought to work from the original documents, which are in Spanish and Portuguese. Until the publication of *The De Soto Chronicles* in 1993, many scholars interested in the location of Mabila relied on the extant English translations of the Biedma, Rangel, Garcilaso, and Elvas accounts (Table 12.1). Although these earlier translations were of variable quality, even a generally good translation can, in crucial places in the text, fail the modern reader whose need for precision is greater than was ever anticipated by the original translator. Clearly, *The De Soto Chronicles* made a lasting contribution to Anglophonic De Soto scholarship not only by pulling together all of the relevant accounts in one convenient source in English but by providing new translations of the principal sources. These translations, especially those of John Worth, are informed by a much more nuanced understanding of the archaeological, geographical, and historical concerns of contemporary scholars. Moreover, their notes and annotations alert the English reader to potential problems with these renderings.[6]

Despite the recent improvement in the quality of the English translations, we considered it prudent to return to the originals in Spanish and Portuguese to reexamine, line by line, particular passages likely to be important to our principal goal of locating the Mabila site. In this exercise, the members of our working group closely examined the original versions of the accounts that specifically describe the itinerary of the De Soto expedition from Cosa to Mabila and from Mabila to Chicasa. Two members of the group are fluent in Spanish (Clayton and Murphy), and we also consulted with John Worth, whose professional preparation and command of the Spanish language make him ideally suited to the task of translating these documents. The group read the relevant sections of the Spanish and Portuguese language accounts together with the English accounts in *The De Soto Chronicles,* discussing the most accurate way to translate some key passages into English.

For example, we focused on geographical nomenclature that could help us locate the site of Piachi, which seems to us to be a key to identifying the Mabila site. We selected for particular scrutiny a number of terms either because they were vaguely stated or because they admitted of multiple meanings in the original Spanish. Two examples illustrate the problem. Rangel describes the town of Piachi as "un pueblo alto, sobre un barranco de un río,

Table 12.1 Translations of the Biedma, Rangel, Garcilaso, and Elvas Accounts

Accounts	Originals	Classic English Translations	English Translations Used in the *De Soto* Chronicles (DC)
Biedma	1857 (1544). Luys Hernández Biedma's account in Buckingham Smith's *Colleción de varios documentos para la historia de la Florida y tierras adyacentes* (London: Truebner).	1866. Buckingham Smith, trans., *Narratives of the Career of Hernando De Soto in the Conquest of Florida.* New York Bradford Club Series No. 5.	1993. John Worth for *DC*. Footnotes by John Worth and Charles Hudson.
Rangel	1851. Rodrigo Rangel's account appeared in Gonzalo Fernández de Oviedo, *Historia general y natural de las Indias* (Madrid: Imprenta de la Real Academia de la Historia).	1904. Edward Gaylord Bourne, *Narratives of the career of Hernando De Soto,* 2 vols. (New York: A. S. Barnes).	1993. John Worth for *DC*. Footnotes by John Worth and Charles Hudson.
Garcilaso	1605. Garcilaso de la Vega, *La Florida del Ynca* (Lisbon: Pedro Crasbeek).	1951. John G. and Jeannette J. Varner, *The Florida of the Inca* (Austin: University of Texas Press).	1935. Charmion Shelby, La Florida of the Inca. Previously unpublished version commissioned for U.S. De Soto Expedition Commission headed by John Swanton.
Elvas	1557. Fidalgo de Elvas, *Relaçam verdadeira dos trabalhos q ho governador dõ Fernãdo de souto e certos fidalgos portugueses passarom no descubrimen to da prouincia da Frolida* (Evora: Andre de Burgos).	1933. James Alexander Robertson, *True relation of the hardships suffered by Governor Fernando De Soto.* Trans. and ed. James Alexander Robertson (DeLand: Florida State Historical Society).	1933. James Alexander Robertson, *True relation of the hardships suffered by Governor Fernando De Soto.* Trans. and ed. James Alexander Robertson (DeLand: Florida State Historical Society). Robertson's notes were updated for *DC* by Dr. John H. Hann.

enriscado."[7] In his *De Soto Chronicles* translation, Worth renders the phrase literally as "a high town, upon the bluff of a rocky river," while pointing out in a footnote that "[t]he term *enriscado,* or craggy, may refer more to the bluff than to the river itself."[8] We suspect that the term *enriscado* probably does refer to the bluff and not to the river and that the phrase was intended to mean *barranco enriscado,* or craggy bluff. This seemingly fine point of translation could end up being a very important detail in determining the location of Piachi.

To check this and other questions of translation, we submitted passages to Juan Carlos González Faraco, a professor of environmental education at the University of Huelva in Spain. Professor González Faraco is a specialist in the ethnography and cultural geography of southern Spain and has extensive experience working in the archives of that region. Therefore, he is intimately familiar with Spanish geographical nomenclature, including that of the sixteenth century. Without alerting him to any of the specific issues of De Soto scholarship surrounding these passages, we asked him simply to explicate and clarify the meanings of questionable Spanish passages in Spanish. In this case, he agreed with our reading of Rangel's description as meaning that the town of Piachi was situated on the craggy bluffs of a river.

A second example of the same exercise concerns the translation of the term *monte.* Several sentences after the passage regarding the "craggy bluff", Rangel describes the movement away from Piachi as follows: "partieron de allí e fueron a un monte." A number of De Soto scholars in the past have argued that *monte* ought to be translated as "mountain," following the translation of Edward G. Bourne who renders this passage as "they departed thence into a mountain."[9] If this were a faithful translation, it would certainly provide a crucial clue for locating Mabila.

Yet, in the *De Soto Chronicles* Worth renders the phrase in question as "they departed from there and went to a forest."[10] *Monte* can indeed mean a natural elevation in the terrain, but it is more commonly used in southern Spain to refer to uncultivated land covered in trees, shrubs, or underbrush. *Monte alto* could be translated as forest in the sense that Worth notes. *Monte bajo* refers to scrublands of bushes, shrubs, and herbs. *Monte* without further specification could refer to either.

We submitted the passage in question to Professor González Faraco, and he responded that given the context, *monte* probably refers to a place covered in vegetation rather than an area of some elevation. In either event, in his opinion, *monte,* if used to describe an elevation, would refer to a gentle rise of no great height. It is worth noting also that in southern Spain when formerly cultivated land is abandoned, or purposely allowed to go fallow, it often reverts to *monte.* It is at least possible that Rangel might be referring to what in Alabama is commonly referred to as an "old field," a formerly cultivated field that is gradually reverting to forest.

Other examples of this approach to translation could be adduced, but our general conclusions after considering the translations are twofold: (1) the Worth translations are reliable guides, although some issues of translation are inherently difficult, perhaps impossible, to resolve because of ambiguities or grammatical lapses in the original texts; (2) although scholars are fortunate to have multiple accounts of the expedition, the kinds of geographical descriptions that could point to distinctive contemporary landmarks on the trail to Mabila are really few in number. Thus, a simple clue to the location of Piachi—that it is a town situated high on a craggy bluff—may be of singular importance in finding Mabila.

Comparing the Narratives from Cosa to Chicasa

To begin our comparison of narratives, we divide the route from Cosa to Chicasa into a series of shorter segments in which we offer detailed comparisons of the route and the events that took place in these segments as described by Biedma, Rangel, and Elvas. For reasons already noted, we have included Garcilaso in this discussion in only the barest way possible. Although he is mentioned from time to time, one should not trust his reconstruction of the route. Also, we have devised an abbreviated comparative travel chart that includes Biedma, Elvas, and Rangel (Table 12.2). In addition, we have drawn a series of schematic maps representing the routes as depicted by the four chroniclers (Figures 12.1–12.4). The maps and table illustrate in graphic form the differences and agreements among the narratives and the discussions that follow elaborate on these details.

From Cosa to Talisi

In the segment of the journey from Cosa to Talisi, the chroniclers only agree on two points—that De Soto detained the cacique of Cosa and that Talisi was a province with a central town also called Talisi. Biedma notes that the direction they took was west/southwest (Figure 12.1). Elvas, in a later passage, specifies that they headed south from Cosa and he is explicit that they were looking for the province of Tascalusa (Figure 12.3).[11] Rangel is silent on this issue of direction (Figure 12.2). According to Garcilaso, from the town of Cosa, the army traveled five days to the town of Talisi, which Garcilaso says was the last town in the province of Cosa (Figure 12.4).

The travel days described for this segment of the expedition vary considerably, with Biedma claiming that it took 5 to 6 days to reach Talisi, Ran-

Table 12.2 Comparative Travel Chart of Biedma, Elvas, and Rangel/Oviedo (R = river, W = west, S = south, N = north)

Route	Biedma (1:232-36)	Elvas (1:94-105)	Rangel/Oviedo (1:285-97)
Cosa to Talisi			
Direction	W & SW	S	—
Travel	5-6	2 to Itaba (pass through Talimu-chusi on the way)	1 day to Talimuchusi
			2 to Itaba (R)
		1 to Ulibahali (R)	"alongside a good river"
			2 to Ulibahali (R)
			"next to a large river"
	To		1 to town "hard by the river"
			1 to Piachi (R)
		2 to Tuasi	"alongside a river"
			2 to Tuasi
			3 to town (palisaded)
			1 to "new town" (R)
	Talisi	5 to Talisi town (R)	"next to the river"
			1 to Talisi (R)
			"next to a large river"
Talisi to Atahachi			
Direction	S	—	—
Travel	—	1 to Casiste	1 to Casiste (R)
		1 to first town of Tascalusa	1 to Caxa "on the bank of the river" (Talisi/Tascalusa border)
	To		1 to Humati, across river (R)
			1 to Uxapita
	"his town"	1 to "cacique's town"	1 to Atahachi
Atahachi to Piachi			
Direction	—	—	—
Travel	— to unnamed town (R)	2 to Piachi (R)	2 to Piachi (R) "upon the craggy bluff of a river"
Piachi to Mabila			
Direction	—	—	—
Travel	To	3 to	2 to town (palisaded)
	Mabila	Mabila	1 to Mabila

Continued on the next page

Table 12.2. *Continued*

Route	Biedma (1:232-36)	Elvas (1:94-105)	Rangel/Oviedo (1:285-97)
Mabila to Apafalaya			
Direction	N	—	—
Travel	10–12	5 via uninhabited land to Apafalaya/ Talicpacana	4 to Talicpacana (R)/ Mosulixa (R)
	to	1 to Zabusta (R)	"very good river" — to Zabusta (R)/Apafalaya (R) "the river of Apafalaya"
Apafalaya to Chicasa			
Direction	N	—	—
Travel	Chicasa (R)	5 to Chicasa (R)	6 to Chicasa (R) "the river of Chicasa"

gel 14 days, and Elvas 10 days (Table 12.2). Biedma says that they traveled through several towns of Cosa before reaching Talisi, but he does not name any of them. Rangel and Elvas generally agree on the towns through which the army passed; both mention the towns of Talimuchusi, Itaba, Ulibahali, Tuasi, and Talisi, and both generally agree on how many days it took to get to each town, that is, from Cosa it took 1 day to get to Talimuchusi, then 1–2 days to Itaba, then 1–2 days to Ulibahali, then 2 days to Tuasi, and finally 5 days to Talisi.

Rangel relates that at the end of the first day of travel after leaving the town of Cosa, they reached the town of Talimuchusi, which was a large town "alongside a good river." Elvas mentions that they passed through Talimuchusi on the first day of travel and slept a half league beyond it near a stream. He also supplies the detail that Talimuchusi was empty when they arrived there. From Talimuchusi, Rangel says they traveled two days to Itaba, while Elvas indicates that it took them only one day to reach Itaba from Talimuchusi. Both Elvas and Rangel describe Itaba as being on a river, and Rangel describes it as a large town. Elvas further specifies that the town was subject to Cosa and that the army had to stay at Itaba six days because the river "which ran hard by the town"[12] was swollen with rain at the time. At the end of six days they crossed this river and slept that night at Ulibahali. Rangel, on the other hand, relates that they stayed in Itaba from August 20–30, and when they left, they spent one night in an oak grove and entered Ulibahali some time the next day.

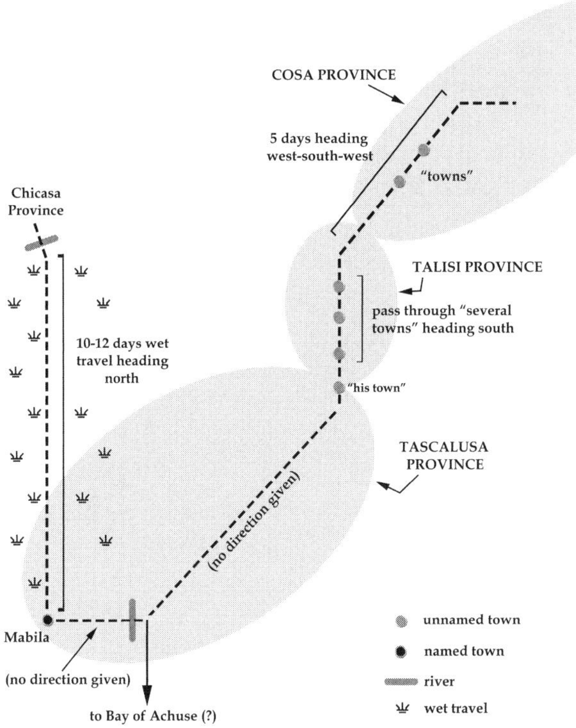

Figure 12.1. The route from Talisi to Apafalaya according to Biedma (drawing by Jeremy Davis).

Elvas and Rangel agree that the main town of Ulibahali was on a river, except that Elvas describes it as a small river and Rangel describes it as a large river. Neither is clear about whether this is the same river they crossed from Itaba or another river. Elvas notes that Ulibahali was a palisaded town and that on the other side of the river was another town, which is where the cacique of Ulibahali was at the time. Both Elvas and Rangel agree that the Indians of Ulibahali had conspired to free the cacique of Cosa, but, according to Rangel, the cacique of Cosa ordered them to lay down their arms. They also concur that the cacique of Ulibahali gave the Spaniards *tamemes* (burden bearers) and Indian women, and that one or two Spaniards remained behind, either willingly or because they became lost. Both remark on the abundance of good grapes in the area.

After leaving Ulibahali, Elvas states that the army spent the first night at a town subject to Ulibahali and the next day they reached another town named

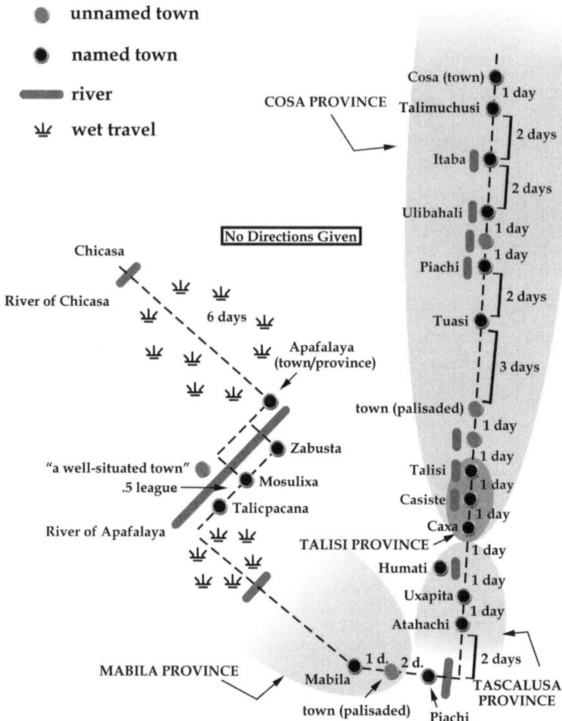

Figure 12.2. The route from Talisi to Apafalaya according to Rangel (drawing by Jeremy Davis).

Tuasi, also subject to the cacique of Ulibahali. Elvas also states that Tuasi was the last town subject to Ulibahali, which would place it on the border between the Ulibahali and Talisi provinces. Rangel, on the other hand, specifies that the army left Ulibahali on September 2 and spent the first night in a "pretty town hard by the river,"[13] and the next day they came to the town of Piachi, also alongside a river. They stayed at Piachi one day, and after leaving this town they spent one night in the open (camping) and arrived at Tuasi the next day. This difference in the number of towns and travel days is the only major discrepancy between Rangel and Elvas concerning this segment of the journey. Rangel then has the army traveling four days from Ulibahali to Tuasi, and Elvas has them traveling only two days and mentions nothing about the unnamed town "hard by the river" and Piachi.

According to Elvas, after leaving Tuasi the army traveled for five days, passing through towns subject to the cacique of the province of Talisi. Rangel

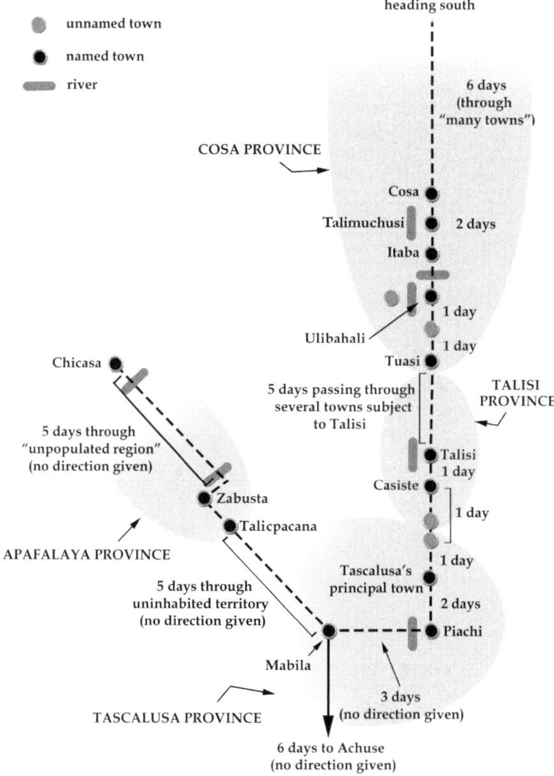

Figure 12.3. The route from Talisi to Apafalaya according to Elvas (drawing by Jeremy Davis).

agrees that there were five days of travel, but he gives more details, saying that after leaving Tuasi, they slept the first two nights in the open, and on the third day they went to an old town that had "double walls and good towers."[14] After traveling the following day, they spent the night in a "new town next to a river."[15] After resting here for much of the day, they left and entered Talisi sometime that same day.

Events at the Town of Talisi

Biedma, Rangel, and Elvas generally agree on the major details of the events at Talisi. As mentioned above, they agree that Talisi was a province, with a central town of the same name. They also agree that when they arrived at Talisi, the people and the cacique had already fled. All also agree that eventu-

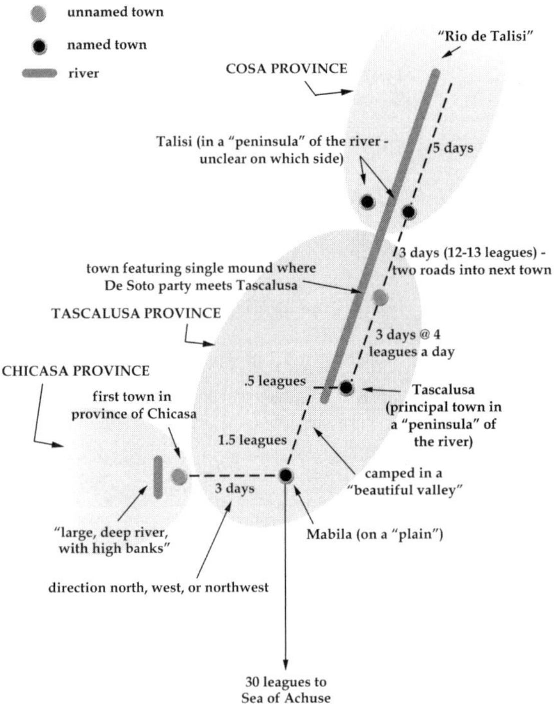

Figure 12.4. The route from Talisi to Apafalaya according to Garcilaso (drawing by Jeremy Davis).

ally the cacique of Talisi met with De Soto and gave De Soto burden bearers, women, and supplies. Biedma gives no additional details and Rangel only describes Talisi as a large town next to a river, with plenty of corn. Elvas says the town of Talisi was a large town near a deep river on the other side of which were other towns. Elvas also mentions that there was maize in abundance, specifying that there was corn on both sides of the river.

Biedma, Rangel, and Elvas are uneven in their details about the relationship between Cosa, Talisi, and Tascalusa. Rangel and Elvas indicate that the cacique of Cosa was released in Talisi, which could be evidence that they had come to the edge of his paramountcy; Biedma does not mention his release nor that De Soto took the cacique as far as Talisi. On the other hand, there is evidence of some kind of cooperative relationship between Talisi and Tascalusa in that Rangel and Elvas agree that Tascalusa's emissaries were allowed to meet De Soto at Talisi. Biedma does not mention anything about Tascalusa while at Talisi. Rangel also indicates that Tascalusa's son was among the group of dignitaries; Elvas does not include this detail.

From Talisi to Atahachi

According to Rangel and Elvas, the army stayed at Talisi 18 to 20 days. Upon leaving the town, Rangel and Elvas explicitly state that the army was headed toward the province of Tascalusa, although neither is clear about the direction they took; Biedma, on the other hand, indicates that they headed south, "drawing near the coast of New Spain."[16]

According to Biedma, from Talisi, the army went south, passing through several towns, to Tascalusa's province, finally stopping at the main town of Tascalusa, where De Soto met the cacique (Table 12.2, Figure 12.1). Biedma gives no indication of days or distance traveled. From Talisi to Atahachi, Rangel and Elvas do not agree on the number of days traveled nor on the number of towns through which the army passed (Table 12.2, Figures 12.2, 12.3). Rangel stipulates five travel days, Elvas only three. In a later passage, Elvas estimates the distance from Cosa to Tascalusa at 60 leagues.

Both Elvas and Rangel agree that it took them one day to get to Casiste from Talisi town, but the details diverge after this. Rangel says that from Casiste, the army arrived at Caxa in one day. He specifies that the town was on a river and at the boundary between the provinces of Talisi and Tascalusa. After leaving Caxa, they marched one day to Humati (which was on the opposite side of the river from their camp), then one more day to Uxapita. The next day they stopped within a league of the main town of Tascalusa. In total, Rangel has the army encountering four towns between Talisi and Atahachi, and he is explicit that Caxa was on the border between the two provinces. According to Elvas, from Talisi they traveled one day to Casiste. The next day, they passed through another town and later that day reached a small town of Tascalusa, where they apparently spent the night. Sometime the next day they arrived within two leagues of the main town of Tascalusa, where they pitched camp. Elvas, then, agrees with Rangel that they entered the province of Tascalusa some time after leaving Casiste, but he does not name Caxa or any other town on the border between the two provinces. Once they moved into the province of Tascalusa, Elvas indicates that they encountered two or three towns, including the principal town. Biedma gives no indication about when they crossed into the province of Tascalusa, but he agrees that De Soto camped on the outskirts of the main town once they arrived there. Garcilaso relates that upon leaving Talisi, they crossed the river of Talisi and traveled three days to an unnamed town where Tascalusa was waiting for De Soto.

Events at Atahachi

All of the chroniclers agree that Tascalusa was a province with a principal town. However, only Rangel recorded the name of the town, which he gives as Atahachi. Biedma does not give any details about the town except to say that the cacique awaited them there in peace. Rangel calls it a "new town"[17] and says that when they arrived in the town, Tascalusa met them on a balcony that was made on a mound to one side of the town plaza. Elvas, on the other hand, describes Tascalusa as meeting them in his dwelling, under a balcony, and that his dwelling was "on an elevated place."[18] All three chroniclers agree that there was a plaza at the town, although Biedma and Elvas give only indirect evidence for it. Both Biedma and Elvas describe the Spaniards as displaying their horsemanship with jousting, horse races, and so forth, which would indicate a large plaza in the town. Rangel mentions a plaza in the passage discussed above, and he also describes De Soto as entering the plaza where Indians danced for them. Obviously these passages about mounds and plazas are important descriptors for the town of Atahachi, and therefore one must scrutinize Elvas's and Rangel's differences. Rangel is explicit about a mound being to one side of the plaza. Elvas's "elevated place" could be just about anything, and one could interpret it to indicate that Atahachi had a mound, or not.

Other details in these passages give some further indications as to the nature of Tascalusa's power and authority and the extent of his domain. For instance, all agree that Tascalusa was a very large man, but only Rangel mentions that he had a son as large as himself who acted as his emissary. All agree that Tascalusa was authoritative, accustomed to being served, and had an indifferent, disdainful attitude toward the Spaniards. However, the chroniclers are not in full agreement over Tascalusa's dominance in the region. Biedma and Rangel agree that De Soto asked for burden bearers (and women, according to Rangel). Biedma specifies that Tascalusa refused to give any at the time and said De Soto could get them in Mabila. Rangel presents a slightly different version, indicating that Tascalusa gave him some burden bearers then, with the promise of more, and women, at Mabila. Interestingly, Elvas does not mention any such demand from De Soto; nor does he mention that Tascalusa told De Soto anything about Mabila at this point.

An important question is whether Mabila was a province subject to Tascalusa or a frontier town in the province of Tascalusa. In other words, were there two provinces (Talisi and Tascalusa) in this area or three (Talisi, Tascalusa, and Mabila)? The chroniclers are not in agreement on this question. Biedma says that while at Atahachi, Tascalusa described Mabila as another town under his domain, while Rangel relates that Tascalusa described Mabila as the province of a principal vassal of his. Elvas does not mention Mabila in these passages, but later he uses the word "vassal" to describe Tascalusa's relationship to the cacique at Mabila. Given this variation we must conclude that these passages are ambiguous on the question.

From Atahachi to Piachi

All of the chroniclers agree that De Soto detained Tascalusa and that he took Tascalusa with him when the army left Atahachi. All also agree that when they left Atahachi they were headed for Mabila, although only Biedma is explicit about this. Rangel and Elvas do not directly mention that the army had this destination in mind when they left Atahachi, but both imply it when they discuss De Soto's sending some soldiers ahead to Mabila to scout out the situation there (an episode Biedma does not recount).

In writing about the route from Atahachi to Piachi, Biedma only says that after leaving Tascalusa's town they traveled an unspecified distance in an unspecified direction before arriving at a large river. It should be noted that Biedma does not mention a town at the river, but his references to local Indians indicate that there most likely was one (Table 12.2, Figure 12.1). Rangel and Elvas are in agreement that it took them two days to get to Piachi (Table 12.2, Figures 12.2, 12.3). Rangel describes Piachi as a "high town" on a craggy bluff overlooking a river.[19] Elvas, on the other hand, says that Piachi was near a large river, which he calls the River of Piachi, but he does not describe the town as situated on a bluff. Because the bluff location may be an important clue in locating Piachi, one must be aware that this detail comes only from Rangel; both Elvas and Biedma fail to mention a bluff.

Rangel and Elvas agree that the town of Piachi was where they crossed a river, although neither gives a clear indication about which side of the river Piachi was on. One might assume that it was on the side of the river on which they were traveling. However, Rangel's tale of the Piachi Indians resisting the Spaniards' crossing could imply that the town of Piachi was on the opposite side of the river from the side on which they were traveling, since the Indians most likely would have staged their resistance to the crossing from the side opposite the Spaniards. Elvas, on the other hand, states that the army arrived at Piachi at the end of their march from Tascalusa's town, implying that Piachi was on the same side of the river as their approach to it.

Both Biedma and Rangel report rumors while here about some survivors of the Narváez expedition who were in Piachi, and apparently because of these rumors, Biedma believed that the River of Piachi ran to the Bay of Achuse. Elvas, on the other hand, does not mention anything about the Narváez expedition, and as we will see, nor does Elvas mention the Bay of Achuse until after the battle of Mabila; Rangel does not mention the bay at all.

One can disentangle the narratives concerning Piachi to get some hints about its organization. Rangel and Elvas agree that it took two days to get to Piachi, and Rangel mentions that the first night they camped in the open. Elvas is silent on the first night out from Atahachi, but like Rangel he does not mention any towns between Atahachi and Piachi. Thus, the evidence in Rangel and Elvas can be taken to indicate that there is at least a two-day journey through an unpopulated region between Atahachi and Piachi. Also, after leaving Piachi, the army traveled for two more days through an unpopulated countryside. Hence, assuming for the moment that Tascalusa and Mabila were two provinces, Piachi may have been an independent town situated between the two, a possibility that leaves the question of the relationship between Tascalusa and Piachi problematic.

The main event at Piachi involved a river crossing. All three chroniclers agree that the army stayed at this location for several days (Biedma specifies two days), although only Biedma and Elvas say they did so in order to build rafts to cross the river, implying, of course, that it was a large river. There are three different versions, however, of the actual river crossing. Biedma does not remark on the army crossing the river, but he intimates that they did so. Rangel writes that the cacique of Piachi resisted their crossing and that they eventually crossed only with difficulty. Elvas, on the other hand, relates that the Indians of Piachi rowed them across the river easily and in safety. All agree that local Indians killed some of De Soto's men while at this location but only after crossing the river. Whether or not these killings were part of Piachi's "resistance" cannot be determined from the narratives and hence do not necessarily indicate that all chroniclers agree that the Indians of Piachi were openly hostile, especially since Elvas explicitly states that they were cooperative. Only Biedma and Elvas report that De Soto held Tascalusa accountable for these killings. Biedma further reports that Tascalusa promised De Soto that he would hand over the killers at Mabila. Since Biedma omits anything about the river crossing, it would be safe to take as fact Elvas's and Rangel's account that the army crossed here. However, the events surrounding the crossing are more difficult to reconcile since Rangel and Elvas actually contradict each other.

Privileging Rangel's account, the cacique's resistance could indicate several things. The resistance could indicate that Piachi was independent of Tascalusa in that the Indians of Piachi were acting carelessly of Tascalusa's well-being given that he was a hostage. Conversely, one could interpret Rangel's story to mean that the Indians of Piachi were in on the conspiracy and used the resistance as a delaying tactic to keep De Soto out of Mabila until the surprise attack was ready. The surprising lack of canoes at this river town, as reported only by Elvas but indirectly supported by Biedma's statement that they had to build rafts to cross the river, lends credence to the latter interpretation—perhaps this was another ruse to delay the army. In either case, we conclude that Piachi's resistance cannot be used as a crucial piece of evidence, especially since there is actual *disagreement* among the narratives about what happened at the river crossing.

Finally, Garcilaso stipulates that after having met Tascalusa, the Spaniards traveled three days at four leagues each day, and on the third day they reached the principal town of Tascalusa, which was also named Tascalusa. After crossing a river, they camped one-half league from the river. As usual any details from Garcilaso are to be considered suspect. Also, the events that Garcilaso describes as taking place at Tascalusa's main town are similar to those described as having taken place at Piachi according to the other chroniclers, and the events in the town where De Soto first met Tascalusa are similar to the events at Atahachi. Hence, it is most likely that Garcilaso conflated or confused Tascalusa's principal town and Piachi.

From Piachi to Mabila

All three chroniclers make short work of the route from Piachi to Mabila. Biedma is most terse, noting only that they arrived at Mabila one day at 9:00 A.M.; he gives no indication of days, direction, or distance traveled. Rangel and Elvas agree that it took the army three days to reach Mabila from Piachi, but neither indicates the direction in which the army traveled (Table 12.2, Figures 12.1–12.3). Rangel says that they left Piachi and entered a scrubland.[20] The context of Rangel's passage and the dates given indicate that the army traveled for one day and spent the night in the scrubland. They then traveled one day to an unnamed palisaded town where they received some chestnut bread (and Rangel comments on the abundance of chestnuts in the area). The next day the army traveled one day to Mabila. According to Rangel, then, the army traveled a total of three days from Piachi to Mabila.

Elvas and Rangel agree that on the third day of travel from Piachi, the army passed through a continuously populated region. Both also agree that a vanguard composed of De Soto and Tascalusa and about forty to forty-five others went ahead to Mabila, but Rangel says that they did so because the rest of the army was delayed by pillaging the populated countryside. Elvas does not indicate any pillaging. Biedma gives no details about the journey from Piachi to Mabila, and no indication in this passage or later that a vanguard went ahead of the main body nor that the army was delayed because of their pillaging. Garcilaso states that it was one and a half leagues from the Spaniards' camp near Tascalusa's principal town (which he may have confused with Piachi) to Mabila, but these figures are not reliable.

Mabila

We now take a closer, comparative look at the events at Mabila, with the analytical aim of locating the town. One clue to the location of Mabila surfaces when Biedma and Elvas relate that at some time during the month-long encampment after the battle De Soto received news that Maldonado's brigantines were at the coast. Biedma reports that they were forty leagues from the sea, and Elvas reports that they heard that Maldonado was waiting for them at the Bay of Achuse, which was a six-day journey from Mabila. Rangel does not mention any such report about ships waiting at the coast. Biedma does not specify the Bay of Achuse here, but one must recall that while at Piachi, Biedma understood the river at Piachi to run to the Bay of Achuse, and both Biedma and Rangel agree that the men heard rumors about some Narváez survivors who had come to Piachi. It is possible to conclude that Maldonado was at the Bay of Achuse some time after the battle of Mabila and that a river that ran into the Bay of Achuse also ran by Piachi.

All the chroniclers agree that Mabila was a palisaded town, although Elvas says it had two gates, while Rangel and Biedma indicate there was only one entrance. Elvas and Biedma state explicitly that Mabila was on an open field and plain, respectively, and Rangel gives indirect evidence for an open environment when he describes the outside of the palisade as a plaza. The three different words used here are distinctions that leave the size of this field, plain, or plaza open to debate. Only Biedma reports that houses outside the palisade had been knocked down; Rangel and Elvas omit this detail.

None mentions Mabila as being near a river or stream. At one point, Elvas notes that the army was so thirsty that some attempted to drink from a bloody pond near the palisade. One could interpret this to mean that there was a scarcity of water, and hence Mabila was at some distance from a stream; however, we would urge caution here since Elvas is the only one to include this detail and since the absence of a river is assumed from omissions and not something explicitly stated in any of the narratives.

There are also suggestive pieces of evidence in De Soto's battle tactics that may be of some help in determining the question of whether Mabila was located at or near a stream. Biedma says that once they were outside the palisade, the mounted soldiers "encircled the entire town."[21] Rangel says that once they were outside the palisade, the army "encircled them [the town] on many sides."[22] And Elvas says that once they were outside the palisade, De Soto ordered the army to "surround" the town.[23] All three cases intimate that De Soto's mounted guard could circle the entire town (although Rangel's "many sides" is unclear in this regard), meaning that Mabila was not right on a stream bank.

This point of agreement, however, gets compromised in later details. Biedma, Elvas, and Rangel agree that De Soto's foot guard assaulted the town, but they vary in terms of how the soldiers entered it. Biedma notes that four squadrons assaulted the town on four sides. Rangel says they cut through the palisade walls and entered the town on three sides. Elvas writes that four companies attacked the town and entered it "from one side and the other."[24] These passages can be interpreted in at least two ways. If one takes these passages literally and as complete descriptions, then the accounts here are not in accord as to whether Mabila was entirely surrounded by a palisade. Biedma's four-sided entrance indicates that it was entirely surrounded; Rangel's three-sided entrance suggests that the town may have been protected on one side by a river and three sides by a palisade. Elvas's statement is ambiguous and cannot be used to corroborate Rangel or Biedma. However, if one takes these passages as variations in what the authors are choosing to emphasize, then there is no contradiction between them, and one could take them to indicate that Mabila was entirely surrounded by a palisade.

In regard to the battle, as we have seen, all agree that De Soto and some of his soldiers entered the town of Mabila and were attacked once inside. All agree that, although the Indians were planning the attack, the battle was sparked spontaneously when Tascalusa left De Soto's presence and refused to return, and in the ensuing altercation a Spaniard injured an Indian. Hence the Spaniards had no time to gather their possessions and possibly some of their horses. All agree that the Spanish possessions were inside the gates and were not retrieved. All agree that the Spaniards set the town on fire. And all agree that the Spanish possessions were lost in the fire. These details are the most unambiguous and have the greatest consensus of all the elements describing the events at Mabila.

The amount of Spanish materials left after the fire, however, is less clear. Of course, how much of the Spanish goods were lost depends on how much had arrived at Mabila at the time of the battle. Biedma does not indicate that the army was divided on the way to Mabila. He relates that the burden bearers unloaded their goods inside the palisade and that after the Spaniards had fled the town, the Indians closed the gates and displayed the goods from the tops of the palisade. He merely says that "all had burned that day."[25] Rangel, on the other hand, is clear that those not in the vanguard did not arrive until after the battle had begun. He does not specify how many goods were at Mabila at the time of the start of the battle or how the goods got inside the palisade walls. He lists nine arrobas of pearls, clothes, ornaments, chalices, wafer molds, and wine as being lost. Elvas, like Rangel, is clear that the main battle line and rear guard arrived after the battle had begun, and he describes the burden bearers as leaving their loads outside the palisade and that once the battle started, the Indians of Mabila rushed outside to collect the loads and free the Indian burden bearers. Elvas lists clothing, pearls, the ornaments for saying mass, and weapons as being lost, and since he notes that the burden bearers were in chains, one could presume that chains were lost as well. With Elvas and Rangel, it seems that only the advance guard's goods were at Mabila when the fighting broke out. In addition, several horses were killed at Mabila; Rangel counts seven and Elvas twelve; Biedma does not tally the number of horses lost. Despite the congruency between Elvas and Rangel on the kinds of things lost, one should not assume that all the Spanish goods and horse tack burned at Mabila were left there after the battle. Since the army camped outside the palisade walls for a month, the survivors undoubtedly scavenged what they could, as they did later after the battle of Chicasa.

The chroniclers are in general agreement over the number of Spanish deaths, 18–22. It is difficult to assess the number of Indian deaths since the chroniclers are surely exaggerating the numbers of 2,500–5,000. They are generally silent on what happened to the Indian corpses, with the exception of Biedma's macabre detail about the Spanish treating their wounds with the fatty tissue of the Indian dead.[26] All agree that many Indians died in the fight and in the fires. None stipulates whether Indian survivors collected their dead for funeral treatments after the battle. However, all indicate that there were Indians moving through the area in the month after the battle, and it is reasonable to suppose that some entered Mabila to collect their dead.

All agree that De Soto camped at Mabila another twenty-seven or twenty-eight days after the battle, although only Elvas explicitly states that they camped in the open, presumably outside the palisade. However, they give conflicting reports about the land around Mabila. Biedma, after the battle, says that the land around Mabila had little food, and in this connection one may recall that Biedma does not give any information about the march to Mabila from Piachi for which Rangel and Elvas report a heavily populated countryside. Rangel only reports that after the battle they burned a good part of the land, although Rangel, when recounting the march from Piachi to Mabila, described the army as spending their second night at an unnamed palisaded town and then pillaging the populated countryside on their third day of travel. Rangel's reference to burning the land would also indicate that the army torched any towns or houses that were nearby. Elvas gives the most detail about the environs when, after the battle, he describes the land around Mabila as populated and fertile. Elvas elaborates that there were some large enclosed towns and a considerable population scattered over the countryside; the scattered houses were one or two crossbow flights apart. He also states that when they left, each man had enough corn for two days, indicating a substantial amount of corn in the vicinity.

As mentioned earlier, Rangel calls Mabila a province under the dominion of Tascalusa, Biedma calls it a town under his authority, and Elvas is ambiguous on the point. It is likewise unclear whether Mabila was the principal town in a province or a heavily fortified frontier town. None mentions a mound at Mabila, which would indicate that it was not the central town of a province; however, one must note that this evidence is based on omission and not something explicitly stated.

The size of Mabila is likewise ambiguous. Only Biedma describes Mabila as a small town; Elvas and Rangel give no indication of the size of the town. Numbers of Indian warriors hiding in Mabila or killed in the battle may be helpful here, although, as we have said, the numbers said to be killed are surely exaggerated. Biedma estimates that there were 5,000 warriors hidden in Mabila. Rangel and Elvas agree with Biedma that there were many warriors hidden in Mabila, but neither specifies the numbers. However, Rangel estimates that 3,000 Indians were killed in the battle, and Elvas estimates that 2,500 Indians were killed. Biedma does not give death figures for the Indians, except to say that none surrendered and that none survived. This would imply that Indian deaths totaled 5,000, the number he says were hidden at Mabila.

From Mabila to Chicasa

From Mabila to Chicasa, Biedma specifies that they headed north; Rangel and Elvas do not specify any direction except, as noted below, Elvas says that De Soto deliberately did not go toward the sea (which was presumably south; see Table 12.2).[27]

According to Elvas, after leaving their month-long encampment at Mabila, they marched in an unspecified direction for five days through uninhabited territory to Talicpacana. From here the army traveled to Zabusta, although whether this was the same day of travel or the next day is unclear (Figure 12.3). Elvas notes that there were towns with plenty of corn and beans in the area of Zabusta. Both towns were in the Apafalaya province. A few leagues from Zabusta they crossed a river, traveling another five days through an unpopulated region to a river on the other side of which lay Chicasa (Table 12.2, Figure 12.3).

Rangel has the army traveling for four days before reaching Talicpacana, but he names more of the towns than Elvas; his sequence is: Talicpacana, Mosulixa, Zabusta, Apafalaya, and Chicasa (Table 12.2, Figure 12.2). Because of ambiguous wording, it is difficult to decipher Rangel's version of this concluding portion of the Alabama journey. As related by Rangel,

> [Four days after leaving Mabila, the Spaniards] arrived at a very good river. [The next day] they went across bad crossings and swamps [to find Talicpacana on a river with another town across the river from it. Three days later they] found a town, a half-league from this one, which is called Moçulixa. . . . [T]he Indians were on the other side of the water, making threats. . . . A piragua was made . . . and they made a large cart to carry it up to Moçulixa, and having launched it in the water . . . they took the land easily. . . . [Three days later] all the army went to a town that is called Zabusta, and there they crossed the river in the piragua and with some canoes that they took there; and they went to take lodging in another town on the other end, because upriver they found another good town and took its lord, who was named Apafalaya, . . . and that bank was called the river of Apafalaya. [Twenty-six days after leaving Mabila, they arrived] at the river of Chicaça, having passed many bad crossings and swamps and rivers and cold weather.[28]

This excerpt reveals the difficulty of comparing the river crossings among the narratives. Biedma found only the crossing of the river at Chicasa worth mentioning. Even though Biedma gives no details about the route to Chicasa, he describes the travel as very difficult because of the cold and because they had to cross "waters" on foot.[29] Biedma's oblique reference to "waters" may indicate that from his perspective no streams between those two rivers constituted a serious enough crossing problem for the army to merit mention. That, however, contrasts with the view of both Elvas and Rangel, who both record that the army made two crossings after leaving Mabila—once at a river in the province of Apafalaya and once at Chicasa, and at both crossings the Spaniards met with Indian resistance.

Elvas relates that the first crossing was at the town of Zabusta, but the Rangel narrative as seen above is more complex. Rangel's reference to "bad crossings and swamps"[30] in the vicinity of Talicpacana (a detail Elvas does not include) probably indicates muddy tributaries rather than the main river. In our interpretation of Rangel, while at Talicpacana, scouts looking for food discovered that the Indians of the town of Mosulixa (somewhere upstream from Talicpacana) had taken a large amount of corn and put it on the other side of the river, and that there were Indians guarding the corn stores and threatening the Spaniards. The Spaniards then built a canoe at Talicpacana as well as a large cart to transport it to Mosulixa. They finished this task on November 29, indicating that they spent at least eight to nine days in and around Talicpacana. After transporting the canoe to Mosulixa, they launched it with sixty armed men who dispersed the Indians on the other side of the river. The contingent then "took the land easily and found plenty of corn."[31] Then, the day after retrieving the corn, the entire army went to Zabusta. Here the full army crossed the river using the canoe they had built as well as some they took from Zabusta. In other words, although two crossings occurred during this time, one involved the contingent of men sent to retrieve the corn and the other occurred when the full army crossed the same river (Figure 12.2).

Elvas, on the other hand, does not mention the town of Mosulixa, although the events he describes at Zabusta are similar to those Rangel relates for Mosulixa. According to Elvas, at Zabusta Indians were on the other side of the river threatening them. They then built a single canoe inside the town of Zabusta in order to hide it from view of the Indians across the river; it took them four days to build it. When it was finished De Soto had some men transport it one-half league upstream, and the next morning they launched it with thirty armed men, causing the Indians making the threats to flee. Afterward, the rest of the army moved upstream a ways before crossing.

After crossing at Zabusta, according to Rangel, the army then marched to the chief's town of Apafalaya, which appears to have been farther up the same river. Rangel called it the river of Apafalaya, and he also remarks that the town was well provisioned. Elvas does not mention a town by the name of Apafalaya. Elvas and Rangel, then, agree on the river crossings between Mabila and Chicasa. They crossed one river at Zabusta (the river of Apafalaya) and another river before entering the province of Chicasa. But the silence of Biedma regarding the difficult and time-consuming crossing of the Apafalaya is hard to understand.

Biedma does not mention the province of Apafalaya at all. Rangel and Elvas agree that it was a province; however, their details about Apafalaya are not in accord. Elvas indicates that they traveled for five days from Mabila through unpopulated lands before arriving at "the province of Apafalaya and the town of Talipataua [Talicpacana],"[32] and then they went to Zabusta. Elvas does not mention a town by the name of Apafalaya, and his wording may indicate that Talicpacana was the main town of the province of Apafalaya.

Elvas relates they left Zabusta and traveled for five days through unpopulated lands to Chicasa. Rangel indicates that the army traveled for four days before reaching first Talicpacana, than Mosulixa, Zabusta, and finally the town of Apafalaya. Of these towns, he only refers to Apafalaya as both a town and a province. Rangel then says they left Apafalaya, taking the cacique with them, and traveled six days to Chicasa, during which time they encountered many bad swamps and crossings (Table 12.2).

Generally, then, both Rangel and Elvas agree that they traveled for three to five days from Mabila before reaching any towns. Both agree that they encountered a province called Apafalaya in the vicinity. Both also agree that there were numerous towns in the area and that they were well provisioned. However, the chroniclers are unclear about whether all or some of these towns were under the single leadership of Apafalaya or whether they were independent polities. Only one cacique (at the town of Apafalaya) is mentioned for this leg of the journey (and only by Rangel). Finally, both agree that once they left this region, the army traveled for five to six days to a river across which lay Chicasa, indicating that the province (or provinces) between Mabila and Chicasa was buffered on both sides by uninhabited territory.

The length of the post-Mabila part of the journey in Alabama is also hard to determine from all four chronicles. Biedma's account (10–12 days) accords well with that of Elvas (10+ days). Rangel's 26 days can be reconciled with Elvas and Biedma only by considering that Biedma and Elvas were counting actual days in travel while Rangel was including total elapsed time. He indicates that they spent perhaps three days in Talicpacana searching for food that they found across the river from Mosulixa, and then eight or nine more days building the canoe. Rangel's actual travel days then may have been 13 to 16, which is closer to Biedma and Elvas's 10 to 12 days. Garcilaso only relates that they traveled three days through "pleasant though uninhabited" country[33] before arriving at Chicasa, but, as always, one needs to be skeptical of his recounting of such details.

Conclusion

As our analysis shows, a comparative approach to reading the De Soto accounts not only yields interesting differences and agreements across the narratives but also forces us to be specific about from whom details are taken, to be clear about whether a detail or episode is contested by another chronicler, to be explicit about any omissions and by whom, and to be ever cognizant of which of the four narratives one is privileging or ignoring in every instance.

Even though researching the sixteenth-century South through the documentary evidence means that scholars cannot always adhere to the standard methods of historiography, this does not mean that the sixteenth century is consigned to historical oblivion. We can reconstruct this important era by articulating careful, comparative analyses of the chronicles with archaeological research. Our working group's contribution to the search for Mabila is a dense comparative analysis of the narratives from which, we hope, those looking for Mabila can construct a series of three or more possible routes and locations that can then be searched. We hope that the fine comparative resolution we have brought to a few pages of each narrative reminds scholars who search such data for particular, painstaking details that these details do not go uncontested across any body of evidence, especially documentary evidence. Through this comparative reading, we hope to remind scholars also that it is always good to keep in mind that no two people see or remember things the same way and that to construct a single narrative from two or more separate sources is fraught with problems; one must be ever mindful of the agreements, disagreements, variability, and omissions across any set of documents.

Notes

We would like to thank Vernon James Knight and The University of Alabama College of Arts and Sciences for inviting us to participate in the workshop and all of the participants who made it a lively, stimulating weekend. We also would like to thank student assistants Megan Batchelor and Erin Phillips for their cheerful help with note-taking and errand-running, and for generally making our job much easier. We are especially grateful to our student assistant Jeremy Davis for rendering our scrawls into expertly done maps.

1. In "Legends of the Adelantado," Lankford analyzes the material in the Garcilaso narrative as a collection of legends generated by the army during their tour, but he concludes that Garcilaso is still not persuasive as historical evidence. See also Galloway, "Incestuous Soto Narratives," 27–39; and Henige, "The Context, Content, and Credibility of *La Florida del Inca,*" 1–23. Our estimation that although Garcilaso is useful in other respects, his narrative cannot be used to reconstruct the expedition's route is in agreement with Charles Hudson in *Knights of Spain, Warriors of the Sun,* 452.

2. The most recent reconstructions of the De Soto route use the four major narratives as well as documentary evidence from other expeditions that retraced Soto's footsteps, specifically the documents from the Tristán de Luna and Juan Pardo expeditions, and much archaeological research. For a summary of this work, see C. Hudson, *Knights of Spain, Warriors of the Sun,* and *The Juan Pardo Expeditions.*

3. For the long-ribbon approach, see chapter 11, this volume.

4. Our goal during the workshop sessions was to read, compare, and contrast the four versions of the route from Cosa to Mabila. From the beginning, our work was collaborative. Braund, Ethridge, and Lankford read aloud, one-by-one, the documents in English, while Clayton and Murphy followed along in the Spanish versions and, with the Elvas text, in the Portuguese version. We only completed the Biedma, Rangel, and Elvas accounts. We did not have time at the conference to read the Garcilaso account. Later, Ethridge read the Shelby translation of Garcilaso and, after a discussion among the group, marginally incorporated the fourth narrative into the group's comparison.

5. For some of this work, see the essays in Galloway, *The Hernando de Soto Expedition,* and Young and Hoffman, *The Expedition of Hernando de Soto West of the Mississippi.*

6. Clayton, Knight, and Moore, *The De Soto Chronicles.*

7. Oviedo y Valdés, *Historia General y Natural de las Indias,* 174.

8. Clayton, Knight, and Moore, *De Soto Chronicles,* 1: 291.

9. Brame, "De Soto in Alabama"; Brannon, "The Route of De Soto from Cosa to Mauvilla,"4; Bourne, *Narratives* 2: 84, online version at http://mith2.umd.edu/eada/html/display.php?docs=ranjel_relation.xml&action=show (accessed July 3, 2007). See also chapter 11, this volume.

10. Clayton, Knight, and Moore, *De Soto Chronicles,* 1: 292.

11. Ibid., 1: 98.

12. Ibid., 1: 94.

13. Ibid., 1: 285.

14. Ibid., 1: 285, 288.

15. Ibid., 1: 288.

16. Ibid., 1: 232.

17. Ibid., 1: 290.

18. Ibid., 1: 95.

19. Ibid., 1: 291. See "Issues of Translation," this chapter, for details about the translation of "craggy bluff."

20. See "Issues of Translation," this chapter, for the translation of *monte* as "scrubland."

21. Clayton, Knight, and Moore, *De Soto Chronicles,* 1: 235.

22. Ibid., 1: 293.

23. Ibid., 1: 101.

24. Ibid.

25. Ibid., 1: 235.

26. This detail is mirrored in Garcilaso's account. Clayton, Knight, and Moore, *De Soto Chronicles,* 2: 349.

27. Garcilaso relates that because of a possible mutiny and his need to deceive his men, De Soto decided not to go to the sea from Mabila. He feared that the army might hear of the ships waiting for them, and he also did not want to backtrack through

the towns that they had already visited. This, of course, could be interpreted to mean that, according to Garcilaso, De Soto headed in a north, west, or northwest direction upon leaving Mabila. The point is worth considering regardless of whether Garcilaso's statements are true.

28. Clayton, Knight, and Moore, *De Soto Chronicles,* 1: 294–96.

29. Ibid., 1: 236. It should be noted that Biedma only mentions rivers twice in the whole Cosa to Chicasa route: the one crossed in Tascalusa's province to get to Mabila and the one crossed to enter the province of Chicasa.

30. Clayton, Knight, and Moore, *De Soto Chronicles,* 1: 294, 296.

31. Ibid., 1: 296.

32. Ibid., 1: 105.

33. Ibid., 2: 362.

13
The Battle of Mabila

Competing Narratives

Kathryn E. Holland Braund

The quest to retrace De Soto's footsteps has fascinated Americans for over three centuries. And we are seekers still—lusting as always for the precise geographic location upon which De Soto and his army (and his pigs) set their feet. Yet, with our eyes so firmly staring downward seeking the route (place), we ignore what is before our eyes: the surviving tales of what happened at Mabila—the constructed narratives of what was remembered and what the chroniclers deemed worthy of inclusion. It is clear that surviving narratives are not passive summations of events but attempts to construct and convey meaning from the memories and perceptions and values of the writers. Indeed, the sources frequently disagree on key "facts." The chroniclers relate their tales for different reasons and purposes. Only one account, that of Biedma, the king's factor, can be considered a legitimate primary source. That of Garcilaso is another matter entirely—a romanticized history of the expedition, purportedly based on interviews with survivors and the author's research. The accounts of Rangel and Elvas were shaped and assembled not only from the memories of participants but by the viewpoints and self-interest of later writers who fashioned them into the forms we have come to know.

The question of the original form of the expedition's records is an important one and begs the question of how and when these accounts and perhaps others that are no longer extant originated. Which members of the expedition were recording events, and in what manner were such records kept? And how did any written account survive the grueling travel and travails of the Spaniards? The events at Mabila provide an additional challenge in regard to these questions. For at Mabila the expedition met with disaster as defiant Indians organized a massive counterattack against the *entrada*. By all accounts, the fire started by the Spaniards to gain the upper hand over their adversaries consumed their baggage, including clothing, communion wafers, and medical supplies.[1] The later testimony of expedition member Alonso de Argote confirms this fact. In a sworn statement supporting the military service of Hernán Suárez de Maçuelas, Argote asserted, on March 9, 1557, that the Indians at Mabila "combatted us with great assertion, so much so that they made us lose the peaceful Indians that we had with us, and come forth from the town where it happened with great damage and the loss of all our clothing and weapons and horses, and in the encounter they killed fourteen Spaniards."[2]

Did this fire affect the record-keepers on the expedition? There is scant evidence of the manner in which record-keeping was undertaken on the expedition. Most likely, Biedma, Rangel, and possibly others carried portable writing desks (*escribanía*). They might have easily procured quills from native birds, but the production of ink would have been a more involved matter. Blotting powder (*ponce*) might have been dispensed with altogether, although substitutes might have presented themselves. Paper would have been carried. The central question in regard to the battle of Mabila must be where the records and diaries were stored: with baggage or on the horses of the writers.[3] De Soto scholars work from faith that the accounts of Biedma, the expedition's factor, and Rangel, the personal secretary of De Soto, were derived from diary entries or notes written as time allowed throughout the expedition. But unless they were carrying their papers on their person, whatever they had recorded up to that point was likely destroyed. Rangel, who with his horse escaped Mabila, must have been carrying his material with him, for his diary-like account is virtually impossible to explain otherwise. But even if their records survived the conflagration, most certainly Biedma and Rangel polished and recast their accounts upon return to Mexico.

In the aftermath of discussions by the historians' group at the Mabila conference, I attempted to briefly analyze the main "story" of each of the major De Soto sources. My intent was to identify the meaning that each writer assigned to events in and around Mabila. Over a decade ago Patricia Galloway called for a "detailed textual analysis" of the major accounts of the expedition.[4] The purpose here is not to answer her challenge but simply to begin the process of examination. Scholars of literary theory, sixteenth-century Spanish literature, and history still have much work to do. In addition to fully accounting for the levels of borrowing, future scholars need to examine the method and motives of the writers, assess their perceptions of events, and scrutinize their interpretations. A thorough analysis would extend to an examination of conflicts among expedition members and challenges to

De Soto's leadership, as well as a more nuanced explanation of events enlightened by a willingness to consider the silences and divergent accounts of specific events, and the contested meanings assigned to these events by the writers.

Others have analyzed the accounts in regard to reliability and derivation.[5] The purpose here is merely to listen to each writer's tale with the hope that more sophisticated analysis of the works will come in time. For now, it is enough to know that separately, these four accounts tell us far more than the composite constructions so frequently employed by modern scholars seeking place over story.

The Factor's Tale: Biedma

Biedma makes clear that he believed that the kidnaping of Tascalusa at Atahachi triggered what followed at Mabila: "because of this he [Tascalusa] committed the ruin that afterward he inflicted on us."[6] According to Biedma, the hostage then promised that at Mabila "he would give us what we requested of him" and the expeditionaries set out for that town along with the chief.[7] Upon arriving at Mabila, Biedma's rather flat and unemotional account notes that the "Indians had demolished all of them [houses outside the palisade] to the ground in order to have the field more clear."[8]

Not intent on overstating the case, Biedma notes that as they entered the town, they did not at first see the armed Indians who were hidden in the houses of the town. Welcome ceremonies and dancing women distracted the Spaniards, until "the Captain of the Governor's guard"[9] followed Tascalusa into a building where he had suddenly retreated. There, he says "those houses were full of Indians, all with bows and arrows, ready to do some treachery."[10] As another Indian passed, De Soto hailed him and the Indian was seized by "a nobleman." When the Indian jerked free, the Spaniard "put hand to his sword and gave him a slash that cut off an arm."[11] Arrows began to fly out of previously cut loopholes. Biedma declares that the attack was a complete surprise, even though signs were obvious as they entered the town: "As we were so unprepared because we thought that we had met them in peace, we suffered so much damage that we were forced to leave, fleeing from the town, and all that the Indians brought us in our loads remained within, as they had unloaded it there."[12] Biedma's statement seems calculated to explain the loss of so much, but he fails to convince us that the Spaniards "had met them in peace"[13] for he makes the obvious signs of hostile intent evident to his readers from the time the expedition approached Mabila.

Once outside the town, De Soto's horsemen encircled the stockade and then some were ordered to dismount and attack, with the objective of setting fire to it, thus burning the town and its inhabitants. Escape through the horsemen would be impossible. Thus, as Biedma informs his readers, the complete destruction of the town and its hostile warriors was justified—the Indians had waged a surprise attack on peaceful Spaniards. Under the rules of war, their destruction was reasonable—and the loss of the expedition's valuable supplies and ill-gotten pearls (as well as the lives of Christians, both Spanish and Indian) was explained. Biedma casts no aspersions on De Soto's leadership. He merely states facts. Even while admitting that the ground around the town had been cleared, obviously in warlike preparation, he maintains that the Spaniards were surprised by treachery. The Spaniards were apparently oblivious to treachery they should have recognized once inside the town, including loopholes in interior walls and what surely must have been a palpable tension that pulsed throughout the town. But no hint of negligence on the part of De Soto escapes from Biedma's pen.

No fact about the "treacherous" Mabilians is as telling as Biedma's final comment on the day, regarding the final Indian survivor who "climbed a tree that was in the wall itself, and removed the cord from the bow and attached it to his neck and to a branch of the tree and hanged himself."[14] In Biedma's tale, the people of the land meant to stop De Soto or perish in the attempt. The Spaniards had triumphed, but the cost was high. Biedma's simple prose offers no hints about the Spanish mood as the sun set on Mabila: "all our supplies were burned, so that not one thing remained. . . . We treated ourselves that night with the adipose tissue of the dead Indians themselves, since we had no other medicine, because all had burned that day."[15]

The captive women took care of the wounded, all of whom survived. The Indians who remained in the area, perhaps eager to rid themselves of the army, informed the Spaniards "that we were up to forty leagues from the sea" and that Spanish ships were there.[16] Biedma reports that many wished to go to the coast, but De Soto "did not dare, for the month of November was already half over and it was very cold, and he felt it advisable to look for a land where he might find provisions in order to be able to winter."[17] In Biedma's hand, suddenly, the region that just weeks before supported a vast population was now "a land of little food."[18] And De Soto's reason for avoiding the coast was noble: seeking to find sustenance for his men, he headed northward. Unstated is the obvious fact that the Spaniards had devastated the region and consumed remaining Indian stores of food.

The Portuguese Gentleman's Tale: Elvas

Elvas, on the other hand, gives a more benign version of the secret attack as he does not relate De Soto's kidnaping of Tascalusa and the continuing threats by the Indians. Elvas only admits that "it afterward appeared" that Tascalusa had ordered a messenger from Piachi "to assemble there all the warriors whom he had in his land."[19] Elvas tells us that after the advance party arrived at Mabila, one of De Soto's men came out of the town to relate that the Indians were "evilly disposed" and "many [Indian] men and many arms had entered the town and they had made great haste to strengthen the stockade."[20] Luis de Moscoso advised caution and suggested that the army remain outside the compound, but a disdainful and decisive De Soto proceeded into the town, to the welcome of Indian "music and singing"[21] with Tascalusa in tow. Once in the town, Tascalusa slipped away to the safety of a house filled with well-armed men. To De Soto's request that he rejoin them, Tascalusa "said that he would not come out of there and that he would not leave that town and that if he [the governor] wished to go in peace he should go immediately and should not insist on trying to take him out of his lands and dominions by force."[22]

Elvas's story is therefore simple: Tascalusa, faced with an indefinite tenure as a hostage, caused his subjects to rise up against De Soto. It is a story of threats and mistreatment of the cacique, and Elvas's pen contrasts the "haughty" and "disdainful" behavior of the Indians with De Soto's patience. Elvas reports that De Soto "endeavored to soothe him with pleasant words."[23] Moreover, De Soto ordered another high-ranking Indian to "pacify him [Tascalusa] with soft words."[24] When the Indian refused, Baltasar de Gallegos seized him by his cloak and "all the Indians straightway rose in revolt,"[25] and then Gallegos stuck the offender with his sword. As De Soto ordered his men out of the town, the Indian burden bearers "set down their loads near the stockade" and were then assisted by the Mabilians who "freed them from their chains and gave them bows and arrows with which to fight. In this way they got possession of all the clothing and pearls, and everything the Christians had and which their Indians were carrying for them."[26] The loss of personal possessions was near complete, for Elvas recalled "inasmuch as the Indians had been peaceful thitherto, some [of the Christians] were bringing their weapons in the packs and were left without arms."[27] By that time, the rest of the army had arrived and the battle was on.

Elvas relates that there were Indian survivors: Indian women who claimed that Tascalusa had left the town at their urging. Elvas's battle proceeds with some differences from other accounts, but the general outline remains: the Spaniards set fire to the town with great loss of Indian life (approximately 2,500 Indians), and 18 Spaniards were killed and 150 were wounded. In addition to the loss of 12 horses (and 70 wounded), "all the clothing carried by the Christians, the ornaments for saying mass, and the pearls were all burned there."[28] Elvas, like the other chroniclers, recognized that the disaster at Mabila had meant the loss of the expedition's supplies, fortune, and link to their Christian God. He holds De Soto blameless for both the beginning of the hostilities and the loss of life and treasure.

The Secretary's Tale: Rangel

In Rangel's telling, the battle of Mabila was not a surprise but the culmination of repeated challenges to the Spaniards, beginning at Piachi, where the chief "was malicious."[29] Rangel relates that at some point De Soto dispatched two scouts to Mabila, who returned to report that "there was a great gathering of armed people in Mabila."[30] Although Rangel does not lay the cause of their difficulties to De Soto's demand for slaves and women, the writer notes that the demands were "unjust,"[31] although given Oviedo's lengthy discourse on the morality of the Spanish conquistadors just a few pages before this episode, this sentiment may more likely originate from Oviedo's hand rather than Rangel's.[32] According to Rangel, as they approached Mabila, the army, apparently taking no notice of the looming threat described by the messenger, spread out "pillaging and scattering themselves,"[33] an action that served only to enrage the Mabilians further as well as to advance their plan. Thus, when he arrived at Mabila, De Soto was accompanied by only forty men on horseback. De Soto, loathe to exhibit weakness, entered the town with his men. De Soto, hardened and experienced in Peru, was a savvy military man who knew and understood his enemies. As Rangel's account tells it, "their [the Indians'] deceits and tricks were understood," and De Soto himself was a master of deceit and trickery.[34]

But as the welcome ceremonies began, with dancing and singing and ball play, the men saw Indians "placing bundles of bows and arrows secretively in some palm leaves, and other Christians saw that the huts were filled high and low with concealed people."[35] At this point De Soto donned his helmet and ordered his men to their horses with instructions to warn the soldiers outside the town. As most of the horsemen exited the town, the Mabilians "took command of the gates of the walls of the town," the "cacique plunged into a hut,"[36] and arrows began to fly at De Soto and a handful of remaining men. One of these, Baltasar de Gallegos, the captain of the guard, sought to apprehend the cacique but was challenged by another Indian, whose arm Gallegos severed; he and Luis de Moscoso found themselves surrounded and fought their way out. Rangel himself was among those left in the town. As the remaining Spaniards, clad in armor and mounted on their horses, fought their way out of the town, Moscoso and Gallegos managed to leave with other soldiers by another gate. Rangel's account of the battle adds important details on the position of key combatants and he praises his fellows in arms: "There was so much virtue and shame this day in all those who found themselves in this first attack and the beginning of this bad day. They fought admirably, and each Christian did his duty as a most valiant soldier."[37]

Valiant or not, the Indians ended up with the town and considerable spoils: "all the property of the Christians and with the horses that they left tied within, which they then killed."[38] As they assembled outside the palisade, De Soto quickly regrouped his troops and as the warriors of Mabila left the palisades, the horsemen began a retreat: "in order to draw them out, they pretended that those on horseback were fleeing at a gallop."[39] Taken in by the ruse, the warriors followed in pursuit only to be cut down and lanced as the horsemen wheeled back toward the town. As they circled the town, the order was given to advance upon it and burn it. This was done, and in the process "the nine arrobas of pearls that they brought were burned, and all the clothes and ornaments and chalices and moulds for wafers, and the wine for saying mass, and they were left like Arabs, empty-handed and with great hardship."[40] Rangel had only praise for the "very honored soldiers" who died, and he left a terrible estimate of the Indian dead for future generations to contemplate: "They killed three thousand Indians, in addition to which there were many others wounded, which they found afterward dead in the huts and by the roads." After dressing the wounds of the surviving men and horses, De Soto's men "burned a great part of the land."[41]

Thus, De Soto's secretary makes clear that the attack was not a surprise but the culmination of challenges that arose as a result of "unjust" actions against the Indians by the Spaniards. Unlike Biedma's justification, Rangel provides none, passing judgment instead on the performance of De Soto's soldiers.

The Inca's Tale: Garcilaso

Garcilaso's tale, on the other hand, is one of sedition and betrayal by the Indians and hints at De Soto's early awareness of their deception and hostility. According to the Inca, Tascalusa went willingly with the army to Mabila, but his friendship was a ruse, which the trusting Spaniards handled by tolerant watchfulness. Finally, according to Garcilaso, after crossing the river, De Soto sent two scouts to Mabila. The Inca then contradicts his earlier assessment of tense relations with the Indians and reports that as De Soto and the vanguard proceeded, the rest of the army "marched scattered through the country hunting and enjoying themselves, quite overlooking the possibility of a battle because of the undisturbed peace that they had enjoyed throughout the summer, up to that time."[42] But De Soto was more cautious and was soon informed that the town was full of armed men and that the Indians had cleared the land around the stockade, "even pulled up the grass roots by hand . . . , a sign that they intend to give us battle and wish to have nothing in their way."[43] Thus, De Soto quietly ordered his men to be on guard; meanwhile Tascalusa and his council debated their strategy. As the Indians were "discussing the death of the Spaniards,"[44] Juan Ortiz was dispatched to the council house to invite Tascalusa to eat with De Soto. After three attempts, another Indian appeared and "spoke with extraordinary arrogance and haughtiness" and denounced the Spaniards as thieves and devils, shouting, "It is only just that they die for it today, being cut to pieces to put an end to their iniquity and tyranny!"[45] As the speaker received a bow and arrows from yet another Indian, Baltasar de Gallegos, who was near and "seeing his treason,"[46] raised his sword and slashed the offending Indian and thus raised the alarm.

Thus, the Inca's tale is told: a secret council, held under the noses of the suspecting but still trusting Spaniards, and the Indians, drawing their weapons first. The Spaniards, at first overcome by this "fierce and bold . . . inundation of Indians," fought "with all good spirit, valor, and strength, defending themselves and withdrawing because it was impossible for them to make a stand and resist the cruel and arrogant violence with which the Indians rushed out of the houses and of the pueblo."[47] In the first round of battle, with the Spaniards retreating, the Mabilians "busied themselves in killing the horses that they found tied and in gathering up all the baggage and possessions belonging to the Christians that had already arrived and was piled against the wall of the pueblo and scattered around the plain, awaiting storage. The enemy got possession of all of this, without anything escaping them except the belongings of Captain André de Vasconcelos, which had not yet arrived."[48]

The Inca tells the tale of battle as one might expect for a man influenced by the values and memories of old soldiers. There are soldiers fighting bravely, with honor, and doing their duty. There is destruction of the Indians and their town. The Inca's Indians—both men and women—are desperate and determined, fighting to kill their enemies and preferring death to Spanish slavery. The Inca invokes compassion for his subjects, who, according to his pen, endure cruelty and fury from their opponents as well as the fire and smoke of battle. And at the end, he asks his readers to consider the condition of the valiant soldiers after the battle. They were soldiers who had fought a defensive battle, conducting themselves as men should—even sparing Indian women who took up weapons against them. More important, they were men who called upon their God who "aided them, by giving them an invincible spirit in that hardship."[49]

Conclusion

Our chroniclers provide us with four tales of the battle of Mabila, different but with common themes. In each of these accounts, De Soto is a force, rather than a presence. We seldom see the man and even then, we are only party to his thoughts through his actions. We also see varying points of view and motives of the narrators, which leaves us with competing, rather than corroborating, narratives. Clearly, all of the chroniclers believed that Tascalusa was responsible for the assault at Mabila, but each interprets the chief's motives differently, resulting in different stories told from different points of view.[50] The narratives are not in full accord on many important points and thus depict the story with Rashomon-like, multiple realities. Even so, it is these four tales—ostensibly told by four men—that reveal Mabila. When we find the site of that town, we will (perhaps) quantify charred remains, reconstruct palisades, and (perhaps) count pearls of wisdom as well as charred ones among our treasures. Yet what can that location add to our understanding of the events at Mabila? Generations of scholars have argued that it is essential to pinpoint the precise route in order to reveal and interpret knowledge about the past. But by relentlessly focusing on place (route) rather than the story (action), we have failed to find Mabila as well as to truly see it. This is not to deny the value of the place but rather to assert that the surviving tales—oftentimes combined and bent to the purpose of fixing place by modern scholars—are perhaps more properly suited for revealing the motives of the participants. It is the task of the next generation of De Soto scholars to take up the challenge and subject these documents to rigorous and sophisticated literary and historical analysis. Then, we will (perhaps) understand the conflicts and tensions within the expedition as well as the impact of these on the events themselves.

Notes

1. See chapter 12, this volume, for similarities and differences among the chroniclers on the specifics of what was lost in the fire.

2. Argote, testimony, courtesy of John E. Worth, University of West Florida, Pensacola. In clarification of this passage, only the horses left in the town were lost. Some escaped and others were not inside the town.

3. George Lankford (personal communication, February 2007) doubts that all the baggage was with the vanguard, and he also speculates that the writers would have had their material with them. For information on writing material used by sixteenth-

century Spaniards, see Deagan, *Artifacts of the Spanish Colonies of Florida and the Caribbean,* vol. 2: *Portable Personal Possessions,* 304–5.

4. Galloway, "Incestuous Soto Narratives," 39.

5. For a discussion of this matter, see chapter 3, this volume. See also Galloway, "Incestuous Soto Narratives," and Altman, "An Official's Report."

6. Clayton, Knight, and Moore, *De Soto Chronicles,* 1: 232.

7. Ibid.

8. Ibid., 1: 233.

9. Ibid.

10. Ibid., 1: 233.

11. Ibid., 1: 235.

12. Ibid.

13. Ibid., 1: 233.

14. Ibid., 1: 235.

15. Ibid., 1: 233.

16. Ibid., 1: 236.

17. Ibid.

18. Ibid.

19. Ibid., 1: 98.

20. Ibid.

21. Ibid.

22. Ibid., 1: 99.

23. Ibid.

24. Ibid.

25. Ibid.

26. Ibid., 1: 100.

27. Ibid.

28. Ibid., 1: 104.

29. Ibid., 1: 291.

30. Ibid., 1: 292.

31. Ibid., 1: 291.

32. Ibid., 1: 295–96.

33. Ibid., 1: 292.

34. Ibid., 1: 264.

35. Ibid., 1: 292.

36. Ibid.

37. Ibid., 1: 293.

38. Ibid.

39. Ibid.

40. Ibid., 1: 294.

41. Ibid.

42. Ibid., 2: 330.

43. Ibid., 2: 332.
44. Ibid., 2: 335.
45. Ibid.
46. Ibid.
47. Ibid., 2: 336.
48. Ibid., 2: 337.
49. Ibid., 2: 348.
50. In his examination of Mabila, Jay Higginbotham has written that "far from concocting an ambush, it seems probable that Taskalusa reacted spontaneously to a baffling situation, to an unexpected turn of events." See Higginbotham, "The Battle of Mauvila, Causes and Consequences," 27. The purpose here, however, is not to reconstruct events or to determine whether the attack on the Spaniards was planned in advance but to understand the story that each chronicler puts forth—and the motives of these writers.

14
Tracing De Soto's Trail to Mabila

Eugene M. Wilson, Douglas E. Jones, and Neal G. Lineback

The charge assigned to our working group at the 2006 "Search for Mabila" conference was to utilize existing information, including both old and new maps, aerial photos, digital images, and other materials not available to or not used by previous De Soto commissions, in an attempt to plot De Soto's route through Alabama to Mabila. The full working group consisted of Eugene M. Wilson (convener), Douglas E. Jones, Neal G. Lineback, E. Mason McGowin, Donald E. Sheppard, and John E. Worth; all members of the working group made important contributions to the findings articulated here. Our ultimate goal was to identify possible routes taken, possible locations for Indian towns and villages mentioned in the Spanish chronicles, and geographic areas within which the site of Mabila is likely to be found.

Our group began its work toward a best-fit hypothesis in locating De Soto's possible routes using the following assumptions: 1) that Atahachi was located near the west side of present-day Montgomery and that De Soto began his westerly march toward Mabila from this town; 2) that there may be other route scenarios that should be explored; 3) that the De Soto expedition would have averaged about four or five leagues (10–13 miles) per day, but on occasion under favorable conditions could extend that distance to six or seven leagues (15–17 miles); 4) that the working group would use the descriptions of terrain, distances, and time of travel between Atahachi and Mabila as related in the *De Soto Chronicles,*[1] as further translated by group member John E. Worth, together with the pre-conference itinerary prepared by Vernon James Knight Jr. (published as chapter 5, this volume); and 5) that, after exploring and describing possible alternative routes and pertinent site locations, members would select best-fit routes to Mabila.

During the September 2006 symposium, our group concluded that the Orrville terrace west and southwest of Selma and Cahaba (formerly spelled

Cahawba) appeared to be the most promising area for the location of the Mabila site complex. As will be seen, in subsequent discussions during the summer of 2007, that working hypothesis was set aside, after two months of archaeological surveys in the Orrville terrace area revealed little evidence of Late Mississippian occupation (see postscript, this volume). Although it fit our understandings at the time, it appears that our placement of Atahachi just west of present Montgomery, on which that conclusion was founded, was incorrect. Consequently, our working group shifted its attention to other route hypotheses proposing a new location for Atahachi downstream from the first, as described below.

This chapter begins with a review of the geology of the region through which De Soto traveled in Alabama, for which it will be understood that primary authorship is by Douglas E. Jones. This is followed by a discussion of the physical geography and natural regions likely impacting De Soto's movements and the locations of related Indian towns, for which the primary author is Eugene M. Wilson. The chapter ends with some best-fit scenarios for De Soto's route and general locations for the village of Mabila, for which the primary author is Neal G. Lineback.

Geologic Overview of De Soto's Route through East and Central Alabama

Hernando de Soto entered northeast Alabama in the fall of 1540 after making a major directional change in his wandering march from Florida by cutting through the Appalachian Mountains in western North Carolina and eastern Tennessee. This movement took the Spanish army across the eroded remnants of the oldest and largest mountain range in eastern North America.[2] The character of the Earth's surface is a mirror of ancient climates, the underlying geologic structure, and the composition of the various rocks involved. Silica-rich rocks resist decomposition and erosion and form ridges and other high ground while soft strata, such as limestone and other sedimentary rocks, more readily decompose to become valleys, stream beds, and fertile soils to be transported by erosion. The geology of any place on earth determines, or helps determine, its terrain, soils and vegetation, stream patterns, and the presence or absence of economic mineral deposits. The grain of the resulting landscape of the southern Appalachians is northeast-southwest, as are the courses of its rivers and streams. Stream beds and their related alluvial deposits generally provide the easiest travel route through rugged terrain.

Created as the result of not less than four episodes of tectonic plate collisions, the Appalachians at their peak development were five miles high and extended northeast-southwest from New England to Alabama. Strata were pushed northwestward by the incoming plates and folded, broken, and altered by terrific heat and pressure, essential elements for the formation of minerals and ore deposits. The results of deformation across this zone ranged from intensely folded, broken, and altered rock on the east (the Piedmont province) to gently tilted and unaltered marine limestone, shale, and sandstone to the west (the Cumberland Plateau province). In between the two is the Valley and Ridge province, distinctive topography generally formed by roughly parallel limestone valleys separated by sandstone ridges.[3] These valley floors have been important migration routes ever since humans appeared in this part of the world. For example, even today, one could walk along one of these valleys from Lake Champlain, New York, almost uninterruptedly to Birmingham, Alabama. De Soto's movement to the west side of the Appalachians placed his expedition in the Valley and Ridge province and the upper reaches of two significant rivers, the Tennessee and the Coosa.

Hudson writes that De Soto traveled down the north bank of the Tennessee River in an effort to reach the populated towns reported to be on the Tallapoosa River to the south.[4] It appears from the physiographic map of the region that the most likely route to this goal would have been for De Soto to leave the Tennessee River valley south of Chattanooga and travel along the east side of Lookout Mountain fifty or sixty miles to the headwaters of the Coosa River around Rome, Georgia. From this point the army probably followed the Coosa, and its considerable number of Indian towns, to central Talladega County where established trails led southeast across the Piedmont into the Tallapoosa drainage some thirty to forty miles away.

It is likely that De Soto's route through northwest Georgia and north-central Alabama was a practical choice. Based on his experience with Pizarro and the Incas in Peru twenty years earlier, De Soto associated gold with mountains. It is well established now that mountains and related mineral deposits indeed are products of tectonic events.

A second justification for this route may have been that prior to entering Alabama the Spanish had learned that most large Indian villages, the source of most of the army's logistical support, were located on elevated river terraces above flood level. Such places provided sandy loam agricultural soils and, frequently, freshwater springs, woodlands for cooking and construction purposes, access to the river for travel and defense, and space for village growth. These attributes were common to most, if not all, Mississippian archaeological sites in the Southeast where terraces were available. These abandoned and elevated stream floodplains are strikingly depicted by yellow and orange colors on modern geologic maps of Alabama.[5]

A significant number of such terraces and related archaeological sites characterize the rivers De Soto encountered in Alabama: the Tennessee, Coosa, Tallapoosa, and Alabama, a few having yielded Spanish artifacts. Any stream, regardless of size, flows downslope from its head, a point or area of origin, to its base level, the lowest point it reaches, another body of water or sea level. In its steeper upper reaches, where the water velocity is higher, streams move heavier particles of rock debris by pushing, rolling, or bouncing them along the bottom of its bed and suspending smaller particles such as sand, silt, and clay. These materials continue to move along until stream velocity decreases and they settle out gradually to become gravel and sand bars, mud flats, and other floodplain features. Normally a well-established stream, in equilibrium, will erode from its upper reaches about the same amount of material that it will deposit farther downstream. A change in a stream's base level has a direct effect on erosion and sedimentation processes.

This phenomenon is best illustrated by the formation of elevated alluvial terraces during the last half-million years of the Pleistocene epoch, the so-called Ice Age. During the principal periods of continental glaciation, worldwide ocean levels fluctuated an average of 350 feet, caused by a combination of shifting precipitation from oceans to increasing weight from growing glaciers and the seesaw rise and fall of the earth's flexible crust to maintain its equilibrium. As the northern part of the North American crust was depressed by the weight of thousands of feet of ice as far south as the present-day Ohio River, its southern counterpart rose. The net result of lower sea level and rising land caused streams to downcut or erode their beds to regain equilibrium. During interglacial periods, when sea levels rose as the glaciers to the north melted and the crust slowly rebounded, vast floodplains were created along stream courses in the south where the crust was sinking in compensation. Consequently, each glacial cycle includes a period of stream erosion and one of deposition and the uplift of the former floodplain by crustal rebound to become an alluvial river terrace. There are six such terrace levels in the Alabama River basin—the only one in the state where such data are available—all representing river floodplains that are now abandoned and uplifted to different elevations, ranging from 100 feet to more than 250, with the youngest at the bottom and the oldest, most eroded one at the highest level.[6]

Any route De Soto followed south toward the Tallapoosa River from the Chattanooga area would have included villages on the Coosa River terraces and ancient foot trails across the heart of the Alabama Piedmont uplands. Between 1835 and 1945, this region supported a large and diverse minerals economy, not the least of which was gold. Along with Georgia and North Carolina in the first few decades of the nineteenth century, gold was discovered in Alabama; more than 40,000 ounces were mined here before the operation ceased a century later.[7]

According to the experts, no archaeological site in Alabama, including those along the Coosa drainage within the Piedmont, has ever yielded a single flake of gold. Maybe the natives did not know about it. Gold was, and still is, hard to find in its pure state. Most of it occurs as ore that requires refinement by crushing and treatment with heat or various chemicals. Most nuggets, flakes, and other small particles of pure gold were derived from the weathering of so-called mother lodes of igneous and metamorphic origins and washed into streams. Since the specific gravity of gold is nineteen times heavier than water, these bits and pieces quickly worked down to the bottom of the stream's bed load of sediments, to be ground, pounded, and aggregated by hard quartz gravel ultimately to become placer deposit gold. If the Mississippians knew about gold, they may have considered it of little value or were unable to smelt it from the ore rock, unlike the Incas, who had developed sufficient metallurgical skills to smelt and cast the metal from local ores.

De Soto and a number of his men had been in Peru with Pizarro and had become rich from the gold artifacts they acquired from the Incas. Apparently, this is what they expected to find in La Florida. In any case, this stretch of the Coosa River where it traverses the Piedmont may have been the closest that De Soto came to gold during his entire odyssey in this part of the New World. This writer (D. E. J.), a geologist, once panned gold dust and a few small nuggets from the creek gravels of the old Rippatoe Placer in Chilton County, only five miles west of the Coosa River. If the army reached the Tallapoosa by a direct land route across the Piedmont, prospecting in any stream encountered along the way likely would have produced some "shows" of the precious metal. Apparently, if such was attempted, it was unsuccessful or unreported.

Just north of present-day Montgomery the Coosa and Tallapoosa rivers join to become the Alabama River, the signatory stream for the celebrated Black Belt region of the Coastal Plain province in Alabama and Mississippi. Underlain by some 1,000 feet of gray to white chalks, limy clays and sands, the Selma Chalk crops out across the state and beyond in an irregular, arcuate band ten to twenty miles wide.[8] These strata, composed of countless billions of ultramicroscopic calcareous algal remains, were deposited in shallow tropical Cretaceous seas that covered much of North America some one hundred million years ago. Two different landforms result from the weathering of these strata. An upper zone of quartz-sandy limestone and hard chalk some two hundred feet thick creates a prominent north-facing ridge or cuesta along the southern boundary of the Black Belt. In contrast, prairie soils and vegetation are developed on the lower eight hundred feet of the nearly pure lime in central and west Alabama and beyond. These prairie soils are almost totally impermeable when wetted but stick to one's feet like glue and dry only by evaporation. Consequently, much of the Black Belt is unsuitable for row crops but is suitable for pasture lands. The natural open prairie surface, sometimes extending over several square miles, was covered primarily with herbaceous plants, including Johnson and other grasses, clover, and coarse weeds. Open cedar brakes and scattered hardwoods, including post oak, hickory, and gum, were common trees. Tall canebrakes were common on lower areas along the Alabama River and its tributary streams. In 1775, William Bartram, in his *Travels,* recorded "expansive . . . grassy plains, or native fields," some with tall grass intermingled with a variety of herbage near the Alabama River.[9] East of Montgomery these chalky sediments gradually change in character to limy mica-rich quartz sands, as streams flowing out of the Piedmont to the north added sediments derived from weathered igneous and metamorphic rocks of the province.

Much of the land surface in the Black Belt consists of Pleistocene terraces superimposed on the prairie surface by the Alabama, Tombigbee, and Black Warrior rivers and ranging in elevation from 100 to 250 feet. These loamy soils were suitable for agricultural purposes as evidenced by the large number of aboriginal sites found thereon.

The character of the Alabama River here is quite different from that of the Coosa. Despite its lime carbonate composition, the impermeable chalk dissolves only slightly in rainwater that becomes a mild carbonic acid with the addition of atmospheric carbon dioxide. In consequence, the river develops distinctive meanders and many steep and high chalk bluffs throughout its passage across the prairie lands.

Based on the concept that animal trails became human trails and, finally, roads and highways, the movement of a Spanish expeditionary force through the Alabama River basin should have been relatively easy. The extent of elevated terraces is such that troop movements should not have been difficult and river crossings infrequent. Based on the 1988 geologic map of Alabama, it appears that one could walk or ride with little difficulty in any sort of weather along the surface of the first or second terraces on the south side of the Alabama River from Montgomery west to Selma. Beyond, into the valleys of the Black Warrior and Tombigbee rivers, the expedition would have encountered a significant change in the terrain. The chalk prairies are replaced by the Fall Line Hills, a north-facing cuesta formed on part of a thick, older layer of marine and non-marine sand and clay strata that underlies the Selma Chalk but also is Late Cretaceous in age. This distinctive physiographic feature divides the Gulf Coastal Plain province from the Appalachian Plateau to the north.

Routes that seem feasible for De Soto's army to have followed through the Black Belt from the Montgomery area to Mabila are along present-day U.S. Highway 80 south of the Alabama River and along the railroad route between this highway and the river (Figure 14.1). These suppositions correlate with the original conclusions of our working group (see below) that the battle site and its related hamlets and post-battle recovery area would have been on the Orrville terrace west and southwest of Cahaba.[10] Furthermore, either route above accommodates the thesis that a northwest march from this point leads to the Black Warrior and Tombigbee river valleys that open the door to Mississippi and Chicasa. Nothing on the geological map of Alabama indicates any geologic or topographic feature that would have prevented or seriously impeded such a movement by the De Soto group through this west Alabama country during the dry fall months.

Physical Geography and Natural Region Impacts on De Soto's Route

After passing through the Appalachian Highlands, the De Soto expedition crossed again onto the Coastal Plain. The expedition departed Talisi, here assumed to be located on the lower Tallapoosa River, and went into the Alabama River valley toward Atahachi. It seems most likely that the route paralleled the general course of the Alabama River following the left bank (facing downstream). Later travelers, among them being Benjamin Hawkins and William Bartram, whose descriptions have become valuable for natural history, followed the same general route toward Mobile.[11] This route fits most closely with the time and distance calculated for towns mentioned in the days following departure from Talisi, based on the Elvas and Rangel accounts. Distances were estimated variously at between four and six leagues (here, one league = 2.47 miles) per day, or about 10 to 15 miles, with 12 miles a direct-line average considering the size and makeup of the entire expedition.

As they moved into the Black Belt region, the Spaniards were entering a broad plain with moderate slopes, bordered by distant hills to the north and south. We have no record of how they perceived this area. Having crossed so much of the Southeast, it may have simply been seen as another region to get through to the next town. The forest would have been familiar—a mixed deciduous-coniferous association (chestnut-oak-pine) on sandy uplands and mainly broadleaf deciduous forest on lowlands. Occasionally, herbaceous-dominated openings, "prairies" or savannas, might have been seen, perhaps

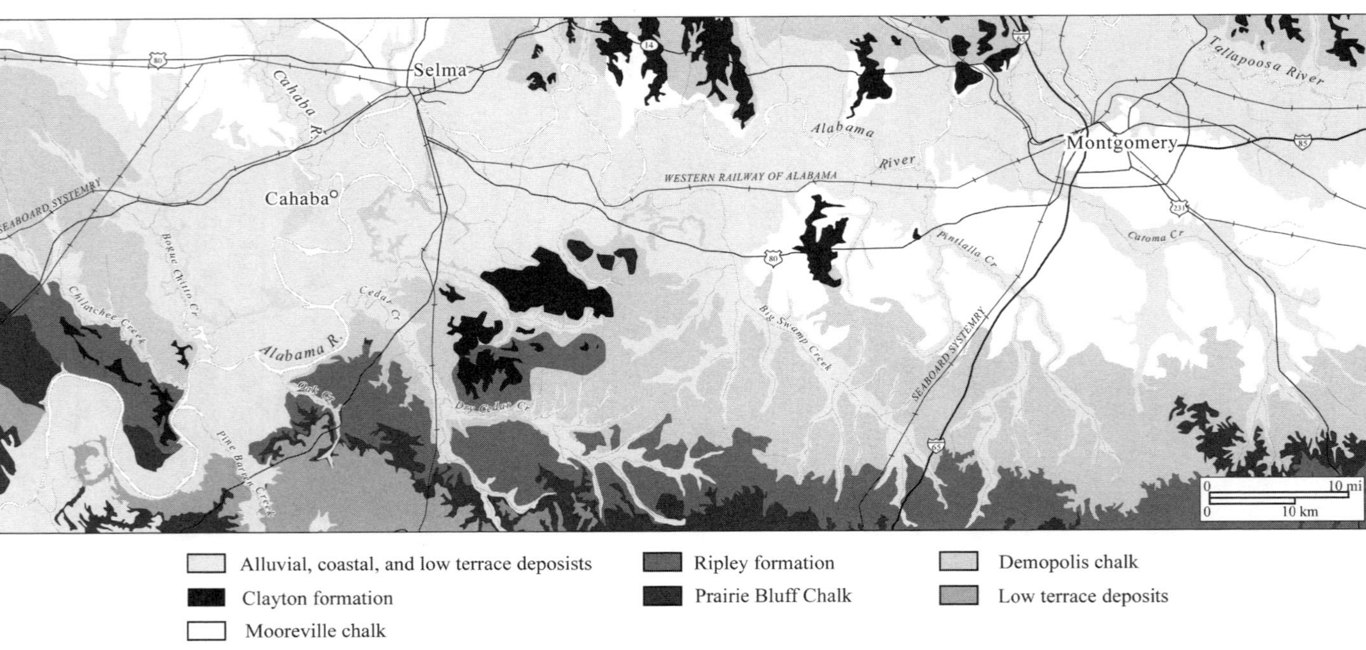

Figure 14.1. Geology of the upper Alabama River and environs in central Alabama.

not appearing much different from the "old fields" seen on previous trails. Wetlands on flat black soil areas and on the active floodplains were often covered with tall canebrakes.

From Montgomery to Selma, the river follows the wide east-west lowland of the Black Belt. The river turns southward at Selma, then flows through uplands and ridges in a more confined valley for about thirty miles. It follows a meandering course entrenched, or cut down into uplands, running close to high bluffs on the outsides of the bends with much lower floodplains or low terraces on the insides of the bends. This pattern of alternating high bluffs and lowlands produces an asymmetrical valley profile between Selma and Prairie Bluff in Wilcox County. Below Prairie Bluff, the valley widens for about fifteen miles, and then resumes the alternating pattern south to the Mobile Delta. The high bluffs are nearly two hundred feet above the river and are typically capped by river terrace sand and gravel and are forested.

We assume that the locations of choice for the more permanent Indian town sites would have been on elevations above the present floodplain. Dispersed settlements parallel to the river with maize fields on the recent floodplain were common in early historic descriptions.[12] The possible locations for Atahachi lie along or near the Alabama River, and include an Indian site in Durant Bend, which is associated with Spanish artifacts. From Atahachi, the De Soto expedition departed on October 12 and went about twenty-five miles to Piachi, which was reached on October 13, the second day of travel. With Atahachi at Durant Bend, this could place Piachi on Elm Bluff or Ripley Bluff, just south of Cedar Creek, opposite Molette Bend.

The physical setting of Piachi was one of the few precise descriptions Rangel recorded, so he must have been impressed. It may have been unusual as the only town up high above a river floodplain, whereas the more common town locations were close to the river. Was Piachi "high" but still low enough for easy access to fields on the floodplain? With regard to a present-day location we might note again how Rangel described the site: "llegaron a Piachi, que es un pueblo alto, sobre un barranco de un río, enriscado."[13] Generally, "we arrived at Piachi, which is a high town, above the valley of a river, rugged" or, more simply, "we arrived at Piachi, a town high on a bluff above a river." Geographically, *barranco* still refers to a steep valley, like a deep ravine or a canyon. Perhaps an impression of the whole river valley was included in Rangel's statement. If so, the only canyon-like section of the river is along the valley at Claiborne Bluff, fifty miles farther south. However, many creeks flowing off high river bluffs are canyon-like: steep, deep, and impressive, smaller than the river but giving the overall effect of a rough or rugged place.

In this middle section of the Alabama River valley, the Piachi site would logically be described as being on a bluff. Here, the cross-valley profile has one very high side and one low side, that is, bluffs located opposite floodplains. The bluffs are, by definition, rough, steep slopes of hills or steep exposures of strata, commonly along rivers.

The translation of *barranco . . . enriscado* as "craggy bluff" seems less accurate: *risco* can be translated as either "bluff" or "cliff."[14] Along the Alabama River we are unlikely to see crags, or projecting peaks of resistant bare rocks, along the ridgelines. Crag, originally a Scottish term, more commonly refers to features shaped by glacial erosion in mountains or by high-altitude freezing and thawing. Alabama River bluffs commonly are covered by high terraces of sand and gravel and are forested. Along the Alabama River, "bluff" best describes the Piachi location.

After leaving the bluff at Piachi, the expedition would have crossed to the opposite side of the river, here assumed to be at Molette Bend. Notations written on early General Land Office survey plats for this area (T14N R8E; T14N R9E) include "open woods," "high level caneland," "oak, ash, hickory, cane, & vines." These notations record different plant communities reflecting local soil and drainage conditions of floodplain and low terrace areas along the river bend.

In this section of the Alabama River valley, crossing the river from any bluff would lead directly across to a low floodplain, not another bluff, since along the meandering channel the bluffs alternate with low floodplain areas. Rangel's statement of October 16, "partieron de alli e fueron a un monte" (we departed from there [Piachi] and went to [or into] a *monte*),[15] means going into woods or woodland, not into mountains or other upland features.[16] Although at low water the river banks are steep and not easily negotiated, they would hardly qualify as uplands, although they would have had some plant cover.

In the middle section of the Alabama is a concentration of Late Mississippian archaeological sites in southern Dallas County and northern Wilcox County designated as the Wilcox segment by Craig Sheldon.[17] Geographically this includes a large river floodplain–low terrace area just south of Molette Bend on the south (left bank) side of the river and adjacent to the bluff, Elm Bluff or Ripley Bluff, where Piachi may have been located. As described in chapter 15 (this volume), within this interesting floodplain and low terrace area the Crenay map of 1733 shows a junction of overland routes connecting the Gulf Coast with the lower Coosa Valley and Ecor Blanc (present-day Demopolis). The map also shows a town symbol for *Vieux* [Old] *Mobiliens* at this route junction. Another Mobilian settlement is shown farther south on the east side of the Mobile Delta.

In this Wilcox segment, ten or more recorded Late Mississippian archaeological sites are located along the Alabama River south of the hills at Prairie Bluff. This is a possible location for Nanipacana, the town and area occupied by the Luna expedition twenty years after De Soto. It is within four days, or not more than about fifty miles distant from Atahachi if the latter is placed at Durant Bend. Possible routes from Atahachi to the Wilcox segment are discussed following this review of geographical areas.

Dallas County climate records show October to be the driest month of the year, with an average of 1.24 to 3.00 inches of rainfall.[18] At low water, creeks and smaller rivers could have been forded easily enough so that no record was made of the De Soto army's crossings except for large streams at which rafts or boats were made or obtained. The Alabama River was wider and deeper, and it was the major obstruction to travel.

Several distinct natural lowland areas that are potential candidates for the location of Mabila are found along the Alabama River. They can be identified with the help of topographic maps, geologic maps, soil survey reports, public land survey plat maps, aerial photos, and satellite images. Each of these aids is useful, but each has limitations.

The most accurate early maps readily available for study are public land survey township plat maps from the General Land Office Records of the Bureau of Land Management. Surveyed in the early 1800s, plat maps were drawn of each township with its thirty-six sections. Many plat maps have interesting details and comments as to land quality for farming, names of trees, outlines of woods, canebrakes, and prairies, streams, river bluffs, Indian town sites, mounds, and trails. Many plats have nothing more than a general outline of streams and most do not have outlines of hills or bluffs away from rivers.

U.S. Geological Survey topographic maps are accurate horizontally and vertically. They commonly employ contour lines that connect points of equal elevation. Thus, land surface forms can be shown, except in the area between the contour lines, so a small contour interval (ten feet or less) is desirable. Shading adds to the depth perception. The planimetric data—human settlement patterns, public land survey lines, and streams—are all included and distances and areas can be accurately measured.

Geologic maps sometimes have contour lines but primarily show the age and types of underlying rocks with a system of colors and patterns. On recent geologic maps of Alabama and its individual counties, shades of green (for Cretaceous age) show the distribution of Black Belt and related formations to the north and south that form lines of hills. Stream deposits of sand and gravel that overlie the bedrock are shown as yellow for Quaternary alluvium. This includes the Recent or Holocene as well as Late Pleistocene floodplain deposits. The latter are extensive, overlying much of the surface of the Black Belt between Montgomery and Selma.

Soil maps are very helpful in locating the extent of natural areas, such as the Black Belt, river floodplains, and terraces. Prior to the mid-1960s, soil types were described in the context of a more geographically oriented system than is the case at present. The older soil maps were made for each county, were colored and very detailed, and included local roads, features, and place-names that now make them useful as historic documents. Over the past forty years, soil survey reports have been expanded to include data useful for forest management, construction, sanitation, and recreation, in addition to chemical and physical properties of soils. The outline of soil types is now printed onto fold-out, large-scale, black-and-white aerial photos instead of one single county map.

Aerial photography and satellite imagery are both valuable for monitoring land use patterns and changes. Since the early 1970s, these have merged to become the separate technical field of remote sensing, combining aerial and satellite systems with satellite global positioning systems (GPS) for accurate point location. Unfortunately, unlike ground-penetrating radar and other surface technologies, airborne remote sensing cannot "see" through trees with sufficient resolution to locate buried features. Where the ground is exposed in dry climates or has been cleared of forest cover, it is possible to identify near-surface patterns, trails, and ruins, particularly after harvest or in a dry season when outlines appear as a result of slight variation in soil moisture.

Early settlers recognized that both the dark prairie soils and soils of river bottomlands, or floodplains soils, had desirable agricultural properties.[19] The largest areas of land purchased by 1843, shown in plat maps of townships T16N 10E and T17N 9E, for example, were located along the banks of the Alabama River and the Cahaba River. Smaller parcels were scattered over the western part of the county and do not clearly show any particular preference. Both the black prairie and bottomland soils are water-sensitive: the bottomlands are subject to flooding, mainly in spring and summer, and the prairie soils have very low permeability. East of the Black Belt region, alluvial, or stream-transported, soil washed from creeks and rivers overlie the limestone. These floodplain and terrace materials are primarily quartz sand and gravel derived from the Appalachian Highlands and result in very different soil properties from those in the Black Prairie soils.

The largest lowland areas in central Alabama include the Black Belt, the Alabama River floodplain, the Cahaba River floodplain, the floodplain of Bogue Chitto Creek, and the low- and mid-level terraces around Orrville and Selma.

The Black Belt west of the Cahaba River is a plain with very low relief, developed on the Selma Chalk with associated black soil and areas of "prairie" vegetation. Where the surface is not eroded, dark soil accumulates as minerals hold organic material in the topsoil. The ground surface is nearly level or gently undulating and stream valleys are broad and shallow. Surface elevations west of Selma range from 230 to 240 feet near Harrell to 120 to 130 feet at Martin Station west of Orrville. The Black Belt extends to the Black Warrior-Tombigbee River and northwestward into Mississippi, and is presumed to be the area crossed by the Spaniards after leaving Mabila toward Chicasa. As a location for human settlement, however, the Black Belt had problems having to do with soil and water.

Permeability in the black prairie soils is so poor that rainwater often accumulates in large pools or ponds, where dense canebrakes once existed. The clay-rich prairie soils become very tenacious when wet; the clay minerals expand, the soil swells, and it becomes very adhesive. This was a serious impediment to travel.[20] Rainwater does not "soak into" the soil, thus shallow well water is not available. In historic times, cisterns and deep artesian wells provided domestic water supplies. Largely because of the impermeable soil, towns and plantation homes in the early 1800s were commonly located on sandy terrace deposits or uplands on the north or south margins of the Black Belt. In the drier months of summer and fall, the prairie soils dry, contract, and become hard. In general, they were productive for cotton if properly cultivated. Today they are primarily used for pasture land and catfish ponds. It would be interesting to study the location of any Late Mississippian sites reported on prairie soils in the Black Belt to understand why these sites were chosen, given the difficulties posed by the soil and water conditions.

The Cahaba River floodplain covers forty-five to fifty square miles and includes many small swamps, ponds, and filled-in channels. A patchwork of small areas of sandy loam soils suitable for agriculture occurs in the central and eastern sides of the plain. The Cahaba River flows along the bluff at the western side of its floodplain, then into the Alabama River. Tributary creeks flow across higher ground from the northern and eastern slopes into the Cahaba. Much of the Cahaba floodplain is cleared or cultivated at present. It has a greater variety of habitats than does the Black Prairie for an agricultural population. In its geographical relation to the Alabama River, it is the western counterpart of the Tallapoosa River to the east.

The Selma terrace covers an area of about 32 square miles and has an elevation of 120 to 150 feet. It occupies a position between the Alabama River floodplain on the south and east, the hilly uplands bordering the north, and the Cahaba River floodplain on the west. It includes an area of prairie soils just north of Selma and terrace and floodplain soils to the west. Presently, much of the surface is cleared or cultivated and includes the Selma metropolitan area.

The Alabama River floodplain and low terraces extend along both sides of the river from Montgomery to Selma and include extensive areas in the elongated river bends. The river bottomlands and low terraces are still productive farmland. The town site of Cahaba lies on a low terrace at the boundary of the Alabama and Cahaba floodplains. For most of its course, the Alabama River is entrenched and is no longer freely meandering. In the early 1800s the river was noted for rapid rise and fall of fifteen to twenty feet after heavy rains. The topography of high terrace bluffs and other hills south of Selma restricts the river floodplain cultivation to the low inner side of the river bends, such as Blackwell Bend, Molette Bend, Gees Bend, and Canton Bend. The valley again widens south of Canton Bend to the Tallahatta hills at the Wilcox-Clarke county line with floodplains along both sides of the river for about fifteen miles.

Terrace deposits are primarily yellow to reddish sand and gravel and occur as step-like, fairly level surfaces above the present floodplain. These deposits overlie the gray limestone of the Selma formations that appear along the river, forming steep, sometimes vertical cliffs. Behind Miller's Ferry Dam the water surface is currently maintained at about 80 feet above sea level. Low terraces include the surface around Old Cahawba Park, 20 to 40 feet above the water level (100 to 120 feet in elevation). The Selma and Orrville surfaces are mid-level, 70 to 90 feet above the water (150 to 170 feet in elevation). Hatcher's Bluff, Whites Bluff, and Red Bluff, the latter just west of Bogue Chitto, are 170 to 180 feet above the water (250 to 260 feet in elevation). It was in this vicinity that Harper gave a good description of the river terraces: "A remarkable topographic feature of this region is a series of high terraces along the Alabama River, principally in Dallas County. . . . Some of them are at least 150 if not 200 feet above the river, and one or two are mesa-like, not abutting against any higher land. Their summits are capped with sandy loam and a few pebbles, but the chalk extends up in them to perhaps 100 feet above the river and makes some high bluffs where the river swings against the terraces, such as Hatcher's Bluff about six miles south of Selma, and Whites Bluff, on the other side of the river."[21]

The bluff opposite Molette Bend is formed on the Demopolis Chalk overlain by the Ripley formation and is not mesa-like. At the river, the bluff is 110 to 120 feet above the water but increases to 330 to 340 feet (410 to 420 feet in elevation) at the small, flat summit at the hamlet of Elm Bluff. This summit and other remnants of high terraces farther back from the present rivers are probably Pliocene-Miocene in age and have elevations to 500 feet.[22] They are shown on geologic maps in orange color (designated as Qt) and are some of the greatest elevations in the Alabama Coastal Plain, indicative of the substantial geologic changes that have occurred over the past several million years.

The Orrville terrace was formed by northward meandering of the ancestral Alabama River during the Pleistocene and is easily identified on topographic maps, aerial photography, and satellite imagery because of the spiraling pattern of crescent-shaped point bar ridges and swales preserved on its surface. It covers about 46 square miles and has a surface elevation of about 150 to 200 feet, locally being slightly higher than the adjacent Black Belt. An archaeological site, now believed to have been destroyed by logging and identified on an early General Land Office map as "Five Indian mounds," was located in township T15N R8E, sections 16 and 21.[23] It was located on the western terrace edge above Bogue Chitto Creek, which drains most of western Dallas County. However, with the primary soil choice of Mississippian culture being bottomland alluvial soils, the low- and mid-level terraces, including the Orrville surface, were probably not used for cultivation. To date, archaeological field surveys have not found evidence of Late Mississippian sites on the Orrville terrace or on the lower Cahaba River floodplain.[24]

The smaller lowlands include the Bogue Chitto and Chilatchee Creek valleys. The Bogue Chitto is a permanent stream that originates in the Fall Line Hills northwest of Selma and flows southward across the Black Belt and into the Alabama River at the south side of Molette Bend. About two to three miles wide, the valley has floodplain soils derived from the Black Prairie and the adjacent river terraces along its lower course. To the west are hills drained by the smaller Chilatchee Creek that forms the boundary between Dallas and Wilcox counties. It is separated from the Bogue Chitto by a narrow terrace ridge that forms Red Bluff on the north side of the Alabama River.

Little evidence for Late Mississippian sites has been found in the vicinity of Selma, a prominent exception being the fortified Mississippian site at Cahaba. This finding constrains possible locations of Piachi south of Selma within the limits of the two-day travel time from Atahachi, assuming a location on or near Durant Bend. If Piachi was situated on the left (east) bank of the Alabama River, the locations that seem most likely include points at Elm Bluff seven miles south of Blackwell Bend opposite Molette Bend, or at locations north or northeast of Camden in Wilcox County.

For the hills to the west of the Bogue Chitto valley around Chilatchee Creek, the original General Land Office survey plat of Township T14 N, R8 E contains a notation of chestnuts ("Broken land oak, chesnut, and pines"). Another interesting association is with the Hatcher's Bluff area, opposite Cahaba, where the home of the U.S. vice president elect (1853) Rufus King was called "Chestnut Hill." Chestnut trees were commonly found in the dry non-calcareous woods, especially on rocky slopes. William Bartram also noted that among other hardwoods was "an abundance of chestnuts on the hills, with Pinus taeda and Pinus lutea," in the "vast open forest" below the Black Belt.[25]

The location of the site of Piachi involves more than just a river crossing because physical conditions on the opposite shore must be met, based on observations by the chroniclers concerning the approach to Mabila and its surroundings. Settlements of this period commonly extended along streams where maize fields were located. Mabila was described as being on a plain or flat area, and it had a pond nearby. Following the battle of Mabila, water and food had to be obtained. Troops who were able roamed about the countryside foraging from any remaining settlements and fields, possibly recrossing the Alabama River in the process. At departure from Mabila, the expedition moved off toward the north with food for two days. This required an area of sufficient density of maize fields that the remaining soldiers and retainers could survive for the three weeks of their recuperation and subsequent travel.

An area meeting most requirements for Mabila is that near Selma along the Alabama River–Cahaba River floodplain. The absence of native and European artifacts contemporary with De Soto in this area, however, seems to have eliminated it from further consideration, although it is one of the most extensive and environmentally diverse regions along the river. The next most favorable areas nearest our posited location for Atahachi are the Bogue Chitto Creek valley, Gees Bend, and the Alabama River floodplain below Prairie Bluff. Wide and level, the Bogue Chitto valley has two areas of artesian springs, or "flowing wells," that could have provided water for domestic use and for a natural or man-made pond. The distances for travel after the river crossing from Piachi over to Molette Bend are sufficient for an unhurried trip to a Mabila site in the valley. It remains to be seen whether sites with Late Mississippian ceramics and Spanish artifacts exist in the Bogue Chitto valley and whether it had the density of population and settlements on the way to

Mabila on October 18 as described in the chronicles. The same applies to the Gees Bend area as well, which has some known sites but has a small floodplain area separated from more populous lowlands downriver.

The largest area of floodplain and associated soils with known Late Mississippian sites lies along the Alabama River below Gees Bend from Prairie Bluff south for about fifteen miles in Sheldon's Wilcox segment.[26] This area is a possible Mabila location if Atahachi was located at Durant Bend. Heading south and southwest from Atahachi on October 12, the army could have made about twelve miles, crossing mostly over continuous low, sandy terrace surfaces, probably covered with a mix of chestnut, oak and pine, and then camped near present-day Berlin. After another nine or ten miles the next day, they could have reached Piachi on an elevated location at the Alabama River. At least, the lead group of horsemen and soldiers could have reached Piachi on the afternoon of October 13. It is possible that October 14 was also a day during which any remaining troops arrived.

The army is believed to have crossed the river on October 16 and, presumably, moved inland some distance. At Elm Bluff or Ripley Bluff, two crossing points seem most likely. One is located at the north end just below Cedar Creek, and a second choice is at the south end of the bluff. This could have been reached on the second day if Atahachi were located farther south within Durant Bend. It is on a low terrace adjacent to a large floodplain with several identified Mississippian archaeological sites and where the Crenay map locates "Mobiliens." To follow the schedule of days, on October 16 the expedition could have moved across Molette Bend as far west as the Bogue Chitto. A travel distance of about fourteen miles would have brought the expedition to the west side of the Alabama River in the vicinity of Prairie Bluff. On the way, chestnut bread was given to Tascalusa at a palisaded town (*pueblo cercado*) they encountered. Chestnuts are noted on the 1800s General Land Office survey maps as growing in this area along Chilatchee Creek. The chronicles do not specifically state that the army camped at the palisaded town, but the town may have been located near Prairie Bluff.

On the morning of October 18, a journey several miles to the south would pass through villages along the way toward Mabila, possibly located on a low terrace nearby—the *llano* of the chronicles—not far from the present Millers Ferry Dam. The broad area of floodplain and associated low-lying soils that extend south along both sides of the river could have provided adequate food for the time following the Mabila battle and beyond. The topography would have made the post-Mabila travel to Chicasa, forty to fifty miles to the northwest, very easy (given dry conditions) over a gently sloping surface with few stream crossings.

After heading northward from Mabila on Sunday, November 14, De Soto's army traveled four days during which no towns were mentioned. On Wednesday, November 17, the fourth day, they "arrived at a very good river." On Thursday, November 18, the expedition "went across bad crossings and swamps and found a town with corn, which was called Talicpacana."[27] These locations were almost certainly on either the Tombigbee or Black Warrior River. By Tuesday, December 14, De Soto arrived at the river of Chicasa and reached the principal Chicasa town in present northeast Mississippi on December 17.

In earlier studies, De Soto route seekers generally followed the westward course across central Alabama to near Selma, then took a long southward-trending route to southern Clarke County for Mabila. That location was possibly influenced by the presence of historic Mobilian towns, the long documented use of Mobilian speech as a lingua franca, and the 1733 Crenay and other maps. In contrast, our current direction is to search farther north from the Mobile Delta, and farther south from the vicinity of Cahaba favored by others,[28] as more information is discovered about Late Mississippian sites. Still, current archaeological data are insufficient to firmly establish the route of De Soto, and other options are still being proposed.

Donald Sheppard, for example, takes the expedition across central Alabama with a somewhat different De Soto itinerary to a possible location for Mabila near Catherine, Alabama, about seven or eight miles northwest of Millers Ferry Dam.[29]

Bruce Trickey proposed a triangulation method for locating Mabila near Grove Hill in Clarke County. Trickey follows authors of previous studies who concurred with a western route from Talisi to Atahachi.[30] Trickey locates Atahachi in Dallas County south of Benton, and brings a fast-moving expedition down to Mabila in southern Clarke County. This requires five full days to cover a straight-line distance of approximately 72 miles from Atahachi to Mabila, instead of three and a half to four days of travel for a total of about 36 to 48 miles as calculated in the present discussion. With two other lines of his triangulation method, the 40 leagues (105 miles) to Achuse (Pensacola) and the other 168 miles to Chicasa (northeast Mississippi), the three lines intersect to place the site of Mabila on an upland west of the Alabama River not far from Grove Hill.[31]

In a more recent study, Caleb Curren proposed a southward De Soto journey after leaving Talisi, based on the direction of travel given by Biedma, evidence from the "De Soto Map," and evidence of known Late Mississippian site locations in southeast Alabama.[32] This proposal would take the De Soto expedition into the headwaters of the Yellow or the Conecuh River toward a Mabila destination farther to the southeast than any hitherto proposed. This direction relies on Biedma's accuracy in noting a southward departure from the province of Talisi. Curren has the De Soto expedition depart the Tallapoosa River at Humati, and thus his locations for Atahachi, Piachi, and Mabila put the expedition a greater distance from a Chicasa location in northeast Mississippi than is presently accepted by most other researchers. To resolve this issue, it would be necessary to shift the locations of the Apafalaya chiefdom and Talicpacana town to the Alabama River in the vicinity of Millers Ferry, where Luna's town of Nanipacana was also possibly located, suggesting the identity of Talicpacana and Nanipacana. Although not addressed by Curren, this reconstruction would in turn affect the Mississippi and Arkansas portions of the expedition as presently understood.

Another issue regarding Curren's proposal is that of travel time. In our opinion, the distances of the proposed locations would require more travel time, or at least a rapid march of fifteen miles per day to accommodate the dates given in the De Soto chronicles. A more refined version of this proposal might better fit the time and distances.

As a result of past and present efforts to find De Soto's route or the Mabila site, we are faced with the need for concrete archaeological evidence. The middle Alabama River seems to have the best possibility for a Mabila location by virtue of the large number of sites and artifacts and by compatible time and distance calculations. Surveys and excavations will have to confirm this or other hypothetical locations.

In the summer of 1559, twenty years after De Soto, an attempt to establish a permanent settlement in La Florida was led by Tristán de Luna.[33] This expedition was large, poorly organized, and cumbersome. It included 500 soldiers, 240 horses, and 1,000 men, women, and children as servants and colonists. Two hurricanes initiated its disastrous history, destroying ships, food, and other supplies. The Luna enterprise almost certainly used the De Soto records and possibly included survivors of the De Soto expedition who helped locate the area of Mabila and Cosa.[34]

Settling in at Achuse, at or near Pensacola, a search party of 200 men under Major Mateo del Sauz was sent out in late September 1559 to find food supplies. Crossing overland 40 leagues to the present Alabama River, the group came to an area of small settlements, the largest of which, with 80 houses, was called Nanipacana. In the neighborhood were ruins of an earlier settlement.

In February 1560, the entire Luna expedition moved north to the Nanipacana area. Still not finding adequate food supplies, Major Sauz was sent out again, toward Cosa, a place noted for its wealth of food according to the De Soto accounts. However, Sauz and his men had great difficulty traveling through the "wilderness" and found Cosa an impoverished region. The possibility is good that it suffered ruin from introduced diseases and/or subsequent warfare from disruption by the De Soto army. The lack of food supplies, the long illness of Luna, and disintegrating leadership ended the enterprise. The last of the Luna expedition left Nanipacana for Bahía Filipina (Mobile Bay) on June 24, 1560. Luna departed Achuse on April 9, 1561, for Havana and Spain.[35]

Future archaeological surveys should eventually find artifacts of both the De Soto and Luna expeditions. Although both periods of occupation were short, a total of approximately 2,000 Europeans were present and both groups should have left evidence of their presence and of their impacts on the local Indian landscape.

Proposed De Soto Routes toward Mabila

Hernando de Soto's contingent of personnel, animals, and supplies entered present-day northeast Alabama in late summer 1540. There are several considerations in determining much about their frequencies of movement and distances of travel over the next few months. Of particular importance are the composition of the army, its reliance on existing trails and stream crossings, its methods of conscripting Indians, the likely speed of its component parts, and its periodic opposition by indigenous chiefdoms along its paths of movement.

According to the De Soto chronicles, De Soto's nine ships arrived on the west coast of Florida in June 1539, carrying approximately 600 men, 220 horses, several dogs, a large herd of Spanish pigs, armor, and weapons, including at least one small cannon. By the time they arrived in Alabama more than a year later, the army had lost only a few of its members, had gained at least one refugee and interpreter, Juan Ortiz, from a previous expedition, and had discarded its cannon.[36]

Only about forty of De Soto's men were mounted on horses, while the remainder walked. Although mounted men were capable of covering daily distances up to twenty miles or more, foot soldiers were limited in daily distances by the weight of their weapons and belongings, their guarding and overseeing Indian porters, their scavenging and reconnoitering, and their herding of pigs. In general, the Spanish army moved only as fast as the slowest contingent, which was probably the group herding the swine.

Although limited pork was available for consumption from the accompanying pigs, the army intended to live mostly off the land, that is, by confiscating Indian foodstuffs for themselves, their horses, and their swine and consuming their own pigs only as a last resort. Although on occasion the Indians may have voluntarily surrendered their foodstuffs to the Spaniards, more often they had to be coerced or their food was simply stolen. Coercing and scavenging for food and looking for precious metals and goods was likely a time-consuming operation for the army, necessitating lengthy stays of several days in villages where food could be assembled and intelligence gathered before moving on.

Indian porters also had to be coerced into transporting supplies and goods, often in leg and neck irons and under guard of the Spaniards, according to the chronicles. In addition, the Spaniards often captured Indian women, forcing them into temporary sexual relationships and forcing their accompaniment at least to another village at some distance. Then some of the Indian porters and women may have been released and others added. Such efforts took time and effort on the part of the Spaniards, slowing the army's movements and scattering the groups out, probably both linearly and laterally across the landscape.

By the time De Soto's army crossed the Blue Ridge and Appalachian mountains, no doubt some of the pigs had been consumed by the Spaniards and some were lost, particularly as they crossed the rugged, heavily forested, and lightly occupied terrain. Swine sows can farrow twice a year, however, with litters of up to eight to twelve piglets. Consequently, the group may have arrived in Alabama near the upper Coosa River valley with at least half as many (if not more) swine as when they arrived at Tampa Bay more than a year prior.

De Soto's swine were Iberian pigs brought from Cuba, perhaps by way of Spain, whose physical characteristics hardly resembled those of modern swine. They might have been from ancestral stock of the present-day European Landrace breed, lean animals with adult body weights of less than 100 pounds (45 kilograms) and long, lanky legs. Their adult physique may have more resembled the peccary or Mexican hog, feral pigs of Florida, or even modern German shepherd dogs than modern commercial pigs (Figures 14.2, 14.3).

Consequently, De Soto's herd of Iberian pigs, including those recently born, could move at a moderately fast pace, except on hot and humid days. Although newborn piglets had to nurse and probably took about a week or two before they could easily keep up with the adults, they were surprisingly agile and mobile. Swine have no sweat glands and must have frequent access to water to cool off in hot weather. Since pigs are proficient swimmers and enjoy water, stream crossings presented little problem for the herd, as they followed the herd's oldest matriarch, perhaps being led by a nose ring by one

Figure 14.2. The physical characteristics of De Soto's Spanish pigs may have resembled those of Thomas Bewick's sketch *Peccary or Mexican Hog* (ca. 1790).

of the foot soldiers. Nonetheless, the herd of swine was probably the slowest moving of all of De Soto's entourage.

When all of the variables affecting travel are assembled and applied to the timing and distances covered by the De Soto army, several important issues become apparent. First, the army likely could not move together as a single unit because the groups moved at different speeds. Nonetheless, although the groups might have been incapable of moving as a unit, the army was not likely disorganized; all groups would have known the location of the others. Because this was a military expedition, Field Marshall Moscoso was in charge of maintaining order, including a vanguard, a main battle line, and a rear guard.[37] The knights always could move fastest and they may have had to wait on the slower-moving followers, which limited the daily distances covered by the entire entourage.

Gathering food would have consumed a considerable amount of time, particularly because De Soto had to be confident of his army's supply, as he had limited knowledge of the availability of food during the next legs of the march. De Soto always feared being ambushed, necessitating that his army take the time to hold porters and women hostage at least until the army could proceed to the next major town. Finally, De Soto and his army were almost frantic to find precious metals, which probably required that any Indian rumor about such booty had to be checked out by sending out scouts to reconnoiter, thus further slowing the army's forward progress.

Figure 14.3. Wild pigs stop near the Kennedy Space Center in Florida (Press Site in the Launch Complex 39 Area) on their daily foraging rounds. Not native to the environment, the pigs are believed to be descended from those brought to Florida by the early Spanish explorers. Without many predators other than humans, the pigs have flourished in the surrounding environs. Photo courtesy of National Aeronautics and Space Administration.

De Soto's main army would have sought the trails of least resistance, probably following existing ridge and terrace trails in low country and valley trails in rugged country. The main body of the army probably tried to avoid most wet lowland floodplain terrain unless it was inhabited and contained Indian villages, because of the canebrakes and because the army would have been forced to cross every tributary stream entering the main streams. Canebrakes would have made it very difficult to maintain control over the herd of pigs, and the numerous stream crossings and wetlands would have slowed all groups.

Preexisting major Indian trails and stream crossings would have provided the most convenient and best routes of connectivity between major Indian towns, while the side trails would have led to small isolated villages. While the main body of the army and the herd of pigs would have followed the main ridge and terrace trails after reaching the lower Coosa River valley, small groups of the mounted vanguard and foot soldiers from the main battle line likely would have taken time to investigate the side trails. Such side forays would have slowed the troops, spread them out over a wide area, and given the herd of swine time to catch up or at least to forage or rest. The hypothesis that the entourage may have been spread out both linearly and laterally during any given day's travel holds great importance for reconstructing events on the day of the battle of Mabila.

On any travel day, it is likely that the group began moving together in the morning, but as the day wore on, the groups would have become more and more spread out. Finally, at the end of the day, the groups would have come together for the night.

Based on geographic data obtained from analyzing the De Soto chronicles, archeologists' work around the Coosa, Tallapoosa, and Alabama rivers, analysis of USGS topographic maps, aerial photos, and digital imagery, and data provided in a host of scientific works involving the length of a Spanish league, our working group concluded that a Spanish league of 2.47 miles should be used to calculate De Soto's travel distances.[38] Travel distances on existing trails, however, would have been considerably different than linear distances between places, given the often difficult terrain and curvilinear trail system, a fact our working group considered in analyzing the topography along the routes.

Consequently, De Soto's army generally would have traveled about four to five leagues (10 to 13 miles) per day on days when stream crossings were particularly easy, when terrain was not particularly difficult, or on the first day of travel after a few days of rest. After the second or third day on the trail, the army generally stayed over in one place for a day or more, perhaps waiting for a few laggards to catch up, but mainly to rest and repair equipment, assemble stores of food, obtain new porters, and generally prepare for another leg of the march.

De Soto was very concerned about his army becoming too scattered, as evidenced by his efforts to wait on small groups lagging behind and his berating individuals who became lost from the column. Whether this resulted from his concern for individuals or his concern about the depletion of his army's strength is not as important to this discussion as the impact it had on the army's forward speed and associated layovers along the trail.

It will be useful here to reiterate the travel sequence from the town of Cosa, with an eye to these concerns. On August 20, 1540, De Soto's army departed the town of Cosa heading south to rendezvous with Captain Maldonado along the coast. De Soto would have traveled south-southwesterly following the northeast-southwest trending topography of the folded Appalachians. He may not have known precisely where to meet Maldonado, but he knew it was along the coast west of his previous winter camp at present-day Tallahassee. Hence, his troops had to move in a generally southerly or southwesterly direction.

Over the next twenty-eight days, the army moved in starts and stops through the Indian agricultural lands in and around the fertile valleys paralleling the Coosa and Tallapoosa rivers. By September 18, the army arrived in the province of Talisi in the lower Tallapoosa River valley lying between the provinces of Cosa and Tascalusa.[39] They stayed in the provincial capital of Talisi for seventeen days, taking advantage of the abundant Indian grain stores harvested during the recent summer, reconnoitering the area, and gaining intelligence about the trail ahead.

As summer days waned and fall approached, De Soto appeared anxious to head toward the coast, particularly since the expedition had failed to find the precious metals—only some freshwater pearls—that the participants sought. He also had learned that the next province of Tascalusa would be neither friendly nor helpful and, in fact, might present a major obstacle to the army's passing. Intelligence gathered while in Talisi about Tascalusa, the feared chief of Tascalusa province, provided reason for concern, but De Soto was using caution by keeping his troops together, avoiding large towns and bivouacking in the open as much as possible.

Until early October, the weather had consisted of typical warm fall days and cool nights, but apparently a fall storm brought enough precipitation to swell the streams and make crossings somewhat more difficult at the time of their stay in Talisi. On October 5, the army left Talisi and proceeded to the small river town of Casiste, and the following day (October 6) they came to the shabby river town of Caxa, located along the borders between the provinces of Talisi and Tascalusa where they turned more sharply westward, following the Alabama River.[40]

Three days were spent reaching the town of Atahachi and the army slept in the open in anticipation of possible hostilities. They entered Atahachi on October 10 and occupied the town for two days.

On October 12, the army left Atahachi for Mabila with chief Tascalusa and a contingent of his men as their guides. De Soto was anxious to reach Mabila, as Chief Tascalusa had convinced him that Mabila would provide much-needed porters for the army. According to Knight, there was a considerable distance of sparsely inhabited territory between Atahachi and Mabila, with only one river town of note, Piachi, located between.[41]

Leaving Atahachi, the army likely followed the topographic grain provided by the southwest-oriented terraces and, as indicated in the previous section, moved parallel to the Alabama River. On fairly level ground with a frequented trail and a strongly desired destination, the Spanish entourage perhaps could have covered ground at an above-average rate. From Atahachi, it took two days to reach Piachi, which was probably at a greater-than-average distance for the army to move in such a short time. After spending the night of October 12 somewhere midway to Piachi, the army reached Piachi on October 13. According to the chronicles, Piachi was located on a high river bluff overlooking the same river (the Alabama River) that flowed past Talisi.

For two days at Piachi (October 14 and 15) the army rested while rafts were built, perhaps because the distances covered in the previous two days of travel had been exceptionally long. And perhaps the group was waiting on the arrival of any laggards before crossing the river.

The army may have crossed the river on either October 15 or 16, but if it was the latter, the army should not have covered much distance on that day. The chief of Piachi contested the river crossing for some unknown reason, and there were casualties during the difficult crossing. At very best, the river crossing would likely have taken in excess of half a day.

On October 16, the army left the area around Piachi and camped in the bush that night. On October 17, they arrived at an unnamed palisaded town in a densely populated region, perhaps in the province of Mabila.[42] At this unnamed town, apparently chestnut bread was served by messengers from the town of Mabila, probably located a few miles away. This may indicate that upland chestnut trees were present at the Mabila site, but not necessarily at the site of the unnamed town, which may have been located on a low terrace devoid of nearby chestnut trees rather than a high terrace where chestnuts were available.

After only a few hours of travel on October 18, the vanguard of about forty cavalry, including De Soto, his guard of crossbowmen, a few footmen, some or all of the Indian porters, and two priests, arrived at the palisaded town of Mabila, located near a densely populated plain.[43]

With regard to our route hypotheses for this travel segment, it is important to recognize that several assumptions regarding the location of Atahachi are possible, each leading to very different conclusions about possible locations for Mabila. Our initial considerations of September 2006 (Route #1) worked from the assumption that Atahachi may have been located at the Charlotte Thompson Indian site near Montgomery. Our subsequent work of June 2007 (Route #2) assumed that Atahachi may have been located at or near Durant Bend. The reasons for these choices are archaeological. These two documented sites are the only ones on the east (south) bank of the Alabama River west of Montgomery that are large native villages with indigenous artifacts of the correct period, that possess a mound (as did Atahachi), and that have also yielded sixteenth-century Spanish artifacts. Both locations for Atahachi have been suggested before, for these reasons.

Our working group initially calculated all distances and sequences of travel along Route #1, encouraged by the "best-fit" scenario and by the widely accepted view that Atahachi must have been located at or near the Charlotte Thompson site. However, in an archaeological survey of February–March 2007, archaeologists found no Late Mississippian sites on the Orrville terrace, predicted by our route hypothesis as the area including Mabila.[44] Because of this report, working group members Wilson, Lineback, and Jones consulted with Vernon James Knight and chose to analyze a second promising route assuming an Atahachi location in Durant Bend, Route #2. This new route from Atahachi to Piachi and Mabila held promising possibilities, and led to an area with much greater archaeological evidence of a densely settled Indian population than Route #1.

It is important, however, to document both successful and unsuccessful efforts to establish De Soto's routes through Alabama to eliminate as much redundancy as possible in future research efforts. Consequently, descriptions of Routes #1 and #2 follow, as well as references to suggested routes by other researchers.

Our working group's Route #1 (Figure 14.4), with Talisi on the Tallapoosa River and Atahachi at the Charlotte Thompson site just west of Montgomery, parallels the present routes of the old Western Railroad of Alabama and U.S. Highway 80 on a terrace south of the Alabama River, some sixty feet above the river. This terrace route is fairly level, dry, and linear, meaning that it would have made for easy traveling, with few streams to cross, and would have been the most direct route westward. Route #1 leads toward the present-day town of Benton, located on the south side of the Alabama River to the south of Days Bend.[45]

Alternative Routes #1a, b, c, d, and e diverge from Benton at the southern end of Days Bend, on to Mabila generally to cross the Alabama River at five different bluff locations (Figure 14.4). Following the crossings of the river, however, all of these proposed alternative routes would begin to converge toward the Orrville terrace (Figure 14.5). However, as noted, preliminary archaeological survey of the Orrville terrace area during February–March 2007 by Ned Jenkins and Teresa Paglione indicated that there were few if any Late Mississippian sites in the predicted area.

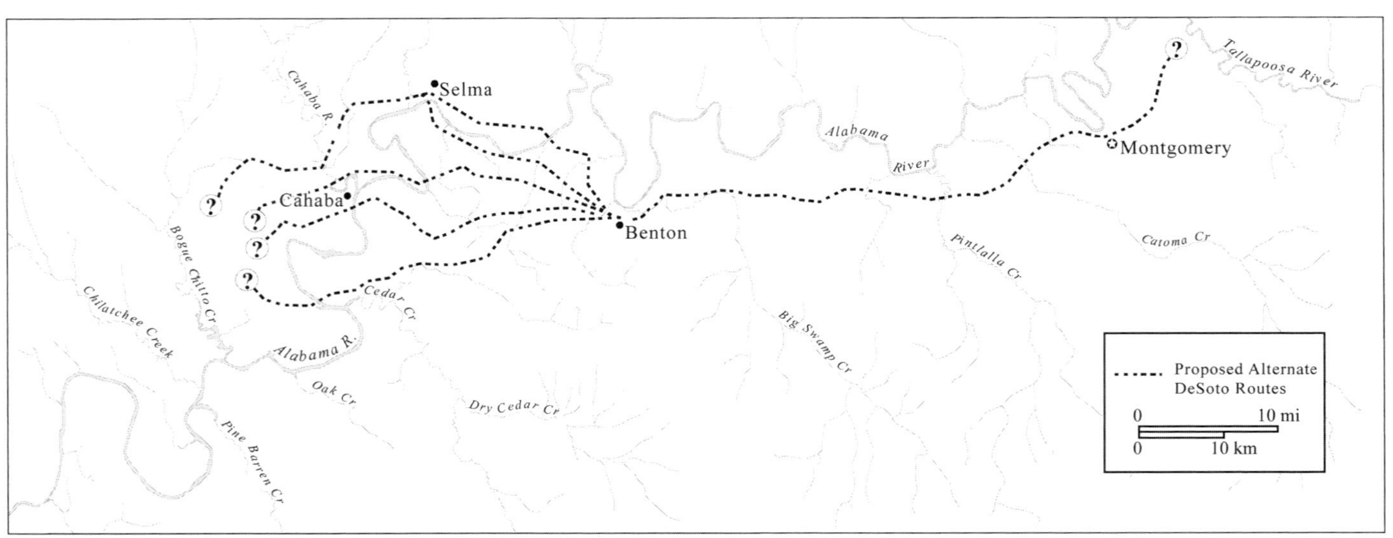

Figure 14.4. Proposed "Route 1" with subroutes, based on a location for Atahachi just west of present-day Montgomery.

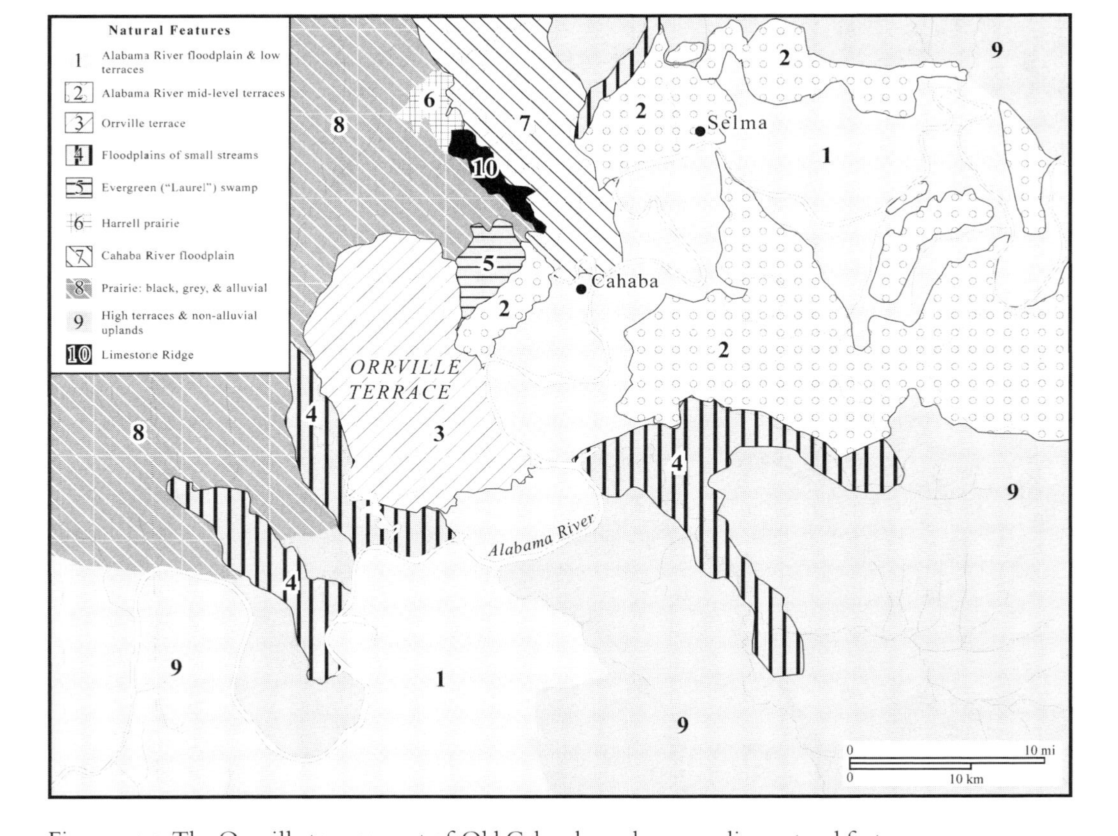

Figure 14.5. The Orrville terrace west of Old Cahawba and surrounding natural features.

Route #2 (Figure 14.6) assumes Atahachi to have been farther west on the Alabama River, at or near Durant Bend. Such a placement would result in De Soto's route being southwesterly after leaving Atahachi, generally paralleling the Alabama River and Alabama Highway 41 toward Camden. According to this proposed route, Piachi would have been located either northeast or southwest of the hills formed by the Ripley Cuesta (Elm Bluff or Ripley Bluff), due west of Richmond on the east side of the Alabama River.

Then, following Route #2a, after crossing the Alabama River, De Soto's army would have traveled west and then southwest to the area on the west bank of the river just south of Millers Ferry. Here occurs a host of previously recorded Mississippian sites, corresponding with the densely populated region described in the De Soto chronicles. According to Route #2a, Mabila might be found within an arc 10–12 miles south and west of Millers Ferry Dam.

After crossing the Alabama River, Route #2b diverges from Route #2a and would have led the army northward up the Bogue Chitto valley for a distance of 5–8 miles. A possible site for Mabila may also be found in this area.

Although we believe it holds somewhat less promise, a final possibility is Route #2c, which diverges from Route #2a by turning southward into Gees Bend. If Mabila is to be found in this area, it would likely occur along the interface between the river floodplain and the first terrace.

Additional scenarios are proposed for De Soto's route through Alabama by other researchers. Members of our working group have cursorily analyzed four other routes (proposed by Caleb Curren, Donald Sheppard, Bruce Trickey, and Andrew Holmes) and have found some points of validity in each.[46] In the end, however, our consensus was that each of these routes possesses at least one major flaw. As do the routes proposed in this document, these routes must stand on their own merits and must withstand the scrutiny of future researchers.

Summary and Conclusions

Members of the working group assigned to explore issues bearing on the physical environment analyzed many sources of information as they sought to identify De Soto's possible route through central Alabama toward the undiscovered town of Mabila. Group members examined the De Soto chronicles in light of old and new maps showing geology, soils, topographic features, Indian sites, and early wagon trails. The group researched aerial photos and

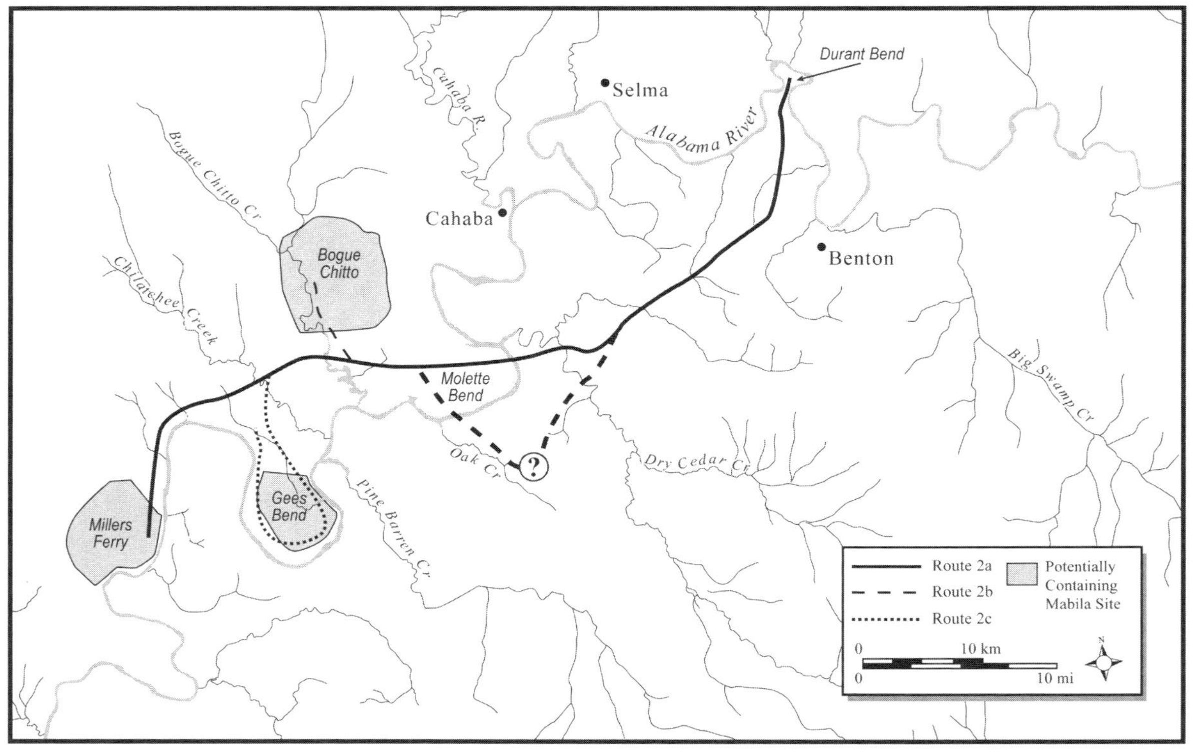

Figure 14.6. Proposed "Route 2" with subroutes, based on a location for Atahachi at or near Durant Bend.

satellite images as well, and used up-to-date archeological site location data in their analyses.

Although the members were not in total agreement, the majority agreed that De Soto's army's route would have been along the south side of the Alabama River from present-day Montgomery, following the trend of the terraces.

Under our Route #1 scenario, as De Soto reached the southern end of Days Bend near present-day Benton, Alabama, five possible subroutes diverge. Three continue generally westward to cross the Alabama River downstream of present-day Selma, the fourth crosses at Selma, and the fifth crosses upstream of Selma on the west side of Durant Bend. All but one of the five (the most southern) seem to converge toward the Mississippian Indian town at Cahaba after crossing the river.

All of these subroutes associated with Route #1, however, point to the Mabila site being located on or around the Orrville terrace, situated only a few miles west and northwest of Cahaba. Productive, alluvial soils cover the terrace and could have provided the quality and quantity of agricultural production and population density described in the chronicles for the area around the town of Mabila. Initial archaeological evidence, however, casts doubt on the Orrville terrace as a likely location for Mabila, despite our initial best-fit model.

Consequently, the principals of our working group refocused their study to include the possibility that Atahachi was located much farther west of Montgomery. They concluded that if the site for Atahachi were located as far west as Durant Bend, where an appropriate archaeological site is known to exist, then the army would have traveled along a series of trails southwestward generally paralleling the Alabama River and approximating Alabama Highway 41 toward Camden. This route would have provided reasonably level topography until the army encountered the hills of the Ripley Cuesta west and north of Pleasant Hill.

Assuming the river crossing at Piachi to have been located at one of two proposed bluff sites opposite Molette Bend, the army could have crossed to the lowland on the other side of the river. Using each of the alternate paths of Route #2, the location of Mabila would be (a) south and southwest of Millers Ferry Dam; (b) in the Bogue Chitto valley; or (c) within Gees Bend.

Clearly, the ultimate test of any of the De Soto route and Mabila site scenarios will depend on field archaeologists to find supporting evidence. In the 467 years that have passed, some of the evidence may have been removed or disturbed by construction and building projects so that today that evidence is underwater or otherwise covered or destroyed. Nonetheless, the total area affected by De Soto's passing through was very large and there should still be ample archaeological evidence awaiting discovery.

Notes

1. Clayton, Knight, and Moore, *De Soto Chronicles.*

2. C. Hudson, *Knights of Spain, Warriors of the Sun.*

3. Lacefield, *Lost Worlds in Alabama Rocks.*

4. C. Hudson, *Knights of Spain, Warriors of the Sun,* 205.

5. Geological Survey of Alabama, *Geologic Map of Alabama.*

6. Szabo, "Quaternary Geology, Alabama River Basin, Alabama."

7. Geological Survey of Alabama, *Gold Deposits in Alabama.*

8. Geological Survey of Alabama, *Geologic Map of Alabama.*

9. Moran et al., *Soil Survey of Dallas County, Alabama,* 3; Bartram, *Travels,* 252.

10. See the introduction to this chapter for the development of our ideas about this portion of the route.

11. Excerpts from their travel notes are included in Erhard Rostlund, "The Myth of a Natural Prairie Belt in Alabama."

12. Kniffen, Gregory, and Stokes, *The Historic Indian Tribes of Louisiana,* 106–09; Phillips, Ford, and Griffin, *Archaeological Survey in the Lower Mississippi Alluvial Valley,* 351–54.

13. Oviedo y Valdéz, *Historia General y Natural de las Indias,* 2: 174.

14. Translation of this passage is discussed elsewhere in "Issues of Translation," chapter 12, this volume.

15. Oviedo y Valdéz, *Historia General y Natural de las Indias,* 2: 174.

16. Translation of this passage is discussed elsewhere in "Issues of Translation," chapter 12, this volume.

17. Chapter 9, this volume.

18. Moran et al., *Soil Survey of Dallas County, Alabama.*

19. This recognition is revealed in letters published in the *Dallas Gazette* during 1853–59 and in the *Cahawba Press* in 1821 and 1825.

20. McGuire, "On the Prairies of Alabama."

21. Harper, *Forests of Alabama,* 156.

22. Maxwell, "Origin and Chronology of Alabama River Terraces."

23. An attempt to relocate these mounds by Ned J. Jenkins and Teresa Paglione during February 2007 found no mounds or other archaeological remains at the indicated location.

24. See postscript, this volume.

25. Bartram, *Travels;* Ballou's *Pictorial Drawing-Room Companion* 15 (1858): 197.

26. Chapter 9, this volume.

27. Clayton, Knight, and Moore, *De Soto Chronicles* 1: 294, 296.

28. C. Hudson, *Knights of Spain, Warriors of the Sun,* 248.

29. Sheppard, "American Conquest."

30. Vernon James Knight Jr., personal communication with the author, December 2006.

31. Trickey, "Mauvilla: A New Approach."

32. Curren, "Going South." This study appeared in 2007 following the Mabila conference and following the preparation of the map of Mabila locations (Figure I.1) in the introduction to the volume.

33. See chapter 4, this volume.

34. C. Hudson, *Knights of Spain, Warriors of the Sun,* 422.

35. Priestley, *The Luna Papers.*

36. C. Hudson, *Knights of Spain, Warriors of the Sun.*

37. Clayton, Knight, and Moore, *De Soto Chronicles,* 1: 57; Knight, personal communication.

38. Chardon, "The Linear League in North America"; Young and Glover, *Measure for Measure.*

39. For the lower Tallapoosa River location of Talisi, see chapter 15, this volume.

40. See chapter 5, this volume.

41. Ibid.

42. Ibid.

43. C. Hudson, *Knights of Spain, Warriors of the Sun,* 236; see chapter 5, this volume.

44. See postscript, this volume.

45. Conversely, any westward route located north of the Alabama River would have crossed very rugged terrain with several deep valleys and many small streams. Additionally, plotting the route based on the De Soto chronicles, any route on the north side of the river would appear contrary to the sequencing of the group's crossing of the Alabama River. Nonetheless, a minority of the working group felt that this route might have merit, although any location of Piachi at a Cahaba River crossing would not fit the "bluff" or river descriptions.

46. Curren, "Going South"; Sheppard, "American Conquest"; Trickey, "Mauvilla: A New Approach"; Baggett, "Archaeologist Says Clarke County Site May Be Lost De Soto Battleground."

15
The Archaeology of Mabila's Cultural Landscape

Gregory A. Waselkov, Linda Derry, and Ned J. Jenkins

The Archaeology Working Group (Linda Derry, Ned J. Jenkins, Vernon J. Knight Jr., Amanda L. Regnier, Craig T. Sheldon Jr., and Gregory A. Waselkov, convener) reexamined without preconceptions the entire range of archaeological evidence for the probable location of Mabila. Earlier hypotheses concerning the location of this Mississippian town and De Soto battle site have advocated places ranging across much of the southern half of Alabama (see introduction, this volume), so we have tried to view afresh the available data. We also have endeavored to retain a degree of separation between historical evidence and archaeological evidence. Most historical archaeologists no longer use artifacts merely to confirm what is written in documents or to search documents for what is found in archaeology. We prefer to treat these two forms of evidence, the documentary and the material, as complementary but distinct—to pay particular attention to areas where these independent sets of data seem to coincide or seem to contradict—and thereby extend the insights of each to achieve a better understanding of the past. We began our reexamination of the evidence at a broad scale and progressed toward an increasingly tighter focus, moving from a regional overview down to site-level resolution. Our goals were to circumscribe a search area, suggest effective search methods, and hypothesize probable archaeological characteristics of the site of Mabila.

Cultural Landscape at the Regional Level

Three decades ago George Lankford pointed out that the clusters of native towns described in the De Soto accounts should correlate with on-the-ground clusters of archaeological sites.[1] Vernon James Knight Jr. used this approach in the 1980s to map the distribution of Late Mississippian sites for the Alabama De Soto Commission, and similar maps have been generated for other sections of De Soto's presumed route through the Southeast.[2] All such efforts suffer from two deficiencies—incomplete site survey data and imprecise estimates of site occupation dates—both of which are serious but susceptible to amelioration. While portions of Alabama remain terra incognita from an archaeological standpoint, certain topographic settings have been systematically searched for sites. In particular, the banks of major rivers are among the most thoroughly surveyed areas of the state. In recent years, few large sites have been newly discovered in such locations, suggesting that most such sites are now known (although the histories of their occupation may not be entirely certain). So for segments of the De Soto route that correspond with major river courses, our survey data are probably acceptable, while for off-river segments our data are more or less inadequate. In the latter case, however, additional site survey offers a means of remediation. Regarding the second critical deficiency in our knowledge, the imprecision of site occupation date estimates, our collective knowledge of artifact chronologies has improved in recent years for the late prehistoric and Protohistoric periods, largely because of interest generated by the De Soto route debate. This refinement of key artifact dates, especially for native pottery types and sixteenth-century Spanish artifacts, has in turn enabled the compilation of ever more accurate site distribution maps.

Considered at the regional scale, our general understanding of mid-sixteenth-century settlement distribution has changed little since the early 1990s, despite the discovery of thousands more prehistoric sites in Alabama, Mississippi, Georgia, and Tennessee during the intervening fifteen years. To the northeast, research by Marvin Smith, David Hally, and colleagues has established the relationship of seven site clusters as elements of the Cosa paramount chiefdom, which reached from the Little Tennessee Valley southwest to the area of Childersburg, in the middle Coosa Valley.[3] And to the northwest, a cluster of sites in and around Clay County, Mississippi, north of Starkville, is considered the likely late prehistoric homeland of the Chickasaws, although the site of Chicasa itself has not yet been located. While Mississippi archaeologists debate individual site attributions to the Chackchiumas, Chickasaws, and Alibamus, the presence of Chickasaw towns in that general vicinity in 1540 seems certain.[4] Those two widely accepted points of reference on the De Soto route, one northeast and the other northwest of Mabila, help us evaluate social identities of site clusters in central and south Alabama (Figure 15.1).

Charles Hudson and colleagues correlated the province of Talisi with the cluster of Kymulga phase sites located east of the Coosa River in southern

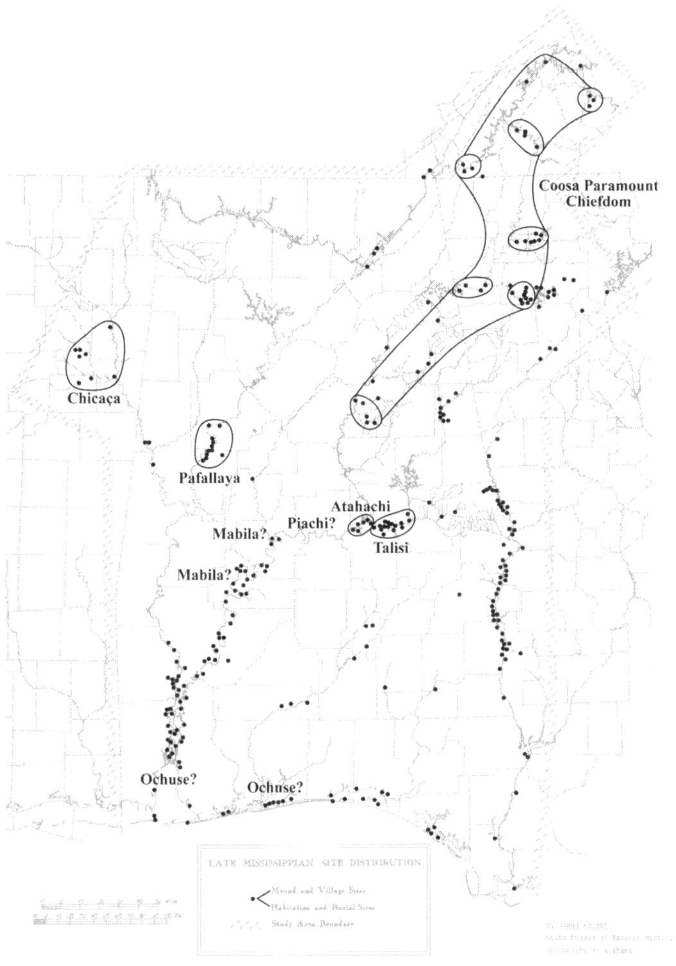

Figure 15.1. Locations of Late Mississippian archaeological site clusters attributed to Chicasa and the Cosa paramount chiefdom, proposed correlations of the Pafallaya, Talisi, and Atahachi chiefdoms with locations of Late Mississippian archaeological site clusters, and possible locations of Piachi, Mabila, and the Bay of Achuse. Cluster boundaries derived from Jay K. Johnson et al., *Protohistoric Chickasaw Settlement Patterns and the De Soto Route in Northeast Mississippi* (report submitted to the National Endowment for the Humanities by the Center for Archaeological Research, University of Mississippi, Oxford, 1991), and David J. Hally, Marvin T. Smith, and James B. Langford Jr., "The Archaeological Reality of de Soto's Coosa," in David Hurst Thomas, ed., *Columbian Consequences,* vol. 2: *Archaeological and Historical Perspectives on the Spanish Borderlands East* (Smithsonian Institution Press, Washington, D.C., 1989); base map data from Vernon J. Knight Jr., *A Summary of Alabama's De Soto Mapping Project and Project Bibliography,* De Soto Working Paper no. 9 (Alabama De Soto Commission, Tuscaloosa, 1988), 32.

Talladega County, Alabama, considered the southernmost site cluster within the Cosa paramount chiefdom.[5] We differ in suggesting that a more likely correlate of Talisi is the large site cluster on the lower Tallapoosa River. Without going into an extended discussion of our reasons, we simply point out that Talisi is described in the De Soto accounts as a province of river towns, not towns scattered along small streams.[6] Furthermore, the provinces of Talisi and Atahachi were separated by no more than one day's march; in contrast, the Kymulga sites had no neighboring cluster that near. Finally, the lower Coosa Valley—which, according to Hudson and colleagues, was traversed by De Soto's army between Cosa and Talisi—is extremely rugged terrain, with little floodplain adjacent to the river and negligible evidence of Late Mississippian inhabitants. An easier north-south route through this region existed farther east, along a drainage divide between the Coosa and upper Tallapoosa rivers, a route followed by a later invading army led by General Andrew Jackson in 1814.

To the west, a major site cluster on the lower Black Warrior River has been identified by virtually all modern scholars of the De Soto route as the most plausible location of the province of Apafalaya, based principally on the distance from the presumed location of the province of Chicasa.[7] Identifying the Apafalaya and Talisi site clusters helps constrain the plausible locations of intervening Atahachi, Piachi, and Mabila.

From this point onward, we make use of Craig Sheldon's update and reevaluation of archaeological site distributions in central and south Alabama (Figure 15.2; see chapter 9, this volume). This recent research has contributed nuance and detail to our understanding of De Soto–era settlement patterns and societal boundaries. While future surveys will certainly find additional sites, a comparison of the 1988 site distribution map and the new map suggests that the overall settlement pattern along the Alabama River is fairly well understood. Settlement during the Late Mississippian and Protohistoric was not even; there are real clusters and real gaps in site distribution. In some instances the site clusters and the intervening areas of sparse occupation along the river that were identified in 1988 are now clearer because the occupation dates of several key sites have been clarified or revised. While we can expect incremental improvements in our knowledge of the riverine sites, particularly by further refinements of chronology, our most pressing need is for thorough surveys of the very large areas on either side of the Alabama River, on smaller drainages and in the Black Belt, where many Late Mississippian and Protohistoric sites must await discovery.

To return to our discussion of the De Soto route, Ned Jenkins has recently posited a correlation between the Atahachi province of the De Soto chronicles

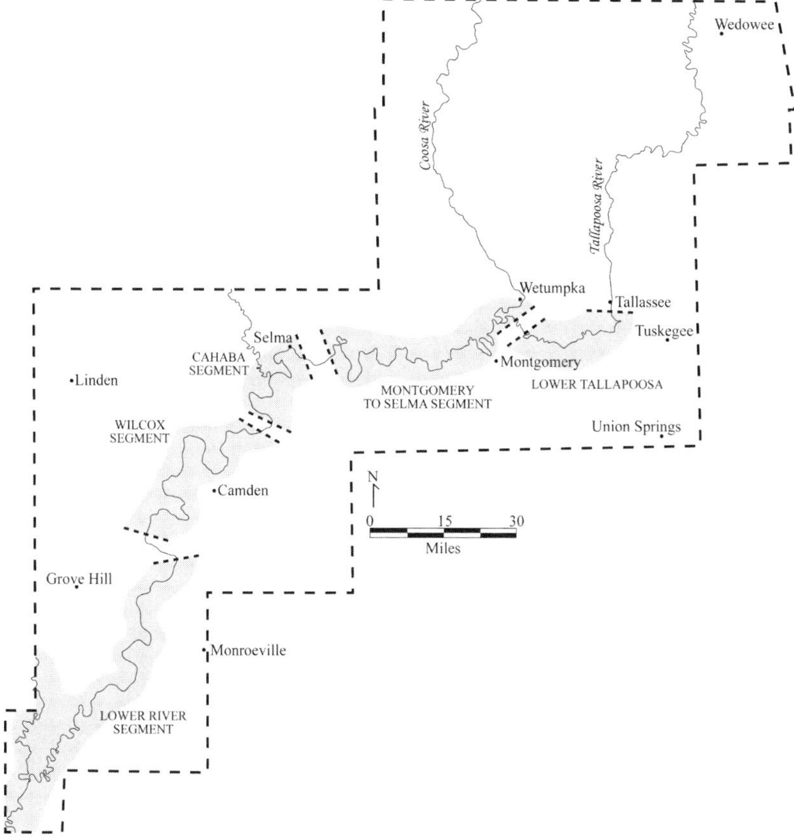

Figure 15.2. Segments of the study area in central and south Alabama defined by clusters or scarcity of Late Mississippian and Protohistoric archaeological sites, based on a 2006 review of Alabama State Site File data by Craig Sheldon (chapter 9, this volume). GIS map by Terance L. Winemiller, Auburn University Montgomery, and Sarah Mattics, University of South Alabama.

and the cluster of Big Eddy phase sites on the upper Alabama River, immediately west of the lower Tallapoosa cluster of Shine II phase sites identified as the province of Talisi.[8] According to Jenkins, the Moundville-related Big Eddy phase appeared along a twenty-five-mile stretch of the upper Alabama River around A.D. 1450 and for the next century retained a cultural identity distinct from the Lamar-related Shine II phase sites found along a thirty-five-mile stretch of the lower Tallapoosa River, with just six miles separating the two chiefdoms. Better definition of the Big Eddy phase ceramic assemblage should be a priority for future research in this area.

The next 104 river-miles (61 straight-line miles) downstream from the westernmost Big Eddy phase site, the Charlotte Thompson mounds, Craig Sheldon (chapter 9, this volume) considers to have been a genuine buffer zone during Late Mississippian times with very sparse occupation. Near the center of this zone, the Durant Bend site (with a ceramic assemblage nearly equally split between Moundville and Pensacola pottery types), a possible candidate for De Soto–era Piachi, has a mound along with evidence of sixteenth-century Spanish contact. Equally intriguing is the presence of a small group of Late Mississippian sites in the vicinity of the lower Cahaba River, including a fortified mound site upon which the early nineteenth-century town of Cahawba was built. Amanda Regnier (chapter 7, this volume) identifies these sites as some of the northernmost of the Pensacola culture, which had a major mound center at Bottle Creek far to the south in the middle of the Mobile-Tensaw Delta. A 1980s survey in the Black Belt west of Cahawba surprisingly revealed the existence of numerous small Protohistoric sites in an environment once thought unattractive to agricultural peoples.[9] Recent surveys in similar habitats in Mississippi have confirmed intensive occupation of the Black Belt during this time period.[10] Considering the spatial relationship of the lower Cahaba Valley sites to the posited locations of Cosa, Talisi, Atahachi, Apafalaya, and Chicasa, this vicinity is an important search area for the site of Mabila.

A very dense concentration of Late Mississippian and Protohistoric sites exists on the middle Alabama River, which Sheldon characterizes as the Wilcox cluster. Sites of the appropriate De Soto–era timeline have been identified as the Furman phase, characterized by a complex ceramic assemblage of diverse origins (though primarily attributable to the Pensacola series) that reflects long-term maintenance of intertown ethnic distinctions (see chapter 7, this volume).[11] This cluster grades into another large, dense concentration of late prehistoric and Protohistoric Pensacola-related sites along the lower Alabama River and in the Mobile-Tensaw Delta, a region favored by Caleb Curren and colleagues for the location of Mabila.[12] However, a location for Mabila in this cluster is too far from the locations we accept for Talisi, Apafalaya, and Chicasa provinces to be plausible, given the daily travel distances that De Soto's army was capable of covering (see chapter 14, this volume).

The foregoing considerations narrowed our search for Mabila to the upper-middle Alabama River vicinity, from Selma to the south end of the Wilcox cluster of sites. Far from this being a radical departure from earlier scholarship, in fact all previous De Soto route interpretations have placed Mabila somewhere on the Alabama Coastal Plain, and most on the Alabama River.

A location west of the Alabama River seems reasonably certain because the Spanish accounts mention only one crossing of a major river, at Piachi, between leaving Atahachi and arriving at Apafalaya.

We maintain that the best-known Late Mississippian archaeological site clusters in the state seem to equate with the "provinces" of the De Soto accounts, given modern refinements of site chronology. Considering research by other archaeologists in the Southeast, particularly in Georgia, on Mississippian chiefdoms and contemporaneous non-stratified societies, we have considerable confidence that these site clusters in Alabama represent discrete political entities. These societies all seem to have been geographically coherent and fairly small, although one of the great benefits of having the De Soto accounts is their descriptions of some higher-order political relationships among groups of simple chiefdoms allied to a paramount chief. Certainly Cosa was one such chief, and Tascalusa may have been another if his authority actually extended beyond Atahachi to Talisi, Piachi, and Mabila, something implied but not terribly clear from the Spanish accounts.

Looking beyond simple geographical proximity, sites within each cluster do tend to share a similar material culture, something that has become increasingly clear over the last few decades, particularly thanks to detailed ceramic analyses at sites along the Tallapoosa and Alabama rivers. Efforts by Regnier, Jenkins, and others to refine pottery chronologies take advantage of that artifact category's stylistic diversity, which reflects cultural sensitivity to spatial, social, and temporal differences. Commonalities in pottery have something to do with ethnic and other measures of social differentiation. As a consequence, distinct archaeological phases (Shine II and Big Eddy) have been proposed that materially distinguish the Talisi and Atahachi clusters (respectively), and recent progress in defining the Furman phase on the middle Alabama River probably describes the material culture of Mabila and related settlements of the 1540 dateline.

Therefore, we suggest a search area for the town of Mabila generally south of Selma, in the parts of Dallas, Wilcox, Perry, and Marengo counties west of the Alabama River. A reconnaissance-level survey, codirected in the field by Ned Jenkins and Teresa Paglione, began in a portion of this area in the spring of 2007 (see postscript, this volume).

Cultural Landscape at the Subregional Level

The descriptive details contained in the chronicles regarding De Soto's approach to Mabila and Mabila itself are reviewed in several chapters in this volume (see chapters 5, 6, and 12). For our purposes, we call attention especially to the estimates given in the accounts of Biedma and Elvas of the distance from Mabila to the Gulf of Mexico port of Achuse, of "up to forty leagues" and "six days' journey," respectively. These estimates have sparked intense debate among modern scholars and constitute the strongest evidence for Mabila's location on the lower Alabama River.[13]

No river is mentioned in connection with Mabila, and the encircling nature of the Spanish attack on the town seems to preclude a riverside location. Perhaps this is reading too much into the written accounts; if the Spaniards attacked a town fronting the river from all land sides, they might have considered it encircled. However, this ambiguity suggests to us the need to consider locations for Mabila away from the Alabama River.

As Knight has argued (chapter 5, this volume), Mabila was situated within a tight cluster of settlements, some of which were "enclosed" or palisaded like Mabila itself, and all of which were burned either during or after the battle. Biedma describes Mabila as situated in a plain, and accounts further suggest that the immediate landscape was open, with scattered houses, fields, roads, and a lake near the town. The vicinity must have been excellent agricultural land, since it sustained De Soto's army for twenty-seven or twenty-eight days, according to Biedma, and they left with two days' provisions.

One line of evidence that has not received much attention in previous attempts to locate Mabila is information available in accounts of central Alabama dating from the eighteenth and nineteenth centuries, several of which have important archaeological implications. One such reference is a map of French colonial Louisiana drafted by the Baron de Crenay, commandant of Mobile, in 1733 (Figure 15.3).[14]

Although Crenay's stay in Louisiana was short, from 1730 to 1733, his position of authority in Mobile gave him access to earlier French maps and travel accounts, as well as to colonists and Indians with firsthand experience in different regions.[15] While we do not know the precise sources of information upon which Crenay relied for his comprehensive map of the colony, his detailed plotting of river bends and other important landmarks on the Alabama River portion is the most accurate found on any French colonial map. In fact, his plot of the Alabama River appeared on many later derivative maps, copied with little or no improvement for years. French military officers routinely traveled the length of the river from Mobile to Fort Toulouse every spring and fall, and their observations probably provided Crenay with river course data. But some place-names must have been solicited from Indians, and a likely source were the Mobilian Indians, who occupied a town bordering the Mobile-Tensaw Delta during that era, from which rowers were hired to propel French military supply boats up- and downstream.[16]

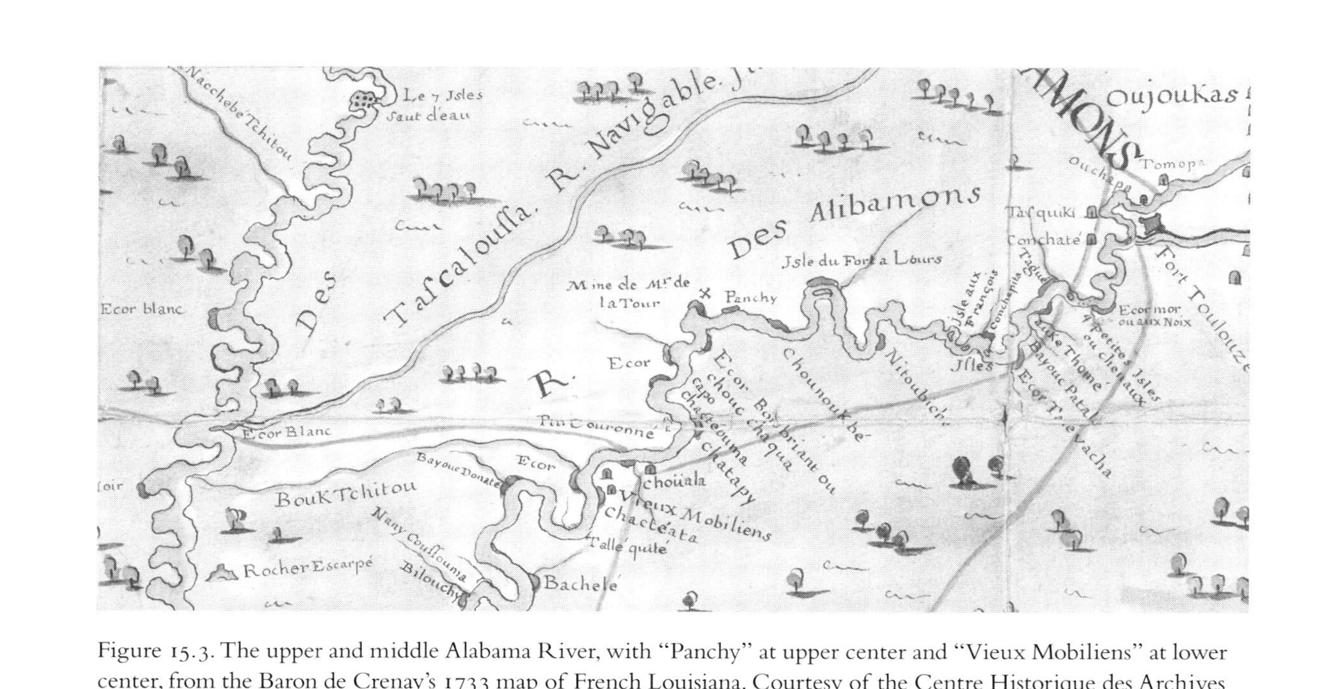

Figure 15.3. The upper and middle Alabama River, with "Panchy" at upper center and "Vieux Mobiliens" at lower center, from the Baron de Crenay's 1733 map of French Louisiana. Courtesy of the Centre Historique des Archives Nationales, Paris.

Though the relationship is not certain, most scholars assume that the Mobilians whom the French encountered along the lower Alabama River in 1700 were descendants of the Mabila Indians who had battled De Soto in 1540. Ceramic similarities spanning the gap bolster that assumption, with lip notching on eighteenth-century Mobilian bowls reminiscent of rim treatment on sixteenth-century Furman phase vessels, both part of the Pensacola pottery tradition. Two notations on Baron de Crenay's 1733 map have sparked interest among De Soto route interpreters. The place-name "Panchy," next to one of Crenay's symbols for bluff (or cut-bank) on the north bank of the upper Alabama River, just east of present-day Selma, could be a nasalized corruption of Piachi, where De Soto's army crossed the river a few days before the battle of Mabila. And, most intriguingly, "Vieux Mobiliens" appears near two village symbols in a bend east of the river. (Cruder manuscript maps of Louisiana drawn by the Delisles around 1700 carry a similar legend, "Vielle Movilla," east of the Alabama River.)[17] French usage of "vieux" implies that this location was the former home of the Mobilians, their old town site. Crenay's placement of the village symbol nearest the phrase corresponds closely with the location of the Liddell archaeological site, 1WX1, an Alabama River phase occupation that may well have been a village site of the Mobilians during the late sixteenth and early seventeenth centuries. Crenay's "Vieux Mobiliens" is not the Mabila of De Soto. However, as the later history of the Mobilians demonstrates, many Indian peoples did move their town sites, particularly in the wake of De Soto. The presence of Mobilians in this area of the middle Alabama River some decades after the destruction of Mabila in 1540 may be a clue to the general whereabouts of that battle site.

Early nineteenth-century written accounts of central Alabama also contain information of archaeological interest. Descriptions of natural vegetation prior to large-scale cotton agriculture and accounts of archaeological discoveries at Cahawba both offer heretofore overlooked insights that may be relevant in the search for Mabila.

The modern landscape of the Black Belt of central Alabama differs radically from that of the mid-sixteenth century, before the creation in the antebellum era of vast monoculture cotton plantations that destroyed most of the region's distinctive forest and prairie habitats. At the very beginning of that massive reworking of the Black Belt environment, in 1817, the federal government established a land office at Cahawba, a newly created town at the confluence of the Cahaba and Alabama rivers. Thomas Freeman, surveyor for the General Land Office, platted the area for settlement and, in the process, created a record of the vegetation before plowing and widespread deforestation. A resurvey of this area in 1845 by James H. Weakley documents the changes wrought by three decades of American settlement, but also adds some additional information on upland habitats that were slowest to be altered by plow agriculture.[18]

Together these surveys offer a view of a mixed forest and patchy prairie landscape created by alkaline soils formed atop chalk geological formations and impacted in still undefined ways by thousands of years of occupation by native Americans. The surveys help us locate former locations of naturally open, level, or gently rolling plains, perhaps like the one Mabila reportedly occupied. A study of General Land Office records for Montgomery County northeast of Cahawba found that the prairies shown on these early survey plats had fewer than ten trees per acre and that these were the same areas that early explorers described as "plains," "savannahs," "native fields," and "prairies."[19]

The English naturalist Philip Henry Gosse spent part of 1838 in Dallas County, east of Cahawba, and left this description of the Black Belt prairies.

> There are in this neighbourhood many prairies,—not the boundless prairies of the West, resembling an ocean solidified and changed to land, but little ones, varying in extent from an acre to a square mile. They are generally so well defined, that the woods environ them on every side like an abrupt wall, and one can hardly be persuaded that these prairies are not clearings made with the axe of the settler. The soil is a very tough and hard clay, and in wet weather the roads running through them are almost impassable, so adhesive are they to the feet of the passengers and the wheels of carriages. . . . There are prairies not very far distant of many miles in extent; the residents on which suffer greatly in dry seasons from the scarcity of water, a want that in a hot climate is peculiarly felt. There are no springs in the prairies, and the inhabitants depend on the rain-water, which, owing to the tenacity of the soil, does not soak into the ground, but accumulates in the hollows until evaporated by the sun. These hollows are sometimes large, and in winter, and during rainy seasons, form permanent ponds of considerable magnitude, but the water is of course very unwholesome.[20]

Until the introduction of artesian wells in the 1840s, a lack of springs and other sources of drinking water limited human settlement away from the major rivers to the vicinities of ponds characteristic of the Black Belt prairies.[21] Perhaps the lake near the stockade of Mabila (mentioned by the Gentleman of Elvas) was such a feature, rather than a borrow pit or permanent natural pond or lake.

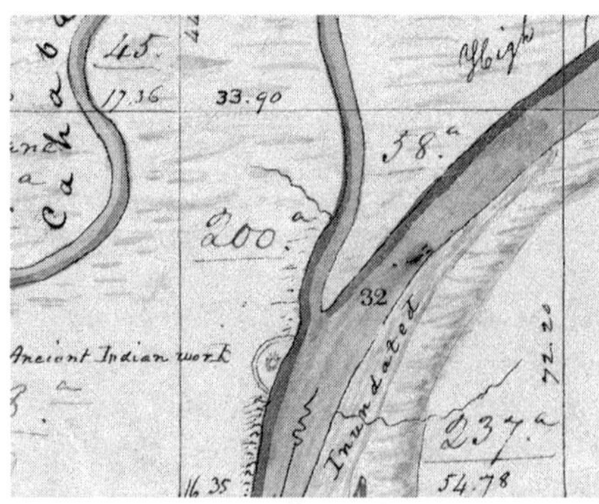

Figure 15.4. Detail of Thomas Freeman's 1817 survey plat showing an "Ancient Indian work" at the confluence of the Cahaba and Alabama rivers. General Land Office Records, National Archives.

Historical sources of this kind also contain hints of archaeological remains that may relate to the Mabila chiefdom. In 1817 surveyor Thomas Freeman recorded a group of five mounds on the northeast side of Bogue Chitto Creek (Township 15N, Range 8E, Sections 16 and 21)[22] and an "old Indian village" (Township 16N, Range 11E, Section 8) on the south bank of the Alabama River within what is now Selmont. Most intriguing is his sketch of an "Ancient Indian work" at the junction of the Alabama and Cahaba rivers (Township 16N, Range 10E, Section 32), where the town of Cahawba, Alabama's first state capital, was established a year later. There Freeman drew a mound inside a semicircle, a configuration recognizable as a defensive ditch or moat, since confirmed by archaeological excavation, that encloses the Furman phase Mississippian village site of 1DS32 (Figure 15.4).[23]

Rather than destroying these aboriginal features, Governor William Wyatt Bibb's plan for Cahawba embraced them. In 1818 the relic Indian landscape was incorporated into the town plan of Alabama's first capital as its centerpiece. A grand vista up the main street terminated at the Indian earthworks; an impressive statehouse would sit atop the mound and the sixteenth-century moat would circumscribe the statehouse grounds. Because of a lack of funds, a temporary building suitable for accommodating the General Assembly was constructed nearby, and the five acres within the earthworks were "reserved" from development for the time being. Before funds for a permanent statehouse materialized, however, the seat of state government moved to Tuscaloosa in 1826. Over the years Governor Bibb's grand landscape plan was forgotten and development encroached on the ancient site.[24]

On August 12, 1859, the *Dallas Gazette* reported that "human bones and brass buttons were found in abundance last year, near the Baptist Church, by the railroad hands, when they were working on the great excavation [for a railroad bed]." The editors of that newspaper speculated that the remains, which were found about two hundred yards outside the moat surrounding the sixteenth-century village, must have long predated the founding of the town in 1818. But by that time the earthworks had already been leveled. Linda Derry's searches in the *Dallas Gazette* turned up a speech delivered in August 1858 from the cowcatcher of a new locomotive parked at the center point of Freeman's 1817 "Ancient Indian work."

> Here, within the circle of our vision, those who have preceded us have selected different places on which to erect works of importance to the societies under their care. Some military race of men, whose name even has fled the eager research of the historian, have here erected their palisades and sunk their deep ditches around a fortress skillfully placed, so as to command this splendid sweep of the Alabama River. . . . Their high mounds, thrown up, perhaps, as memorials of some great event, and used for sacrificial altars, and for the resting places of their dead, have all given away before the appropriating energy of this generation. We have gathered their labors and heaped them together in the embankment for the Railroad, where their curious pottery, their crude implements of warfare, and their bones mingle in a singular tribute to the superiority of their successors in the dominion of this soil.[25]

Documentary research also led to the discovery of remnants of the Furman phase mound. An 1860 newspaper account described construction of a warehouse where the mound once stood.[26] During the Civil War this warehouse was converted into a prison for captured Union soldiers. One soldier's account describes the earthen warehouse floor being two to three feet higher than the surrounding ground.[27] Modern test excavations have confirmed that the lower two feet of mound deposits were left to form the floor of the warehouse.[28]

So, in the final analysis, we now know that a sizable, fortified, mid-sixteenth-century Indian town was located at the mouth of the Cahaba River, and that much of that site is intact beneath the remains of the early nineteenth-century town of Cahawba. While its riverside location seems to make this site an unlikely candidate for Mabila itself, that possibility deserves further investigation. Alternatively, these remains could be the unnamed palisaded town where the Spaniards received chestnut bread the night before the battle of Mabila.

The Site of Mabila

What will the site of Mabila look like? Biedma describes Mabila as "small"; judging from the size range of palisaded Mississippian towns known elsewhere in the Southeast, "small" probably means two to five acres in extent. The site belonged to a tight cluster of towns, at least one other of which was palisaded, within a circumference of perhaps twelve or fifteen miles. Numerous farmsteads were present between the larger towns, and archaeological remains of these should be evident.

As summarized by Jenkins (chapter 6, this volume), we expect archaeological evidence of a Mississippian-style daubed palisade with towers and gates (some or all perhaps burned); a central interior plaza; a substantial number of burned houses of Late Mississippian style with evidence of habitation at the time of their destruction (not abandoned prior to burning, as was more commonly the case); and demolished structures outside the palisade, torn down prior to the battle. Lots of daub (fired clay) will be present throughout the site, particularly on house floors and along the palisade (and in the dry moat, if there was one).

Previous efforts to pinpoint De Soto's route and Indian towns along that route have relied heavily on the distribution of sixteenth-century Spanish artifacts across the Southeast. Since Spanish artifacts were presumably lost and abandoned by the army all along its line of march, and other artifacts were given to Indians as presents, traded to them, and stolen by them, one would certainly expect the army's route to correspond at least in a general way with finds of Spanish artifacts of the appropriate period. However, three decades of research based on that line of reasoning have demonstrated that sixteenth-century Spanish artifacts have turned up in a great many more places than could possibly all fall along the De Soto route. For route reconstruction, these data have some severe limitations—particularly their easy portability, their potential for reuse, and their tendency to be deposited in native graves—that make them unreliable at the level of site survey. Their absence at sites along a proposed route would certainly raise doubts about the validity of that route hypothesis, but the presence of Spanish goods is not sufficient evidence of a route location.

On the other hand, the different nature of Spanish-Indian interaction at Mabila creates a very different set of expectations regarding the kinds and quantities of artifacts anticipated at the site of the battle (see chapter 8, this volume). The violent and rapid end to the town's existence, the presence of much of the Spaniards' baggage inside Mabila during its destruction, and the limited abilities of the army to retrieve and repair what was lost or damaged during the battle all must have contributed to the loss or abandonment of considerable quantities of Spanish goods. The army's long stay in the vicinity after the battle undoubtedly involved efforts to salvage weapons and other valuables in the burned house ruins of Mabila, and native survivors of the battle may have made similar efforts. But the success rate of their efforts at salvage, while difficult for us to evaluate, is not likely to have approached the level of systematic recovery attained by modern archaeologists. Thus we anticipate finding a lot of broken and fire-damaged Spanish artifacts at the site of Mabila. These ought to include damaged and melted brass and iron artifacts of all sorts, crossbow bolt tips, links of iron chains, links of chain mail, and iron horse gear. In particular, the loss of horses during the battle may have made excess harness and saddle parts redundant and subject to recycling or discard.

The artifact assemblage left by the Indians at Mabila would of course include a wide range of domestic items destroyed when the town was burned. If our current understanding of Late Mississippian material culture is correct, this would include Furman phase ceramics and a great many small triangular stone arrow points used by the thousands of warriors said to have participated in the battle. Treatment of the remains of the twenty-some Spaniards and the very numerous Indians who were killed during the battle or died later from their wounds is not specified in written accounts. Presumably De Soto's Spanish dead would have been given Christian burials, but whether the Indians were left unburied or were disposed of in some fashion is unknown. We expect many human remains to be found inside the burned houses.

Most of central Alabama has been plowed, much of it intensively for a century or more. Therefore, the site of Mabila is very probably plowed, although perhaps now in pasture or trees. Some locations in the Alabama River floodplain have received substantial quantities of flood-borne soil deposits in historic times, which potentially could bury sites at considerable depths. The site of Mabila, however, may be located well away from the river in a place with little or no modern flood-borne deposition. Consequently, we suspect that Mabila's archaeological evidence will be visible either on the ground surface, if presently plowed, or just beneath the surface. Site features are likely limited to the top few feet, and intensive plowing will almost certainly have degraded the upper parts of features.

What survey and excavation methods will lead to identification of the Mabila site? An initial reconnaissance survey (see postscript, this volume) has already begun to test various search methods. An informant survey of the entire search area, focusing on farmers as well as collectors, is an efficient means of acquiring existing knowledge of sites known to locals. Analysis of existing collections can help eliminate sites that are too early and too late, while perhaps providing leads to the existence of Mississippian sites of appropriate date. Remote sensing will probably be limited in value because of heavy present-day ground cover, at least until a likely site is found. One exception might be early aerial photos (ca. 1930s–1950s), taken before the reversion of many large fields to forest. Aerial photos of plowed fields containing fortified Mississippian sites have often revealed evidence of moats, stockades, mounds, and large semisubterranean structures.

Based on our knowledge of Late Mississippian settlement preferences, the survey should target sandy/silty loam soils and prairies. Field surveys should draw on the recommendations of project geographers regarding high-probability locations. Initial efforts should employ non-probabilistic reconnaissance at first, because Mabila existed as part of a tight cluster of contemporary Mississippian settlements. A reconnaissance survey is likely to find a cluster, while perhaps missing many individual sites. Once Mississippian sites are found, adjacent locations should be surveyed more intensively for additional sites in a possible cluster.

How will we know when we find Mabila? Sheldon (chapter 9, this volume) outlines necessary and sufficient conditions that will be helpful in its identification. Once candidate archaeological sites have been located by surveys, test excavations should focus on daub concentrations and the remains of burned structures. A wide array of remote sensing (including ground-penetrating radar, magnetometry, earth conductivity, and resistivity) can be deployed to evaluate individual sites that meet initial expectations. Remote sensing should be able to locate anticipated features of Mabila, such as a palisade, burned structures, and numerous burials. These noninvasive methods can then help direct further test excavations and eventually full-scale excavations to fully investigate likely candidates for Mabila. A definitive, widely accepted identification of Mabila will probably depend on the recovery of Spanish weaponry along with the remains of Indians inside burned structures within a palisaded town site.

Notes

1. Lankford, "A New Look at DeSoto's Route through Alabama."

2. Knight, *A Summary of Alabama's De Soto Mapping Project and Project Bibliography;* for similar maps, see Hally, Smith, and Langford, "The Archaeological Reality of de Soto's Coosa"; Johnson et al., *Protohistoric Chickasaw Settlement Patterns.*

3. Hally, Smith, and Langford, "The Archaeological Reality of de Soto's Coosa"; M. Smith, *Coosa,* 2, 86.

4. Johnson et al., *Protohistoric Chickasaw Settlement Patterns;* Morgan, "Historic Period Chickasaw Indians" and *The Mississippi De Soto Trail Mapping Project.*

5. DePratter, Hudson, and T. Smith, "The Hernando de Soto Expedition," 121;

C. Hudson, *Knights of Spain, Warriors of the Sun,* 228–29; cf. J. Hudson, *Looking for De Soto.*

6. C. Hudson, *Critique of Little and Curren's Reconstruction of De Soto's Route through Alabama* and *De Soto in Alabama;* cf. Little and Curren, "Conquest Archaeology of Alabama," 178–79. The archaeological rationale for an alternative route of march is presented in Jenkins, "Tracing the Origins of the Early Creeks."

7. Hudson, Smith, and DePratter, "The Hernando de Soto Expedition," 183–91; C. Hudson, *Knights of Spain, Warriors of the Sun,* 250–60; Curren, *The Route of the Soto Army through Alabama;* Little and Curren, "Conquest Archaeology of Alabama," 184–85.

8. Ned J. Jenkins, "Tracing the Early Origins of the Creeks: The Moundville Connection" (unpublished manuscript in possession of the author, 2006).

9. Patterson, "Archaeological Reconnaissance of Selected Areas."

10. Rafferty, "Prehistoric Settlement Patterning."

11. Regnier, "Late Mississippian Coalescence in the Alabama River Valley."

12. Curren, *The Route of the Soto Army through Alabama* and *Archeology in the Mauvila Chiefdom;* Little and Curren, "Conquest Archaeology of Alabama"; Trickey, "Mauvilla: A New Approach"; Little and Harrelson, *Pine Log Creek.*

13. For the estimate by Biedma, see chapter 1, this volume; for that of Elvas, see Elvas, "The Account by a Gentleman from Elvas," 1: 104; for the debate over the distance, see Trickey, "Mauvilla: A New Approach."

14. Crenay, "Carte de partie de la Louisianne."

15. Galloway, *Practicing Ethnohistory,* 149–51, 160.

16. Waselkov and Gums, *Plantation Archaeology at Rivière aux Chiens,* 17.

17. See Galloway, *Choctaw Genesis,* 245–49.

18. Original Survey Plat, Township 16 N, Range 10 East, surveyed by Thomas Freeman, 1817 (DM ID #65643), and Dependent Resurvey Plat, Township 16 North, Range 10 East, surveyed by James W. Weakley, 1845 (DM ID #65647), Land District of Alabama, St. Stephens Meridian, General Land Office Records, Bureau of Land Management, Washington, D.C.

19. Rankin and Davis, "Woody Vegetation"; John A. Barone, "Historical Presence and Distribution of Prairies."

20. Gosse, *Letters from Alabama,* 75, 80–81.

21. Cobb, "Alabama's Wonder of the Earth"; Schmitz, Wax, and Peacock, "Water-Resource Controls on Human Habitation."

22. Recent archaeological survey by Ned Jenkins and Teresa Paglione found no site in this location, suggesting the possibility that Freeman misplaced the site on his map.

23. Chase, "An Archeological Evaluation at Old Cahaba, Alabama"; Knight, *Archaeological Test Excavations;* Martin, "Archaeological Investigations of an Aboriginal Defensive Ditch," 60–74.

24. Derry, "Southern Town Plans," 22, 25.

25. "Inauguration of the 'Cahaba,'" *Dallas Gazette,* August 20, 1858.

26. "Cahaba Warehouse," *Dallas Gazette,* July 12, 1860; Dallas County Probate Office, Deed Books 1862: T-400.

27. Hawes, *Cahaba,* 19.

28. Derry, "Southern Town Plans," 19–20.

Postscript

Vernon James Knight Jr.

I want to emphasize that the main purpose of this book is to espouse a method rather than to reach any hard conclusions. My colleagues and I are convinced that the method advocated, which combines expertise from several disciplines in an open dialogue about evidence and procedures, is the most productive way to proceed to a solution of the Mabila mystery. Nonetheless, chapters 14 and 15 already tout specific search areas for Mabila. These reconstructions, like all others that precede them, are best phrased as working hypotheses. Because they have fairly obvious on-the-ground consequences, such ideas immediately suggest field testing to validate, invalidate, or refine them, and that, too, is part of the process.

In the weeks following the September 2006 conference, members of the group were highly motivated to organize an archaeological survey. For readers who may be unfamiliar with archaeological fieldwork, there is far more to it than might at first be imagined. A few casual field trips will not do. To do it the right way requires considerable resources and institutional commitment, not to mention time, and most of us have employment that keeps us otherwise quite busy. Once the commitment is made, all areas surveyed have to be accurately plotted on digital maps. All artifacts found, whether or not they have anything to do with De Soto, have to be washed, cataloged, and analyzed. All archaeological sites found, whether or not they have anything to do with De Soto, have to be officially registered in the Alabama State Site File and the Alabama Online Cultural Resources Database.[1] And the results have to be reported in some accessible way so that interested parties can learn from them. At the present time, there is no ready source of grant funds for such an undertaking.

With all of this firmly in mind, conference participants Linda Derry, Ned Jenkins, Mason McGowin, Craig Sheldon, and Vernon James Knight, together with USDA–Natural Resources Conservation Service archaeologist Teresa Paglione, convened at the John Tyler Morgan house in Selma on January 5, 2007, to discuss the organization of a survey. Professor Sheldon took the lead in proposing a survey design that would combine the resources of the Alabama Historical Commission, the USDA–Natural Resources Conservation Service, The University of Alabama, Auburn University in Montgomery, and volunteers from the central Alabama area including conference participant Mason McGowin. The proposed survey would be conducted during weekends in February and March 2007 and would be codirected by Ned Jenkins and Teresa Paglione, both veteran archaeological surveyors familiar with the area. Their superiors at the Alabama Historical Commission and the USDA–Natural Resources Conservation Service agreed to release them for the survey and, in the case of the USDA–Natural Resources Conservation Service, to provide a much-needed field vehicle. The survey would begin within the northern part of the search area suggested by the archaeologists during the Mabila conference, and one specifically favored by the "physical environment" working group, namely the Orrville terrace landform and adjacent environs immediately west of Cahaba.[2] Elsewhere, specific candidates for the location of the town of Piachi would also be visited and tested.

Having adopted this survey design, the survey was set in motion, and at this writing the initial season's fieldwork is complete. Numerous new archaeological sites were recorded, and two candidate sites for De Soto–period occupation were subjected to intensive testing, one by The University of Alabama and the other by Troy State University.

One survey result can already be reported: no good candidate for Mabila was found. Although this sounds like a negative result, in reality it is actually quite helpful to be able to rule out some candidate areas and therefore to make positive progress in narrowing down the possibilities. It is extremely important not to jump to conclusions, and there is still a great deal to do. With these results in hand, the group will evaluate which route hypotheses, if any, might now be reasonably set aside and which deserve new scrutiny. As reported in chapter 14, authors Wilson, Jones, and Lineback have already made some progress along these lines. In this manner, the group will make recommendations as to new areas that merit coverage in the next survey attempt.

Notes

1. See chapter 9, this volume.
2. See "Route 1," chapter 14, this volume.

Bibliography

Adorno, Rolena. "Álvar Nuñez Cabeza de Vaca, Relación." Paper presented at "Counter-Conquests and Captivities," Early Ibero/Anglo Americanist Summit, Tucson, May 16–19, 2002. http://www.mith2.umd.edu/summit/Proceedings/Adorno2.htm (accessed July 3, 2007).

Allan, Jean. "Moundville's Fortifications." Paper presented at the 56th Annual Meeting of the Southeastern Archaeological Conference, Pensacola, Fla., 1999.

Altman, Ida. "An Official's Report: The Hernández de Biedma Account." In Patricia K. Galloway, ed., *The Hernando de Soto Expedition: History, Historiography, and "Discovery" in the Southeast,* 3–10. University of Nebraska Press, Lincoln, 1997.

Ambrose, Stephen E. *Undaunted Courage: Meriwether Lewis, Thomas Jefferson, and the Opening of the American West.* Simon and Schuster, New York, 1997.

Anderson, David G. *The Savannah River Chiefdoms.* University of Alabama Press, Tuscaloosa, 1994.

———. "Stability and Change in Chiefdom-Level Societies: An Examination of Mississippian Political Evolution on the South Atlantic Slope." In Mark Williams and Gary Shapiro, eds., *Lamar Archaeology: Mississippian Chiefdoms in the Deep South,* 187–213. University of Alabama Press, Tuscaloosa, 1990.

Argote, Alonso de. Testimony regarding military service of Hernán Suárez de Maçuelas, Mexico City, March 9, 1557. Archivo General de Indias, Seville, Patronato 77, No. 1, Ramo 1.

Arnold, J. Barto III, and Robert S. Weddle. *The Nautical Archeology of Padre Island: The Spanish Shipwrecks of 1554.* Academic Press, New York, 1978.

Arnold, J. Barto III, David R. Watson, and Donald H. Keith. "The Padre Island Crossbows." *Historical Archaeology* 29, no. 2 (1995): 4–19.

Atchison, Robert B. Jr. *Archaeological Survey in the Lower Cahaba Drainage.* Report of Investigations 53. Office of Archaeological Research, University of Alabama, Tuscaloosa, 1987.

Avalle-Arce, Juan Bautista de. "Gonzalo Fernández Oviedo y Valdés: Chronicler of the Indies." In Patricia K. Galloway, ed., *The Hernando de Soto Expedition: History, Historiography, and "Discovery" in the Southeast,* 369–79. University of Nebraska Press, Lincoln, 1997.

Avellaneda, Ignacio. *Los Sobrevivientes de La Florida: The Survivors of the De Soto Expedition.* Ed. Bruce S. Chappell. Research Publications of the P. K. Yonge Library of Florida History, no. 2. University of Florida Libraries, Gainesville, 1990.

Badger, R. Reid, and Lawrence A. Clayton, eds. *Alabama and the Borderlands: From Prehistory to Statehood.* University of Alabama Press, University, 1985.

Baggett, Connie. "Archaeologist Says Clarke County Site May Be Lost De Soto Battleground." *Mobile Press-Register,* May 24, 2007.

Ball, Timothy H. *A Glance into the Great South-East, or Clarke County, Alabama, and Its Surroundings: From 1540–1877.* 1882; repr. Willo Publishing Company, Tuscaloosa, Alabama, 1962.

Barone, John A. "Historical Presence and Distribution of Prairies in the Black Belt of Mississippi and Alabama." *Castanea* 10, no. 3 (2005): 170–83.

Bartram, William. *The Travels of William Bartram, Naturalist Edition.* Ed. Francis Harper. Yale University Press, New Haven, 1958; repr., University of Georgia Press, Athens, 1998.

Beck, Robin A., David G. Moore, and Christopher B. Rodning. "Identifying Fort San Juan: A Sixteenth-Century Spanish Occupation at the Berry Site, North Carolina." *Southeastern Archaeology* 25, no. 1 (2006): 65–77.

Biedma, Luys Hernández de. "Relación de la Isla de La Florida." *Colleción de Documentos Ineditos Relativos al Descubrimiento, Conquista, y Colonización de las Posesiones Españolas en América y Occeanía,* vol. 3. Imprenta Manuel B. de Quiros, Madrid, 1865.

———. "Relation of the Island of Florida." In Lawrence A. Clayton, Vernon James Knight Jr., and Edward C. Moore, eds., *The De Soto Chronicles: The Expedition of Hernando de Soto to North America in 1539–1543,* 1: 221–46. University of Alabama Press, Tuscaloosa, 1993.

Blake, Alan. *A Proposed Route for the Hernando de Soto Expedition, Based on Physiography and Geology, Part III—Chiaha to Mabila, Part IV—Mabila to the Mississippi River.* De Soto Working Paper no. 6. Alabama De Soto Commission, Tuscaloosa, 1988.

Blakely, Robert L., ed. *The King Site: Continuity and Contact in Sixteenth-Century Georgia.* University of Georgia Press, Athens, 1988.

Blitz, John H. *Ancient Chiefdoms of the Tombigbee.* University of Alabama Press, Tuscaloosa, 1993.

———. "Mississippian Chiefdoms and the Fission-Fusion Process." *American Antiquity* 64 (1999): 577–92.

Boston, Barbara. "The 'De Soto Map.'" *Mid-America* 23 (1941): 236–50.

Bourne, Edward G., ed. *Narratives of the Career of Hernando de Soto.* 2 vols. Allerton Book Company, New York, 1904; repr. ed. 1922.

Brain, Jeffrey P. "The Archaeology of the De Soto Expedition." In R. Badger and L. Clayton, eds., *Alabama and the Borderlands: From Prehistory to Statehood,* 96–107. University of Alabama Press, Tuscaloosa, 1985.

———. "Artifacts of the Adelantado." *Conference on Historic Site Archaeology Papers 1973* 8 (1975): 129–38.

———. "Introduction: Update of De Soto Studies since the United States De Soto Expedition Commission Report." In John R. Swanton, *Final Report of the United States De Soto Expedition Commission,* xi–lxxii. Reprinted with an introduction by Jeffrey P. Brain. Smithsonian Institution Press, Washington, D.C., 1985.

———. *Tunica Treasure.* Peabody Museum, Harvard University, Cambridge, Mass., 1979.

Brain, Jeffrey P., and Charles R. Ewen. "Introduction to Bibliography of De Soto Studies." In Lawrence A. Clayton, Vernon James Knight Jr., and Edward C. Moore, eds., *The De Soto Chronicles: The Expedition of Hernando de Soto to North America in 1539–1543,* 2: 507–14. University of Alabama Press, Tuscaloosa, 1993.

Brame, James Y. "De Soto in Alabama, 1540." *Arrow Points* 13 (1928): 33–39, 47–54, 63–71.

Brannon, Peter A. "The Route of De Soto from Cosa to Mauvilla." *Arrow Points* 2, no. 1 (1921): 3–8.

Bratten, John R. "Buried Secrets: Analyses in the Emanuel Point Ship Laboratory." *Gulf South Historical Review* 14, no. 1 (1998): 31–45.

Brose, David S. "Modeling Site Locations." In David S. Brose, Ned J. Jenkins, and Russell Weisman, eds., *Cultural Resources Reconnaissance Study of the Black Warrior–Tombigbee System Corridor, Alabama.* Vol. 1: *Archaeology,* 157–206. Center for Archaeological Studies, University of South Alabama, Mobile, 1983.

Brown, Ian W., ed. *Bottle Creek: A Pensacola Culture Site in South Alabama.* University of Alabama Press, Tuscaloosa, 2003.

Brown, Ian W., and Richard S. Fuller, eds. "Bottle Creek Research: Working Papers on the Bottle Creek Site (1Ba2), Baldwin County, Alabama." *Journal of Alabama Archaeology* 39, nos. 1–2 (1993): 1–169.

Brown, M. L. *Firearms in Colonial America: The Impact on History and Technology, 1492–1792.* Smithsonian Institution Press, Washington, D.C., 1980.

Bullen, Ripley P. "De Soto's Ucita and the Terra Ceia Site." *Florida Historical Quarterly* 30, no. 4 (1952): 317–23.

Castro, Daniel. *Another Face of Empire: Bartolomé de las Casas, Indigenous Rights, and Ecclesiastical Imperialism.* Duke University Press, Durham, 2007.

Chang Rodríguez, Raquel, ed. Introduction to *Beyond Books and Borders: Garcilaso de la Vega and La Florida del Inca.* Bucknell University Press, Lewisburg, Penn., 2006.

Chardon, Roland. "The Linear League in North America." *Annals, Association of American Geographers* 70, no. 2 (1980): 129–53.

Chase, David W. "An Archeological Evaluation at Old Cahaba, Alabama." Manuscript on file at Old Cahawba Archaeological Park, Selma, Ala., 1982.

———. "A Brief Synopsis of Central Alabama Prehistory." Paper presented at the winter meeting of the Alabama Archaeological Society, 1979. Copy on file at the Archaeology Laboratory, Auburn University–Montgomery, Ala.

———. "Prehistoric Pottery of Central Alabama." *Journal of Alabama Archaeology* 44, nos. 1–2 (1998): 52–98.

Clayton, Lawrence A., Vernon James Knight Jr., and Edward C. Moore, eds. *The De Soto Chronicles: The Expedition of Hernando de Soto to North America in 1539–1543.* 2 vols. University of Alabama Press, Tuscaloosa, 1993.

Cobb, Nicholas H. Jr. "Alabama's Wonder of the Earth." *Alabama Review* 49 (1996): 163–80.

Cottier, John W. *Archaeological Salvage Investigations in the Miller's Ferry Lock and Dam Reservoir.* Report to the National Park Service, Department of Anthropology, University of Alabama, 1968. Copy on file at Office of Archaeological Research, University of Alabama, Tuscaloosa.

Cottier, John W., and Craig T. Sheldon. *Interim Report of an Archaeological Survey of U.S. Army Corps of Engineers Properties along the Alabama River.* Report submitted to the U.S. Army Corps of Engineers, Mobile District. Department of Sociology and Anthropology, Auburn University, Auburn, Ala., 1980. Copy on file at Department of Sociology and Anthropology, Auburn University.

Crenay, Baron de. "Carte de partie de la Louisianne qui comprend le Cours du Missisipy depuis son embouchure jusques aux Arcansas, celuy des rivieres de la Mobille depuis la Baye jusqu au Fort de Toulouse: Des Pascagoula de la riviere aux Perles. Le tout relevé par estime Fait a la Mobille Mars 1733 par les soins et recherches de Monsieur le Baron de Crenay Lieutenant pour le Roy et commandant a la Mobille." Dépot des Fortifications des Colonies, no. 1A, Louisiane. Centre Historique des Archives Nationales, Archives Nationales, Paris.

Cumming, William P., and Louis De Vorsey Jr. *The Southeast in Early Maps.* 3rd ed. University of North Carolina Press, Chapel Hill, 1998.

Curren, Caleb B. "The Alabama River Phase: A Review." In Caleb B. Curren Jr., ed., *Archaeology in Southwestern Alabama: A Collection of Papers,* 95–102. Alabama-Tombigbee Regional Commission, Camden, Ala., 1982.

———. *Archaeology in the Mauvila Chiefdom.* Mobile Historic Development Commission, Mobile, Alabama, 1992.

———. "Going South towards the Sea: A Radical New Look at Soto's Route through South Alabama." *Archeology Ink, an Online Research Journal,* June 2007, 1–19. http://archeologyink.com/Going%20South.htm (accessed September 7, 2007).

———. *The Protohistoric Period in Central Alabama.* Alabama-Tombigbee Regional Commission, Camden, Ala., 1984.

———. *The Route of the Soto Army through Alabama.* De Soto Working Paper no. 3. Alabama De Soto Commission, Tuscaloosa, 1987.

Curren, Caleb, and Janet Lloyd. *Archaeological Survey in Southwest Alabama, 1984–1987.* Technical Report 1. Alabama-Tombigbee Regional Commission, Camden, Ala., 1987.

Damp, Jonathan E. "The Summer of 1540: Archaeology of the Battle of Hawikku." *Archaeology Southwest* 19, no. 1 (2005): 4–5.

Deagan, Kathleen A. *Artifacts of the Spanish Colonies of Florida and the Caribbean, 1500–1800. Vol. 1: Ceramics, Glassware, and Beads.* Smithsonian Institution Press, Washington, D.C., 1987.

———. *Artifacts of the Spanish Colonies of Florida and the Caribbean, 1500–1800. Vol. 2: Portable Personal Possessions.* Smithsonian Institution Press, Washington, D.C., 2002.

Deagan, Kathleen A., and José María Cruxent. *Columbus's Outpost among the Taínos: Spain and America at La Isabela, 1493–1498.* Yale University Press, New Haven, 2002.

DeJarnette, David L., and Asael T. Hansen. *The Archaeology of the Childersburg Site, Alabama.* Notes in Anthropology 6. Florida State University, Tallahassee, 1960.

DePratter, Chester B., and Marvin T. Smith. "Sixteenth-Century European Trade in the Southeastern United States: Evidence from the Juan Pardo Expeditions (1566–1568)." In Henry F. Dobyns, ed., *Spanish Colonial Frontier Research,* 67–78. Spanish Borderlands Research no. 1. Center for Anthropological Studies, Albuquerque, N.M., 1980.

DePratter, Chester B., Charles Hudson, and Marvin T. Smith. "The Hernando de Soto Expedition: From Chiaha to Mabila." In R. Badger and L. Clayton, eds., *Alabama and the Borderlands: From Prehistory to Statehood*, 108–27. University of Alabama Press, University, 1985.

Derry, Linda. "Southern Town Plans, Storytelling, and Historical Archaeology." In Amy L. Young, ed., *Archaeology of Southern Urban Landscapes,* 14–29. University of Alabama Press, Tuscaloosa, 2000.

De Vorsey, Louis Jr. "Silent Witnesses: Native American Maps." *Georgia Review* 46 (Winter 1992): 709–26.

Diamond, Jared M. *Guns, Germs and Steel: The Fates of Human Societies*. W. W. Norton, New York, 1997.

Dickens, Roy S. Jr. "Archaeology in the Jones Bluff Reservoir of Central Alabama." *Journal of Alabama Archaeology* 17, no. 1 (1971): 1–114.

Dickens, Roy S. Jr., Edward L. Prince, and Joseph L. Benthall. *Archaeological Investigations in the Jones Bluff Reservoir of the Alabama River.* Report submitted to the National Park Service, Department of Anthropology, University of Alabama, Tuscaloosa, 1968. Copy on file at Office of Archaeological Research, University of Alabama, Tuscaloosa.

Dowling, Lee. "*La Florida del Inca:* Garcilaso's Literary Sources." In Patricia K. Galloway, ed., *The Hernando de Soto Expedition: History, Historiography, and "Discovery" in the Southeast,* 98–154. University of Nebraska Press, Lincoln, 1997.

Duncan, David Ewing. *Hernando de Soto: A Savage Quest in the Americas*. Crown, New York, 1995.

Durand, José. "La Biblioteca del Inca." *Nueva Revista de Filologia Hispanica* 2 (1948): 239–64.

Elbl, Martin Malcolm, and Ivana Elbl. "The Gentleman of Elvas and His Publisher." In Patricia K. Galloway, ed., *The Hernando de Soto Expedition: History, Historiography, and "Discovery" in the Southeast,* 45–97. University of Nebraska Press, Lincoln, 1997.

Elvas, Fidalgo de. "The Account by a Gentleman from Elvas." In Lawrence A. Clayton, Vernon James Knight Jr., and Edward C. Moore, eds., *The De Soto Chronicles: The Expedition of Hernando de Soto to North America in 1539–1543,* 1: 19–219. University of Alabama Press, Tuscaloosa, 1993.

———. *Relaçam Verdadeira dos Trabalhos que ho Gouernador don Fernando de Souto e Certos Fidalgos Portugueses Passarom no Descobrimento da Prouincia da Frolida [Florida]. Agora Nouamente Feita per hun Fidalgo D Eluas*. Ed. André de Burgos. Evora, Portugal, 1557. Reprinted in facsimile in James A. Robertson, ed. and trans., *True Relation of the Hardships Suffered by Governor Fernando de Soto & Certain Portuguese Gentlemen during the Discovery of the Province of Florida:*

Now Newly Set Forth by a Gentleman of Elvas. Publications of the Florida State Historical Society, no. 11. De Land, and Yale University Press, New Haven, 1932.

Ewen, Charles R. "Anhaica: Discovery of Hernando de Soto's 1539–1540 Winter Camp." In Jerald T. Milanich and Susan Milbrath, eds., *First Encounters: Spanish Explorations in the Caribbean and the United States, 1492–1570,* 110–18. University Presses of Florida, Gainesville, 1989.

Ewen, Charles R., and John H. Hann. *Hernando de Soto among the Apalachees: The Archaeology of the First Winter Encampment.* University Presses of Florida, Gainesville, 1998.

Fleming, Victor K. Jr. "Historic Aboriginal Occupation of the Guntersville Basin, Alabama." Master's thesis, Department of Anthropology, University of Alabama, Tuscaloosa, 1976.

Flint, Richard, and Shirley Cushing Flint, eds. *The Coronado Expedition: From the Distance of 460 Years.* University of New Mexico Press, Albuquerque, 2003.

Freide, Juan, and Benjamin Keen, eds. and contribs. *Bartolomé de las Casas in History: Toward an Understanding of the Man and His Work.* University of Northern Illinois Press, DeKalb, 1971.

Fuller, Richard S. "The Bear Point Phase of the Pensacola Variant: The Protohistoric Period in Southwest Alabama." *Florida Anthropologist* 38, nos. 1–2 (1985): 150–55.

———. "Out of the Moundville Shadow: The Origin and Evolution of Pensacola Culture." In Ian W. Brown, ed., *Bottle Creek: A Pensacola Culture Site in South Alabama,* 27–62. University of Alabama Press, Tuscaloosa, 2003.

Fuller, Richard S., and Ian W. Brown. *The Mound Island Project: An Archaeological Survey in the Mobile-Tensaw Delta.* Bulletin 19. Alabama Museum of Natural History, Tuscaloosa, 1998.

Fuller, Richard S., Diane E. Silvia, and N. R. Stowe. *The Forks Project: An Investigation of the Late Prehistoric–Early Historic Transition in the Alabama-Tombigbee Confluence Basin.* Report submitted to the Alabama Historical Commission, University of South Alabama, Mobile, 1984. Copy on file at the Center for Archaeological Studies, University of South Alabama, Mobile.

Fundaburk, Emma L. *Southeastern Indians, Life Portraits: A Catalogue of Pictures, 1564–1860.* Scarecrow Reprint Corporation, Metuchen, N.J., 1969.

Galloway, Patricia. "The Archaeology of Ethnohistorical Narrative." In David Hurst Thomas, ed., *Columbian Consequences.* Vol. 3: *The Spanish Borderlands in Pan-American Perspective,* 453–69. Smithsonian Institution Press, Washington, D.C., 1991.

———. *Choctaw Genesis, 1500–1700.* University of Nebraska Press, Lincoln, 1995.

———. "*La Florida*'s Route through Maps: From Soto to the Present." In Raquel

Chang-Rodríguez, ed., *Beyond Books and Borders: Garcilaso de la Vega and La Florida del Inca,* 75–90. Bucknell University Press, Lewisburg, Pa., 2006.

——, ed. *The Hernando de Soto Expedition: History, Historiography, and "Discovery" in the Southeast.* University of Nebraska Press, Lincoln, 1997.

——. "The Incestuous Soto Narratives." In Patricia K. Galloway, ed., *The Hernando de Soto Expedition: History, Historiography, and "Discovery" in the Southeast,* 11–44. University of Nebraska Press, Lincoln, 1997.

——. *Practicing Ethnohistory: Mining Archives, Hearing Testimony, Constructing Narrative.* University of Nebraska Press, Lincoln, 2006.

——. "Review of *The Juan Pardo Expeditions: Exploration of the Carolinas and Tennessee, 1566–1568,* by Charles Hudson." *Journal of Southern History* 58 (1992): 327–28.

Garcilaso de la Vega, El Inca. *La Florida del Inca.* Ed. Sylvia L. Hinton. Cronicas de América 22. Heroes, Madrid, 1986.

——. "La Florida." In Lawrence A. Clayton, Vernon James Knight Jr., and Edward C. Moore, eds., *The De Soto Chronicles: The Expedition of Hernando de Soto to North America in 1539–1543,* 2: 25–559. University of Alabama Press, Tuscaloosa, 1993.

Gatschet, Albert S. *A Migration Legend of the Creek Indians, with a Linguistic, Historic, and Ethnohistoric Introduction.* Vol. 1. Ed. D. G. Brinton. Brinton's Library of Aboriginal American Literature, No. IV. Philadelphia, 1884.

Geological Survey of Alabama. *Geologic Map of Alabama.* Special Map 220. Geological Survey of Alabama, University, 1988.

——. *Gold Deposits in Alabama.* Bulletin 136. Geological Survey of Alabama, University, 1989.

Gosse, Philip Henry. *Letters from Alabama, (U.S.) Chiefly Relating to Natural History.* Morgan and Chase, London, 1859.

Graham, Bennett. *A Preliminary Report of Salvage Archaeology in the Claiborne Lock and Dam Reservoir.* Report submitted to the National Park Service, Department of Anthropology, University of Alabama, 1967. Copy on file at Office of Archaeological Research, University of Alabama, Tuscaloosa.

Greenblatt, Stephen. *Marvelous Possessions: The Wonder of the New World.* University of Chicago Press, Chicago, 1991.

Gutierrez, Gustavo, O.P. *Las Casas: In Search of the Poor of Jesus Christ.* Trans. Robert R. Barr. Orbis Books, Maryknoll, N.Y., 1993.

Hally, David J. "Archaeology and Settlement Plan of the King Site." In Robert L. Blakeley, ed. *The King Site: Continuity and Contact in Sixteenth-Century Georgia,* 1–16. University of Georgia Press, Athens, 1988.

——. "An Overview of Lamar Culture." In David J. Hally, ed., *Ocmulgee Archaeology, 1936–1986,* 144–74. University of Georgia Press, Athens, 1994.

———. "The Settlement Patterns of Mississippian Chiefdoms in Northern Georgia." In Brian R. Billman and Gary M. Feinman, eds., *Settlement Pattern Studies in the Americas: Fifty Years since Virú,* 96–115. Smithsonian Institution Press, Washington, D.C., 1999.

———. "The Territorial Size of Mississippian Chiefdoms." In James A. Stoltman, ed., *Archaeology of Eastern North America: Papers in Honor of Stephen Williams,* 143–68. Archaeological Report no. 25. Mississippi Department of Archives and History, Jackson, 1993.

Hally, David J., Marvin T. Smith, and James B. Langford Jr. "The Archaeological Reality of de Soto's Coosa." In David Hurst Thomas, ed., *Columbian Consequences.* Vol. 2: *Archaeological and Historical Perspectives on the Spanish Borderlands East,* 121–38. Smithsonian Institution Press, Washington, D.C., 1989.

Hamilton, Peter J., and Thomas M. Owen, eds. "Topographic Notes and Observations on the Alabama River, August, 1814, by Major Howell Tatum." *Transactions of the Alabama Historical Society, 1897–1898.* Montgomery, 1898.

Hammerstedt, Scott W. "Late Woodland and Mississippian Settlement of the Black Warrior Valley: A Preliminary Assessment." *Journal of Alabama Archaeology* 47, no. 1 (2001): 1–45.

Hanke, Lewis. *The Spanish Struggle for Justice in the Conquest of America.* Southern Methodist University Press, Dallas, 2002.

Harper, Roland M. *Forests of Alabama.* Monograph 10. Geological Survey of Alabama, University, 1943.

Hartman, Gayle Harrison. "Where Coronado Camped." *Archaeology Southwest* 19, no. 1 (2005): 12.

Hawes, Jesse. *Cahaba: A Story of Captive Boys in Blue.* Burr Printing House, New York, 1888.

Hemming, John. *The Conquest of the Incas.* Harcourt, Brace, Jovanovich, New York, 1970.

Henige, David. "The Context, Content, and Credibility of *La Florida de Ynca.*" *The Americas* 43 (1986): 1–23.

———. "Proxy Data, Historical Method, and the de Soto Expedition." In Gloria A. Young and Michael P. Hoffman, eds., *The Expedition of Hernando de Soto West of the Mississippi, 1541–1543,* 155–72. University of Arkansas Press, Fayetteville, 1993.

———. "'So Unbelievable It Has to Be True': Inca Garcilaso in Two Worlds." In Patricia K. Galloway, ed., *The Hernando de Soto Expedition: History, Historiography, and "Discovery" in the Southeast,* 155–77. University of Nebraska Press, Lincoln, 1997.

Higginbotham, Jay. "The Battle of Mauvila, Causes and Consequences." *Gulf Coast Historical Review* 6 (1991): 19–33.

——. *Mauvila.* A. B. Bahr and Company, Mobile, Ala., 2000.

Hoffman, Paul E. "Discovery and Early Cartography in the Northern Gulf Coast." In Alfred E. Lemmon, John T. Magill, and Jason R. Wiese, eds. *Charting Louisiana: Five Hundred Years of Maps,* 7–39. Historic New Orleans Collection, New Orleans, 2003.

——. "Introduction: The De Soto Expedition, a Cultural Crossroads." In Lawrence A. Clayton, Vernon James Knight Jr., and Edward C. Moore, eds., *The De Soto Chronicles: The Expedition of Hernando de Soto to North America in 1539–1543,* 1: 1–17. University of Alabama Press, Tuscaloosa, 1993.

——. *A New Andalucia and a Way to the Orient: The American Southeast during the Sixteenth Century.* Louisiana State University Press, Baton Rouge, 1990.

Holmes, Nicholas H. Jr., and Charles E. Bates. "A Comparison of Trace Elements Present in Two Iron Objects from a Mississippian Site in South Alabama with Those of Spanish, French, and American Irons." *Journal of Alabama Archaeology* 42, no. 2 (1996): 154–71.

Hubbert, Charles M., and Richard A. Wright. "Lalakala, the Fishing Place: Another Way of Seeing the Archaeology of the Rother L. Harris Reservoir." *Journal of Alabama Archaeology* 33, no. 1 (1987): 1–109.

Hudson, Charles. *Critique of Little and Curren's Reconstruction of De Soto's Route through Alabama.* De Soto Working Paper no. 12. Alabama De Soto Commission, Tuscaloosa, 1988.

——. *De Soto in Alabama.* De Soto Working Paper no. 10. Alabama De Soto Commission, Tuscaloosa, 1989.

——. *Knights of Spain, Warriors of the Sun: Hernando de Soto and the South's Ancient Chiefdoms.* University of Georgia Press, Athens, 1997.

——. *The Juan Pardo Expeditions: Exploration of the Carolinas and Tennessee, 1566–1568.* 2nd ed. University of Alabama Press, Tuscaloosa, 2005.

Hudson, Charles, Marvin T. Smith, and Chester B. DePratter. "The Hernando de Soto Expedition: From Mabila to the Mississippi River." In David H. Dye and Cheryl Anne Cox, eds., *Towns and Temples along the Mississippi,* 183–91. University of Alabama Press, Tuscaloosa, 1990.

Hudson, Charles, Marvin T. Smith, Chester B. DePratter, and Emilia Kelley. "The Tristán de Luna Expedition, 1559–1561." *Southeastern Archaeology* 81 (1989): 31–45.

Hudson, Joyce Rockwood. *Looking for De Soto: A Search through the South for the Spaniard's Trail.* University of Georgia Press, Athens, 1993.

Jackson, Harvey H. III. *Rivers of History: Life on the Coosa, Tallapoosa, Cahaba, and Alabama.* University of Alabama Press, Tuscaloosa, 1995.

Jenkins, Ned J. *Archaeology of the Gainesville Lake Area: Synthesis.* Report of Investigations 23, Office of Archaeological Research. University of Alabama, Tuscaloosa, 1982.

———. "Ceramic Summary Descriptions and Chronology." In David S. Brose, Ned J. Jenkins, and Russell Weisman, eds., *Cultural Resources Reconnaissance Study of the Black Warrior–Tombigbee System Corridor, Alabama.* Vol. 1: *Archaeology,* 73–156. Center for Archaeological Studies, University of South Alabama, Mobile, 1983.

———. "Early Creek Origins: The Moundville Connection." Paper presented at the 61st annual meeting of the Southeastern Archaeological Conference, St. Louis, Mo., 2004.

———. "Tracing the Origins of the Early Creeks, 1050–1700 CE." In Robbie Ethridge and Sheri Shuck-Hall, *Mapping the Mississippian Shatter Zone: The Colonial Indian Slave Trade and Regional Instability in the American South.* University of Nebraska Press, Lincoln, forthcoming.

Jenkins, Ned J., and Richard A. Krause. *The Tombigbee Watershed in Southeastern Prehistory.* University of Alabama Press, Tuscaloosa, 1986.

Jenkins, Ned J., and Teresa A. Paglione. *An Archaeological Reconnaissance of the Lower Alabama River.* Report submitted to the Alabama Historical Commission. Department of Sociology, Auburn University–Montgomery, 1980.

Jenkins, Ned J., Cailup B. Curren, and Mark F. DeLeon. *Archaeological Site Survey of the Demopolis and Gainesville Lake Navigation Channels and Additional Construction Areas.* Report submitted to the U.S. National Park Service by the Department of Anthropology, University of Alabama, 1975.

Jeter, Marvin D. *An Archaeological Survey in the Area East of Selma, Alabama, 1971–1972.* Report of the Selma Area Archaeological Project, University of Alabama at Birmingham, 1973.

Johnson, Jay K., G. R. Lehmann, James R. Atkinson, Susan L. Scott, and A. Shea. *Protohistoric Chickasaw Settlement Patterns and the De Soto Route in Northeast Mississippi.* Report submitted to the National Endowment for the Humanities by the Center for Archaeological Research, University of Mississippi, Oxford, 1991.

Jones, Douglas E., ed. *The Highway Route of the De Soto Trail in Alabama.* De Soto Working Paper no. 8. Alabama De Soto Commission, Tuscaloosa, 1988.

Kelso, William M. *Jamestown: The Buried Truth.* University of Virginia Press, Charlottesville, 2006.

———. *Jamestown Rediscovery I: Search for 1607 James Fort.* Association for the Preservation of Virginia Antiquities, Jamestown, Va., 1995.

Kniffen, Fred B., Hiram F. Gregory, and George A. Stokes. *The Historic Indian Tribes of Louisiana: From 1542 to the Present.* Louisiana State University Press, Baton Rouge, 1987.

Knight, Vernon J. Jr. "Aboriginal Pottery of the Coosa and Tallapoosa River Valleys." *Journal of Alabama Archaeology* 44, nos. 1–2 (1998): 188–207.

———. *Archaeological Test Excavations at the Site of Old Cahawba, March, 1987.* Report submitted to the Alabama De Soto Commission, the Alabama Historical Commission, and the Alabama State Museum of Natural History, Tuscaloosa, 1987.

——. "Cultural Complexes of the Alabama Piedmont: An Initial Statement." *Journal of Alabama Archaeology* 26, no. 1 (1980): 1–27.

——. *East Alabama Archaeological Survey—1985 Season.* Report of Investigations 47. Office of Archaeological Research, University of Alabama, Tuscaloosa, 1985.

——. Introduction to *Archaeological Survey and Excavations in the Coosa River Valley, Alabama,* 1–6. Bulletin 15. Alabama Museum of Natural History, Tuscaloosa, 1993.

——. *A Summary of Alabama's De Soto Mapping Project and Project Bibliography.* De Soto Working Paper no. 9. Alabama De Soto Commission, Tuscaloosa, 1988.

——. *Tukabatchee: Archaeological Investigations at an Historic Creek Town, Elmore County, Alabama: 1984.* Report of Investigations 45. Office of Archaeological Research, University of Alabama, Tuscaloosa, 1985.

Knight, Vernon J. Jr., and John W. O'Hear. *Archaeological Investigations in the Rother L. Harris Reservoir: 1975.* Report submitted to Alabama Power Company. Department of Anthropology, University of Alabama, Tuscaloosa, 1975. Copy on file at Office of Archaeological Research, University of Alabama, Tuscaloosa.

Knight, Vernon J. Jr., and Vincas P. Steponaitis. "A New History of Moundville." In Vernon James Knight Jr. and Vincas P. Steponaitis, eds., *Archaeology of the Moundville Chiefdom,* 1–25. Smithsonian Institution Press, Washington, D.C., 1998.

Knight, Vernon J. Jr., Gloria Cole, and Richard Walling. *Archaeological Reconnaissance of the Coosa and Tallapoosa River Valleys, East Alabama: 1983.* Report of Investigations 43. Office of Archaeological Research, University of Alabama, Tuscaloosa, 1984.

Lacefield, Jim. Lost Worlds in Alabama Rocks: A Guide to the State's Ancient Life and Landscapes. Alabama Geological Society, University, 2000.

Lafferty, Robert J. "An Analysis of Prehistoric Southeastern Fortifications." Master's thesis. Department of Anthropology, Southern Illinois University, Carbondale, 1973.

Lankford, George E. III. "A New Look at DeSoto's Route through Alabama." *Journal of Alabama Archaeology* 23, no. 1 (1977): 10–36.

——. "Legends of the Adelantado." In Gloria A. Young and Michael P. Hoffman, eds., *The Expedition of Hernando de Soto West of the Mississippi, 1541–1543,* 173–91. University of Arkansas Press, Fayetteville, 1993.

Las Casas, Bartolomé. *Fray Bartolomé de las Casas: Obras Completas.* 14 vols. Fundación "Instituto Bartolomé de las Casas" de los Dominicos de Andalucia. Alianza, Madrid, ca. 1988–98.

Lemmon, Alfred E., John T. Magill, and Jason R. Wiese, eds. *Charting Louisiana: Five Hundred Years of Maps.* Historic New Orleans Collection, New Orleans, 2003.

Lewis, R. Barry, Charles Stout, and Cameron B. Wesson. "The Design of Mississippian Towns." In R. Barry Lewis and Charles Stout, eds., *Mississippian Towns and Sacred Places,* 1–21. University of Alabama Press, Tuscaloosa, 1997.

Lewis, Theodore H., ed. "The Narrative of the Expedition of Hernando de Soto by the Gentleman of Elvas." In F. W. Hodge and T. H. Lewis, eds., *Spanish Explorers in the Southern United States, 1528–1543.* Charles Scribner's Sons, New York, 1907.

Little, Keith J., and Caleb Curren. "Conquest Archaeology of Alabama." In David Hurst Thomas, ed., *Columbian Consequences.* Vol. 2: *Archaeological Perspectives on the Spanish Borderlands East,* 169–95. Smithsonian Institution Press, Washington, D.C., 1990.

Little, Keith J., and Kevin Harrelson. *Pine Log Creek: Ethnohistoric Archaeology in the Alabama-Tombigbee Confluence Basin.* Research Series No. 3. Archaeological Resource Laboratory, Jacksonville State University, Jacksonville, Ala., 2005.

Lockhart, James. *Men of Cajamarca: A Social and Biographical Study of the First Conquerors of Peru.* University of Texas Press, Austin, 1972.

Lyon, Eugene. "The Cañete Fragment: Another Narrative of Hernando de Soto." In Lawrence A. Clayton, Vernon James Knight Jr., and Edward C. Moore, eds., *The De Soto Chronicles: The Expedition of Hernando de Soto to North America in 1539–1543,* 1: 307–10. University of Alabama Press, Tuscaloosa, 1993.

Mallios, Seth. *The Deadly Politics of Giving: Exchange and Violence at Ajacan, Roanoke, and Jamestown.* University of Alabama Press, Tuscaloosa, 2006.

Martin, Troy O. "Archaeological Investigations of an Aboriginal Defensive Ditch at Site 1Ds32." *Journal of Alabama Archaeology* 35 (2005): 60–84.

Maxwell, R. W. Jr. "Origin and Chronology of Alabama River Terraces." *Transactions, Gulf Coast Association of Geological Societies* 31 (1971): 83–95.

McGuire, W. W. "On the Prairies of Alabama." *American Journal of Science* 26 (1834): 93–98.

Merediz, Eyda, and Santa Arias, eds. and contribs. *Teaching Las Casas.* Modern Language Association, New York, 2008.

Michaelis, Ronald F. *Old Domestic Base-Metal Candlesticks.* Antique Collectors' Club, Woodbridge, Suffolk, U.K., 1978.

Milanich, Jerald T. "The European Entrada into La Florida: An Overview." In David Hurst Thomas, ed., *Columbian Consequences.* Vol. 2: *Archaeological Per-*

spectives on the Spanish Borderlands East, 3–29. Smithsonian Institution Press, Washington, D.C., 1990.

Moore, Clarence B. "Certain Aboriginal Remains of the Alabama River." *Journal of the Academy of Natural Sciences of Philadelphia,* 2nd ser., 11, no. 3 (1899): 288–347.

———. "Certain Aboriginal Remains of the Lower Tombigbee River." *Journal of the Academy of Natural Sciences of Philadelphia,* 2nd ser., 13, no. 2 (1905): 246–78.

Moore, Edward C. Foreword to Lawrence A. Clayton, Vernon James Knight Jr., and Edward C. Moore, eds., *The De Soto Chronicles: The Expedition of Hernando de Soto to North America in 1539–1543,* 2: ix–x. University of Alabama Press, Tuscaloosa, 1993.

Moran, W. J., et al. *Soil Survey of Dallas County, Alabama.* Bureau of Chemistry and Soils, U.S. Department of Agriculture, Washington, D.C., 1938.

Morgan, David. *The Mississippi De Soto Trail Mapping Project.* Archaeological Report No. 26. Mississippi Department of Archives and History, Jackson, 1996.

Morgan, David W. "Historic Period Chickasaw Indians: Chronology and Settlement Patterns." *Mississippi Archaeology* 31 (1996): 1–39.

Morse, Dan F. "Archaeology and the Population of Arkansas in 1541–1543." In Gloria A. Young and Michael P. Hoffman, eds., *The Expedition of Hernando De Soto West of the Mississippi, 1541–1543: Proceedings of the De Soto Symposia 1988 and 1990,* 29–35. University of Arkansas Press, Fayetteville, 1993.

Nabokov, Peter, and Robert Easton. *Native American Architecture.* Oxford University Press, New York, 2005.

Nance, C. Roger. *The Archaeological Sequence at Durant Bend, Dallas County, Alabama.* Special Publication no. 2. Alabama Archaeological Society, 1976.

Nielsen, Jerry J. *Archaeological Investigations of Three Additional Sites in the Claiborne Lock and Dam Reservoir.* Report submitted to the National Park Service, Department of Anthropology, University of Alabama, 1969. Copy on file at Office of Archaeological Research, University of Alabama, Tuscaloosa.

Oakley, Carey B., and G. Michael Watson. *Cultural Resources Inventory of the Jones Bluff Lake, Alabama River, Alabama.* Report of Investigations 4, Office of Archaeological Research, University of Alabama, Tuscaloosa, 1977.

Oviedo y Valdés, Gonzalo Fernández de. *Historia General y Natural de las Indias.* Ed. José Amador de los Rios. 4 vols. Real Academia de la Historia, Madrid, 1851–54.

———. *Historia General y Natural de las Indias.* Ed. J. Natalicio González. 14 vols. Asunción del Paraguay, 1944–45.

———. *Historia General y Natural de las Indias.* Ed. Juan Perez de Tudela Bueso.

5 vols. 2nd ed. Bibioteca de Autores Españoles desde la Formación del Lenguaje Hasta Nuestros Días, Ediciones Atlas, Madrid, 1992.

Owen, Thomas M., comp. *Handbook of the Alabama Anthropological Society.* Alabama Anthropological Society, Montgomery, 1910.

———. "Prehistoric Works." In *Publications of the Alabama Historical Society, Miscellaneous Collections,* 1: 357–74. Alabama History Commission, 1901.

Parish, Helen Rand, ed. *Bartolomé de las Casas: The Only Way.* Trans. Francis Patrick Sullivan. Paulist Press, New York and Mahwah, N.J., 1992.

Parry, J. H. *The Age of Reconnaissance: Discovery, Exploration and Settlement, 1450–1650.* University of California Press, Berkeley, 1963.

Patterson, Paul. "Archaeological Reconnaissance of Selected Areas of the Black Prairie Region of West Central Alabama." *Journal of Alabama Archaeology* 36, no. 2 (1990): 99–132.

Payne-Gallwey, Ralph. *The Book of the Crossbow.* Dover, New York, 1995.

Peebles, Christopher S., ed. *Prehistoric Agricultural Communities in West Central Alabama: Excavations in the Lubbub Creek Archaeological Locality.* Vol. 1. Report submitted to the U.S. Army Corps of Engineers, Mobile District. University of Michigan Museum of Anthropology, Ann Arbor, 1983.

Phillips, Carla Rahn, and William D. Phillips Jr. *The Worlds of Christopher Columbus.* Cambridge University Press, Cambridge, 1992.

Phillips, Philip, James A. Ford, and James B. Griffin. *Archaeological Survey in the Lower Mississippi Alluvial Valley, 1940–1947.* Papers of the Peabody Museum of Archaeology and Ethnology, vol. 25. Harvard University, Cambridge, Mass., 1951.

Pickett, Albert James. *History of Alabama and Incidentally of Georgia and Mississippi, from the Earliest Period.* 1851; repr., Birmingham Book and Magazine Company, Birmingham, Ala., 1962.

Priestley, Herbert Ingram, ed. and trans. *The Luna Papers: Documents Relating to the Expedition of Don Tristán de Luna y Arellano for the Conquest of La Florida in 1559–1561.* 2 vols. Florida State Historical Society, De Land, 1928.

Rafferty, Janet. "Prehistoric Settlement Patterning on the Mississippi Black Prairie." In Evan Peacock and Timothy Schauwecker, eds., *Blackland Prairies of the Gulf Coastal Plain: Nature, Culture, and Sustainability,* 167–93. University of Alabama Press, Tuscaloosa, 2003.

Rangel, Rodrigo. "Account of the Northern Conquest and Discovery of Hernando de Soto." In Lawrence A. Clayton, Vernon James Knight Jr., and Edward C. Moore, eds., *The De Soto Chronicles: The Expedition of Hernando de Soto to North America in 1539–1543,* 1: 247–306. University of Alabama Press, Tuscaloosa, 1993.

Rankin, H. Taylor, and D. E. Davis. "Woody Vegetation in the Black Belt Prairie of Montgomery County, Alabama, in 1845–46." *Ecology* 52, no. 4 (1971): 716–19.

Raudzens, George, ed. and contrib. *Technology, Disease, and Colonial Conquest, Sixteenth to Eighteenth Centuries: Essays Reappraising the Guns and Germs Theories.* Brill, Leiden and Boston, 2001.

Regnier, Amanda L. "Late Mississippian Coalescence in the Alabama River Valley." Paper presented at the 63rd annual meeting of the Southeastern Archaeological Conference, Little Rock, Ark., 2005.

———. "A Stylistic Analysis of Burial Urns from the Protohistoric Period of Central Alabama." *Southeastern Archaeology* 25, no. 1 (2006): 121–34.

Robertson, James A. "Review of The Luna Papers: Documents Relating to the Expedition of Don Tristan de Luna y Arellano for the Conquest of La Florida in 1559–1561, by Herbert Ingram Priestley." *Hispanic American Historical Review* 10 (1930): 64–67.

———, ed. and trans. *True Relation of the Hardships Suffered by Governor Fernando de Soto & Certain Portuguese Gentlemen during the Discovery of the Province of Florida: Now Newly Set Forth by a Gentleman of Elvas.* Publications of the Florida State Historical Society, no. 11. De Land, and Yale University Press, New Haven, 1932.

Rostlund, Erhard. "The Myth of a Natural Prairie Belt in Alabama: An Interpretation of Historical Records." *Annals of the Association of American Geographers* 47, no. 4 (1957): 392–411.

Scarry, C. Margaret. *Excavations on the Northwest Riverbank at Moundville: Investigations of a Moundville I Residential Area.* Report of Investigation 72. Office of Archaeological Research, University of Alabama Museums, Tuscaloosa, 1995.

Schiffer, Peter, Nancy Schiffer, and Herbert Schiffer. *The Brass Book: American, English, and European, Fifteenth Century through 1850.* Schiffer Publishing, Exton, Pa., 1978.

Schmitz, Darrel W., Charles L. Wax, and Evan Peacock. "Water-Resource Controls on Human Habitation in the Black Prairie of North-Central Mississippi." In Evan Peacock and Timothy Schauwecker, eds., *Blackland Prairies of the Gulf Coastal Plain,* 194–211. University of Alabama Press, Tuscaloosa, 2003.

Schroedl, Gerald F. "Mississippian Towns in the Eastern Tennessee Valley." In R. Barry Lewis and Charles Stout, eds. *Mississippian Towns and Sacred Places,* 64–93. University of Alabama Press, Tuscaloosa, 1997.

Sheldon, Craig T. Jr. "Anthropological Society Field Activities." In *Cataloguing and Documenting the Historic Creek Archaeological Collections at the Alabama De-*

partment of Archives and History. Final Report to the National Science Foundation (BNS-8507469). Montgomery, 1987. Copy on file at the Alabama Department of Archives and History, Montgomery.

———. Introduction to *The Southern and Central Alabama Expeditions of Clarence Bloomfield Moore,* 1–114. University of Alabama Press, Tuscaloosa, 2001.

———, ed. *The Southern and Central Alabama Expeditions of Clarence Bloomfield Moore.* University of Alabama Press, Tuscaloosa, 2001.

———. "Where Bartram Sat: Historic Creek Indian Architecture in the Eighteenth Century." Paper presented at the Bartram Trail Conference Biennial Meeting. Montgomery, Ala., 2003.

Sheldon, Craig T. Jr., David W. Chase, Gregory A. Waselkov, Teresa Paglione, and Elisabeth Sheldon. *Cultural Resource Assessment of the Demopolis Lake Reservoir: Fee Owned Lands.* Auburn University Archaeological Monograph 6. Department of Sociology and Anthropology, Auburn University, Auburn, Ala., 1982.

Sheppard, Donald E. "American Conquest." http://www.floridahistory.com/inset44.html (accessed September 7, 2007).

Smith, Buckingham, trans. *De Soto's Conquest of Florida.* Bradford Club, New York, 1866.

Smith, Marvin T. *Archaeology of Aboriginal Culture Change in the Interior Southeast: Depopulation during the Early Historic Period.* University Press of Florida, Gainesville, 1987.

———. *Coosa: The Rise and Fall of a Southeastern Mississippian Chiefdom.* University of Florida Press, Gainesville, 2000.

———. *Historic Period Indian Archaeology of Northern Georgia.* Georgia Archaeological Research Design Paper no. 7, Laboratory of Archaeology Series Report no. 30. University of Georgia, Athens, 1992.

———. "The Route of DeSoto through Tennessee, Georgia, and Alabama: The Evidence from Material Culture." *Early Georgia* 4, nos. 1 and 2 (1976): 27–48.

———. "A Sixteenth-Century Coin from Southeast Alabama." *Journal of Alabama Archaeology* 30, no. 1 (1984): 56–59.

Smith, Marvin T., and Mary Elizabeth Good. *Early Sixteenth-Century Glass Beads in the Spanish Colonial Trade.* Cottonlandia Museum, Greenwood, Miss., 1982.

Smith, Marvin T., and Stephen A. Kowalewski. "Tentative Identification of a Prehistoric 'Province' in Piedmont Georgia." *Early Georgia* 8, nos. 1 and 2 (1980): 1–13.

Smith, Roger C., John R. Bratten, J. Cozzi, and Keith Plaskett. *The Emanuel Point Ship Archaeological Investigations, 1997–1998.* Report of Investigations 68. Archaeology Institute, University of West Florida, Pensacola, 1998.

South, Stanley, Russell K. Skowronek, and Richard E. Johnson. *Spanish Artifacts from Santa Elena.* Anthropological Studies 7. Occasional Papers of the South Carolina Institute of Archaeology and Anthropology, University of South Carolina, Columbia, 1988.

Steponaitis, Vincas P. *Ceramics, Chronology, and Community Patterns: An Archaeological Study at Moundville.* Academic Press, New York, 1983.

Stowe, Noel R. "The Pensacola Variant and the Bottle Creek Phase." *Florida Anthropologist* 38, nos. 1–2 (1985): 144–49.

Sturtevant, William C. Foreword to John R. Swanton, *Final Report of the United States De Soto Expedition Commission,* v–ix. Reprinted with an introduction by Jeffrey P. Brain. Smithsonian Institution Press, Washington, D.C., 1985.

Swanton, John R. "De Soto's Line of March from the Viewpoint of an Ethnologist." *Proceedings of the Mississippi Valley Historical Association* 5 (1912): 147–57.

———. *Early History of the Creek Indians and Their Neighbors.* Bulletin 73, Bureau of American Ethnology. Smithsonian Institution, Washington, D.C., 1922.

———. "Ethnological Value of the De Soto Narratives." *American Anthropologist* 34 (1932): 570–90.

———. *Final Report of the United States De Soto Expedition Commission.* House Document No. 71, 76th Cong., 1st Sess. GPO, Washington, D.C., 1939.

———. *Indian Tribes of the Lower Mississippi Valley and Adjacent Coast of the Gulf of Mexico.* Bulletin 43, Bureau of American Ethnology. Smithsonian Institution, Washington, D.C., 1911.

———. "The Landing Place of De Soto." *Science* 80 (1934): 336–37.

———. "The Relation of the Southeast to General Culture Problems of American Pre-History." In *Conference on Southern Pre-History,* 60–74. Committee on State Archaeological Surveys, Division of Anthropology and Psychology, National Research Council, Washington, D.C., 1932.

———. "Tracing De Soto's Route." In *Explorations and Field-Work of the Smithsonian Institution in 1934,* 77–80. Smithsonian Institution, Washington, D.C., 1935.

Szabo, Michael W. "Quaternary Geology, Alabama River Basin, Alabama." Master's thesis, Department of Geology, University of Alabama, Tuscaloosa, 1972.

Thomas, Cyrus. *Report on Mound Explorations of the Bureau of Ethnology.* Annual Report for 1890–91, Bureau of American Ethnology. Smithsonian Institution, Washington, D.C., 1894.

Trickey, E. Bruce. "Mauvilla: A New Approach." *Journal of Alabama Archaeology* 41 (1995): 79–87.

Turner, Daymond. "The Aborted First Printing of the Second Part of Oviedo's

General and Natural History of the Indies." *Huntington Library Quarterly* 46 (1983): 105–25.

United States Army Corps of Engineers. "Alabama River from Junction to Hurricane Bluff Bar, Sheet No. 1," and "Alabama River from Hurricane Bluff Bar to Wetumpka, Sheet No. 2." In *United States Army Corps of Engineers, Annual Report of the Chief of Engineers.* Washington, D.C., 1884.

———. "Map of the Coosa River from Lock No 4 Ala. to Greensport Ala." In *Annual Report, U.S. Engineer's Office, Corps of Engineers.* Montgomery, Ala., 1890.

———. "Map of the Coosa River from Wetumpka Ala. to Lock No 4 Ala." In *Annual Report, U.S. Engineer's Office, Corps of Engineers.* Montgomery, Ala., 1889.

Vargas Machuca, Bernardo de. *Milicia y Descripción de las Indias.* Madrid, 1599.

Varner, John G., and Jeanette J. Varner, eds. and trans., *The Florida of the Inca.* University of Texas Press, Austin, 1951.

Vogt, George W. *Standard Catalog of Mexican Coins, Paper Money and Medals.* Ed. Colin R. Bruce II. Krause Publications, Iola, Wisc., 1981.

Wagner, Henry Raup, and Helen Rand Parish. *The Life and Writings of Bartolomé de las Casas.* University of New Mexico Press, Albuquerque, 1967.

Waselkov, Gregory A. *Coosa Valley Archaeology.* 2 vols. Report submitted to the U.S. Army Corps of Engineers, Mobile District. Auburn University Archaeological Monograph 2. Department of Sociology and Anthropology, Auburn University, Auburn, Ala., 1980.

———. "A History of the Alabama Anthropological Society." *Southeastern Archaeology* 13, no. 1 (1994): 64–76.

———. *Lower Tallapoosa River Cultural Resources Survey, Phase I Report.* Department of Sociology and Anthropology, Auburn University, Auburn, Ala., 1981. Copy on file at Auburn University Archaeology Laboratory, Auburn, Ala.

Waselkov, Gregory A., and Bonnie L. Gums. *Plantation Archaeology at Rivière aux Chiens, ca. 1725–1848.* Center for Archaeology Studies, University of South Alabama, Mobile, 2000.

Waselkov, Gregory A., and Kathryn E. Holland Braund, eds. *William Bartram and the Southeastern Indians.* University of Nebraska Press, Lincoln, 1995.

Weber, David J. *The Spanish Frontier in North America.* Yale University Press, New Haven, 1992.

Welch, Paul D. "Outlying Sites within the Moundville Chiefdom." In Vernon J. Knight Jr. and Vincas P. Steponaitis, eds., *Archaeology of the Moundville Chiefdom,* 133–66. University of Alabama Press, Tuscaloosa, 1998.

Wesson, Cameron B. "Mississippian Sacred Landscapes: The View from Alabama." In R. Barry Lewis and Charles Stout, eds., *Mississippian Towns and Sacred Places,* 93–122. University of Alabama Press, Tuscaloosa, 1997.

Young, Gloria A., and Michael P. Hoffman, eds. *The Expedition of Hernando de Soto West of the Mississippi, 1541–1543.* University of Arkansas Press, Fayetteville, 1993.

Young, R. A., and T. J. Glover. *Measure for Measure.* Sequoia Publications, Littleton, Col., 1996.

Contributors

Kathryn E. Holland Braund, professor of history at Auburn University, specializes in the early history of the Creek and Seminole Indians. She is the author of *Deerskins and Duffels: Creek Indian Trade with Anglo-America, 1685–1815* and other works on the historic Indians of the Southeast.

Lawrence A. Clayton, professor in the Department of History at The University of Alabama, is a historian specializing in Latin America and the early Hispanic period in the Americas. He is coeditor of *The De Soto Chronicles* and coauthor of *A History of Modern Latin America.*

Linda Derry, site director at Old Cahawba Archaeological Park, Alabama Historical Commission, is a historical archaeologist specializing in community archaeology and archaeological interpretation. She is coeditor of *Archaeologists and Local Communities: Partners in Exploring the Past.*

Robbie Ethridge, associate professor in the Department of Sociology and Anthropology at the University of Mississippi, is a cultural anthropologist and ethnohistorian specializing in the history of the Indians of the American South. She is the author of *Creek Country* and coeditor of *The Transformation of the Southeastern Indians, Light on the Path* and the forthcoming *Mapping the Mississippian Shatter Zone.*

Ned J. Jenkins, director of Fort Toulouse/Jackson State Park, is an archaeologist specializing in the southeastern United States. He is coauthor of *The Tombigbee Watershed in Southeastern Prehistory.*

Douglas E. Jones, professor emeritus of geology, served as department chair, dean of the College of Arts and Sciences, and other higher administrative positions at The University of Alabama. He served as director of The University of Alabama Museums, including Moundville Archaeological Park, and as chairman of the Alabama De Soto Commission during the

1980s. He is coauthor of *Vertebrate Fossils of Alabama* and editor of *Explorations into Highland New Guinea, 1930–1935*.

Vernon James Knight Jr., professor in the Department of Anthropology at The University of Alabama, is an archaeologist specializing in the prehistory and early history of the southeastern United States and Caribbean. He is coeditor of *The De Soto Chronicles* and *Archaeology of the Moundville Chiefdom*.

George E. Lankford is a folklorist who retired in 2001 from Lyon College in Batesville, Arkansas, where he was Pauline M. and Brooks Bradley Professor in the Social Sciences and chair of the Social Sciences Division. He is author of *Native American Legends,* a study of southeastern myths, *Bearing Witness,* a collection of Arkansas slave narratives, *Reachable Stars,* a study of North American Indian astronomical myths, and *Looking for Lost Lore,* a series of studies of prehistoric myths, rituals, and art.

Neal G. Lineback is a former geography professor at The University of Alabama and is currently professor emeritus at Appalachian State University. He is editor of the *Atlas of Alabama,* has authored or coauthored more than one hundred publications, and currently writes a nationally syndicated news column called *Geography in the News*.

Michael D. Murphy, professor and chair of anthropology at The University of Alabama, is a cultural anthropologist who specializes in vernacular Catholicism and protected landscapes in southern Spain. He is coeditor of *El Rocío: Análisis Culturales e Históricos* and author of "Catholicism" in *Religion and Culture: An Anthropological Focus*.

Amanda L. Regnier is a member of the Oklahoma Archeological Survey research faculty at the University of Oklahoma. She has published articles about Late Mississippian and Protohistoric occupations and ceramics in the Alabama River Valley.

Craig T. Sheldon Jr., Distinguished Research Associate Professor of Anthropology at Auburn University Montgomery, is an archaeologist with research interests in the late prehistoric and Early Historic periods of the southeastern United States. He is coauthor of "French Habitations at the Alabama Post, ca. 1720–1763" in *Archeologiques Collections Hors-Series,* and author of the introduction to the *Southern and Central Alabama Expeditions of Clarence Bloomfield Moore*.

Gregory A. Waselkov, professor of anthropology at the University of South Alabama, specializes in French colonial archaeology and the ethnohistory of southeastern North America. He is coeditor of the revised and expanded edition of *Powhatan's Mantle: Indians in the Colonial Southeast* and author of *A Conquering Spirit: Fort Mims and the Redstick War of 1813–1814*.

Eugene M. Wilson, professor emeritus of geography in the Department of Earth Sciences, University of South Alabama, specializes in the geography and history of the Gulf Coast and Caribbean region.

John E. Worth, assistant professor of anthropology at the University of West Florida, is an archaeologist and ethnohistorian specializing in the European colonial era in the southeastern United States and Cuba. He is author of *The Struggle for the Georgia Coast* and *The Timucuan Chiefdoms of Spanish Florida.*

Index